Combating Gender Violence
in and around schools

Combating Gender Violence
in and around schools

edited by Fiona Leach and
Claudia Mitchell

Trentham Books
Stoke on Trent, UK and Sterling, USA

Trentham Books Limited
Westview House   22883 Quicksilver Drive
734 London Road   Sterling
Oakhill   VA 20166-2012
Stoke on Trent   USA
Staffordshire
England ST4 5NP

First published 2006

British Library Cataloguing-in-Publication Data
A catalogue record for this book is available from the British Library

ISBN-13: 978 1 85856 388 6
ISBN-10: 1 85856 388 7

Designed and typeset by Trentham Print Design Ltd, Chester
and printed in Great Britain by Cromwell Press Ltd, Trowbridge

Contents

CONTENTS

Acknowledgements

That there is enough material to fill a book like *Combating Gender Violence in and around Schools* several times over is a shocking indictment of the nature of schooling around the world. The contributions to this volume do however offer a sense of hope by showing that, through the combined efforts of researchers and activists, it is possible to confront and combat the problem.

We are particularly grateful to Sara Humphreys for her editorial assistance (and also her chapter), Faisal Islam for checking references and Lindsay Cornish for her assistance in creating the index. Finally, we thank Gillian Klein of Trentham Books for her enthusiasm, efficiency and commitment in seeing the project through to fruition.

Fiona Leach and Claudia Mitchell

Preface

The clear and unavoidable message from the *United Nations Secretary General's Study on Violence against Children* is that no violence against children is justifiable; all violence against children is preventable. The study is certainly not pointing fingers at particular regions. Violence against children is a global problem and no Government can feel complacent. In every region, in stark contradiction of human rights norms and children's developmental needs, much violence against girls and boys remains legal, state-authorised and socially approved – even in places that are supposed to protect them, like schools.

Children spend more time under the care of adults in pre-schools, schools, vocational centres and other places of learning than they do anywhere else outside of their homes. Like parents, the adults who oversee, manage and staff these places have a duty to provide safe and nurturing environments that support and promote children's learning and development. They also have a duty to make sure that such development prepares children for life as responsible adults, guided by values of non-violence, gender equality, non-discrimination, tolerance and mutual respect. These are also the values that Governments embrace when they ratify the Convention on the Rights of the Child and other international human rights conventions, along with obligations to protect children from all forms of violence, in schools and elsewhere.

Violence in schools can be prevented and must not be tolerated. Giving children access to education of the highest quality can be the social vaccine against violence in all of society. The reality for many millions of children, however, is that schools expose them to violence and, in so doing, deny them their right to education. Violence in and around schools makes it difficult for girls (and also boys) to get to and from school, to learn effectively while in school, and to remain in school long enough to reap all the benefits of education.

It has to be recognised that virtually all forms of violence against children are entrenched in gender roles and inequities that follow children throughout their short childhood and formative years into adulthood. Even before they are born, girls are prepared for different, and generally lower, expectations than their male peers; and boys are socialised towards power and violence as a viable strategy to deal with conflict. By being victims, perpetrators and witnesses of violence, children learn that violence is an acceptable way for the strong and aggressive to get what they want from the comparatively weak, passive or peaceful. Thus girls, and boys, learn from an early age the rules of the game of life.

Whether perpetrated by adults or children, almost all violence in schools reflects a hidden curriculum that promotes gender inequality and stereotyping. For example, boys taunt each other about their lack of masculinity and harass girls with verbal and physical gestures that are sexual in nature. Corporal punishment is harsher and more frequent for boys than for girls. Sexual aggression by male teachers and boys is often dismissed as 'just boys being boys'. Girls are blamed for 'asking for it'. The implicit messages are that males should be tough, assertive, sexually predatory and ready for life in a rough-and-tumble world but females should be delicate, passive, sexually pure and sheltered. These behaviours and messages often make schools unsafe and uncomfortable for girls and are prominent among the reasons why, in many developing countries, adolescent girls are far less likely to attend school than adolescent boys.

Importantly, focusing on girls alone would not only appear to blame the victim – as if it were all her fault – but would risk overlooking a truly sustainable solution: a solution which must bring men and boys fully on board to speak out and take action in support of equity for girls and women.

As this book attests, there is clearly a need to recognise that girls and boys are affected by violence in their daily life no matter where they live – in both the real and virtual (internet) world. This means that the analysis of this impact must be intelligently integrated into policy and practice to promote safe and non-violent families and communities where children live and play and develop their potential. It also means conducting the research and public debate on such issues as how gender roles prevent or protect girls and boys from violence; how traditional practices affect girls and boys; how parenting practices are applied to girls and boys; how families and communities have failed to prevent sexual violence; and what changes are required to make a difference.

As the chapters on strategies for change in *Combating Gender Violence in and around Schools* suggest, active engagement is also needed, and this means strengthening children's knowledge, including knowledge of their rights and an openness towards diversity and tolerance, and their skills in support of healthy and effective negotiation, and peaceful and non-violent conflict resolution. This means listening to girls and to boys, and working with others who are responsible for finding sustainable solutions and ensuring that schools are safe and welcoming, effective and dynamic places for girls and for boys to learn and develop.

A coordinated, systematic and human rights-based national response to violence against children is needed, one which takes account of gender and gives special attention to vulnerable groups of children. The case studies provided in this book, along with a description of strategies help to map out ways of developing comprehensive and targeted services and programmes. Finally, it must be said that schools neither create society's problems alone nor can they solve them alone. The concerted efforts of many sectors and individuals is needed to stop gender violence in schools.

Professor Paulo Sérgio Pinheiro
Independent Expert for the UN Study on Violence against Children

PART 1

**GENDER VIOLENCE IN AND AROUND
SCHOOLS: INTERNATIONAL
PERSPECTIVES**

1

Situating the study of gender violence in and around schools

Fiona Leach and Claudia Mitchell

Liberia: Young girls are still being sexually exploited by aid workers and peacekeepers despite pledges to stamp out such abuse, according to Save the Children. As people displaced by the civil war return to their villages, government officials and teachers are contributing to the abuse. Teachers have demanded sex in lieu of school fees, or even just to give good grades. (from http://news.bbc.co.uk/1/hi/world/africa/4983440.stm)

South Africa: According to a recent study by Reshma Sathiparsad in KwaZulu-Natal, schoolboys believe it is acceptable to beat their female partners to keep them in line. To one boy, beating a girl meant there were 'slim chances of her misbehaving', to another it meant you loved her because if you didn't you wouldn't bother to do it. (from *The Witness*, www.witness.co.za, April 6, 2006)

India: The police arrested a 50-year-old primary schoolteacher in Hardwar, Northern India, accused of sexual misconduct and abuse of eight boys aged between six and 10 years. It was reported that he had been forcing them into sexual misconduct during the lunch hour and assaulting them if they resisted his attempts. (from *The Tribune*, Chandigarh, 24 March 2005)

United Kingdom: Dozens of deaf girls and boys were victims of one of Britain's most predatory paedophiles, who was allowed to work at a specialist boarding school for several decades, even though he had been prosecuted for sex offences. One victim, now aged 49, was repeatedly raped as a four-year-old while other children slept, but could not call out. (from *The Observer*, 14 May 2006)

3

Genesis of the book

Combating gender violence in and around schools comes out of our own work on gender violence in countries including South Africa, Zimbabwe, Zambia, Swaziland, Malawi, Ghana, Botswana, Rwanda and the Gambia over the last decade. This work has ranged from conducting country studies (Leach *et al*, 2003; Mitchell and Kanyangara, 2006) through to debating methodological issues (Leach, 2006), designing and testing school-based interventions (Mlamleli *et al*, 2001), providing a global overview of current knowledge (Dunne *et al*, 2006) and disseminating information on research findings and interventions through the internet and newsletters (id21). What is exciting about this work is a sense of an expanding community of practitioners, academics, activists, non-governmental and governmental agencies committed to the idea that children should have the right to learn in safe spaces. Underlying this growing network is a commitment to the notion that teachers and young people can be active agents in addressing gender violence both in and beyond school. It is in this context that we began to imagine an edited book that would draw on the work being done in this area in diverse settings across the world.

While the genesis of the book was a relatively straightforward process of identifying researchers, activists and practitioners we knew were doing interesting work on gender violence among young people, putting the book together has been more complicated. We were committed to the idea of highlighting a range of interventions and strategies for combating gender violence. We also wanted to cover a spectrum of geographical and political contexts, including situations where children and young people are particularly vulnerable, for example as refugees, victims of armed conflict or as AIDS orphans. What we found, however, is that there are no easy solutions, and that most work has been directed at identifying types of gender violence rather than developing interventions.

We also found that when researchers have shifted their focus, for example to the study of gender violence in the *primary* school (Deevia Bhana's chapter from South Africa) or to working with young men (eg the chapters by Gary Barker *et al* and Seshradi and Chandran from Brazil and India), new issues emerge. The question of what to include under the umbrella term 'gender violence', and how to label it, has presented its own problems, as noted below. Finally, while we found many examples documenting work in Sub-Saharan Africa, and especially in South Africa where a number of interventions are under way, there is a dearth of studies from other regions. But the process of identifying these new dimensions to the problem suggests a blurring of boundaries between issues and interventions, as the act of identifying issues can in itself constitute an intervention. The chapters in the book are therefore not easily separated into those that explore problems and those that offer solutions. At the same time, this overlap provides recognition that enhancing our understanding of the issues through empirical research has a direct bearing on how we develop appropriate interventions.

Notwithstanding the growing array of emerging issues and new country contexts explored in this book, we have identified interventions which, while not generic, can nonetheless be read as *strategies* for change. These include participatory approaches which involve young people themselves in the research and/or design and implementation of programmes, some of which address adolescent hyper-masculinity. Other approaches place teachers at the heart of the process of bringing about change in schools. We do not suggest that these interventions are replicable but we hope they will generate ideas and possibilities that can be transformed into context-specific strategies and solutions.

A global context

The case studies and interventions described here are not meant to sit outside existing work on gender and schooling. Indeed, we hope that the book will make a contribution to understanding the barriers to achieving equality of opportunity and outcomes in education, especially in countries where universal basic education has not yet been achieved and where gender gaps in educational participation remain wide. Recognition of the negative impact of widespread gender violence in schools on efforts to improve pupil enrolment, retention and achievement is long overdue. If the universally agreed targets on education contained in the Millennium Development Goals are to be achieved – universal access to primary education and gender equality at all levels of education by 2015 – this issue cannot be ignored.

We are accustomed to viewing the school as a benign institution, a safe and pupil-friendly place where children acquire valuable knowledge and skills and develop constructive relationships in preparation for adult life. But media reports such as those sketched out at the start of this chapter and recent ethnographic studies have made us aware that schools can also be sites of violence and that this is a global phenomenon. Less well recognised is the understanding that acts of violence in schools, as in other institutional settings, have their origins in forms of social inequality, including gender inequality.

That violence against children in and around schools is finally being recognised as a worldwide phenomenon is evident in the two-year global *Study on Violence against Children* commissioned by the Secretary-General of the United Nations (United Nations, 2006). This involved consultations with children as well as other key stakeholders in the nine regions of the world. In its final form, it examines the scale and nature of violence against children in school – as well as in the home, on the streets and at work – covering bullying, gang violence, corporal punishment and gender violence, in a range of contexts across countries and regions, across ages from nursery school up, and targeting both boys and girls. Most importantly, it is intended to provide a platform for action by governments through its recommendations concerning the policy implications of making schools safe for teachers and pupils. Our book adds to this study by providing a gender perspective on issues of violence previously discussed in genderless terms. It also offers case studies of new and emerging aspects of gender violence, for example, cyber-bullying, exploratory studies in countries such as Russia and Pakistan, where little attention has been paid until now to gender violence in schools, and, most importantly, examples of interventions and strategies for change.

Gender violence is a particularly problematic area to research due to the sensitivities of investigating sexual matters, particularly when children are involved. The reluctance to investigate sexual violence, and gender inequalities more generally, has kept it largely unrecognised and invisible. This book seeks to confront the silence surrounding gender violence in and around schools and to provide a more coherent and in-depth understanding of the issues, offering opportunities for further research and real possibilities for reducing its scope and harmful effects.

Definitions

We define 'gender violence' broadly in this book. In the school context, it includes physical, verbal, emotional and psychological forms of violence, covering violent acts perpetrated by pupils on other pupils, by teachers on pupils (including corporal punishment) and by pupils on teachers.[1] *Fear* of violence, especially for girls, often from youths and adult men not associated with the school, is also important, as are more subtle forms of violence originating in unequal gender relations in contemporary society, which the school environment all too often fosters and helps perpetuate.

Agreeing on terminology for the contributors to use in the book was challenging so we have, on the whole, left intact the terms as they used them. While acknowledging that there is much overlap, we feel it necessary to draw out the

nuances of meaning implicit in certain terms because the way we conceptualise and label the problem has implications for the types of strategies considered to be effective in dealing with it.

Bullying: The literature on violence in schools, and the policies and interventions developed to address it, most commonly use 'bullying' to refer to
pupil-on-pupil violence. Although the term is useful in that it highlights the
intentional and repeated nature of such behaviour, it is gender-neutral and
therefore discourages recognition of the fact that girls and boys, whether as
perpetrators or victims, experience violence in different ways. The concept of
bullying also puts the onus on the individual – as deviant – rather than on
societal influences which may encourage bullying behaviour. As Stein (2003)
points out, defining school violence as bullying also conveniently sidesteps
human rights legislation that is applicable in cases of sexual harassment and
abuse.

Most of our contributors chose to avoid the term 'bullying' and opted instead
for gender-specific or gender-sensitive terms. The principal ones are explained below.

Gender violence, gender-based violence and sexual violence: Some authors
have used the term 'gender-based' or 'gender-related' violence. This suggests
that some forms of violence are not gendered and that their cause is unrelated
to socially-sanctioned norms of male and female behaviour. On the whole,
however, we take the view that violence always has a gender dimension, even
if other factors such as race, religion, physical appearance, ability *etc* may be
more salient in a particular incident. The term 'sexual violence' is used by
some authors to categorise incidents of an overtly sexual nature, such as
forced sex or rape.

Sexual abuse, sexual harassment and gendered harassment: Sexual abuse
implies sexual exploitation of a child by an adult (and sometimes by another
child or adolescent) by virtue of his/her superior power, and for his/her own
benefit or gratification. 'Abuse' is a widely recognised legal term, which
focuses on the power imbalance within the abusive relationship. In contrast,
sexual harassment is more usually associated with adult victims, eg pupils in
higher education and employees in the workplace, although, as this book
reveals, children and adolescents also engage in sexual harassment. When
developing a gender equity policy for the South Africa government in the
1990s, Wolpe *et al* (1997) defined it as involving unsolicited acts of physical
intimacy, unsolicited demands – whether directly or by implication – for
sexual favours, remarks with sexual connotations and any unwelcome

conduct of a sexual nature with intent to offend, humiliate or intimidate. In this book, Elizabeth Meyer has chosen to use the term 'gendered harassment', suggesting that forms of harassment are not always overtly sexual and may include those that reinforce the traditional gender roles of heterosexual masculinity and femininity in subtle and hidden ways.

Organisation of the book

The book has three main parts. Part 1 focuses on mapping out some of the broader issues surrounding gender violence in schools. This introductory chapter is followed by Erika George's account of the international commitments on equality of access to primary education, and on the elimination of violence against women, in particular in relation to regions of the world where girls continue to be seriously disadvantaged in terms of educational participation. Fiona Leach then provides an historical overview of research into gender violence in schools in developing country contexts.

Part 2 presents case studies from across the world of gender violence in and around schools. These include chapters which explore neglected or unrecognised manifestations of school violence in settings where there is already a substantial body of research on this topic. First, Shaheen Shariff and Rachel Gouin present a new and particularly unpleasant form of school-related gender violence, namely cyber-bullying. They draw on a number of North American court cases to show how ill-prepared the school and justice systems are to deal with it and how reluctant schools have been to recognise their responsibility in addressing it. Next, Elizabeth Meyer explores a longstanding but largely ignored aspect of violence in North American schools, namely homophobic violence and violence directed at individuals whose behaviour does not fit with heterosexual norms. The third chapter, by Neil Duncan, examines girl-on-girl violence in English schools and suggests that, contrary to public perception, physical violence may be an integral part of social relations between some groups of girls. In the fourth, Sara Humphreys explores corporal punishment as a gendered practice, drawing on research data from Botswana to show that female and male teachers and pupils relate to and experience corporal punishment differently, and that this needs to be acknowledged before effective strategies can be designed to eradicate the practice.

These chapters are followed by original research from several countries where the phenomenon of violence in schools has scarcely been explored to date, and its gendered dimensions not at all. The first, by Olga Zdravomyslova and Irina Gorshkova, comes from Russia, where until recently the public resisted any discussion of gender issues, despite emerging evidence of high levels of domestic violence. The authors invited first year university students to record their recent memories of school violence, and found that it is widespread and, as elsewhere, largely perpetrated by males on females and accepted as routine. Nazish Brohi and Anbreen Ajaib note the same lack of gender-aware research in Pakistan, but focus on how the 'overarching constellation of violence' faced by women in Pakistani society permeates the school system, with the silence surrounding any offence against women making schoolgirls even more vulnerable to sexual harassment and assault. A related set of vulnerabilities is highlighted by Kay Standing, Sara Parker and Laxmi Dhital, who document the impact of armed conflict on children in Nepal. Both boys and girls are exposed to violence from government and rebel forces, such as kidnapping and recruitment as child soldiers or messengers, but girls face the additional risk, and daily fear, of rape or of being forced to become a militant's temporary wife.

Part 3 documents some of the interventions which have been tried out in efforts to combat gender violence in school or among school-age young people. These include (1) those that directly draw on the voices of young people themselves, (2) those that challenge dominant versions of masculinities, and (3) those that place teachers – both pre-service and in-service – at the centre of change. There are several commonalities across the interventions in these categories. The idea of participation and engagement is at the centre of much of this work, as we see in the significance of media and arts-based approaches in 'giving voice' to participants. In particular we look at work with photo-voice, video, drawing, theatre and film as tools for change. Reflection itself is critical. Finally, a curriculum for addressing gender violence is vital – and for other interventions which are sustained and wide-ranging – regardless of whether it is at the level of working with teachers or learners.

Part 3 begins with several youth-focused chapters which use visual, media-based and other participatory approaches to give voice to young people. Claudia Mitchell, Shannon Walsh and Relebohile Moletsane draw on examples from Southern Africa to look at the ways in which cultural production through drawing, photography and video can give young people a voice to 'see for themselves' and even more importantly to 'speak for themselves'. Monica Mak describes a drawing-to-video intervention from South Africa and examines the participatory aspects of video production and screening, including the potential for audience engagement. Arguing for the idea of what might be described as body-across-the curriculum, June Larkin and Carla Rice describe a curriculum project based on the idea of 'body equity', a term they use 'to capture and convey an approach that promotes acceptance and inclusion of diverse bodies in schools' (p131). As they note, by emphasising body *equity* over body *image*, it is possible to shift the focus from changing body images to creating equitable school cultures.

These chapters lead into the next section entitled 'challenging masculinities'. Shekhar Seshradi and Vinay Chandran describe the ways film has been used in India to interrogate dominant views of masculinity with young boys and to offer alternative forms of gender behaviour at an early age. Gary Barker and colleagues at PROMUNDO discuss their work in Latin America and India, where conventional male views of women and men are challenged in workshops and social marketing campaigns with the aim of encouraging more gender-equitable attitudes and behaviour. Robert Morrell and Gethwana Makhaye describe the success of several projects with boys and young men in South Africa which focus on challenging constructions of masculinity. Their assumption is that, since masculinity is constructed, it can be changed through programmes which give boys the opportunity to talk about themselves, develop a language of introspection and self-interrogation, learn humility and self-respect, and affirm the importance of responsible living. Martin Mills illuminates the way in which current policy in education in Australia is being driven by concerns over the under-achievement of boys, at the risk of undermining efforts at achieving gender equality and eliminating violence against girls in school. Finally, Deevia Bhana, in her work with learners in a primary school in South Africa, places on the agenda the significance of interrogating masculinity and power relations in the primary classroom and playground. She argues that starting this process early is in itself an intervention.

The last section of Part 3 highlights interventions with teachers and other school personnel in Kenya, Uganda, and several countries in West Africa: Ghana, Sierra Leone and Guinea. The work takes on what might be described as a 'starting with ourselves' approach. Lucy Stackpool-Moore and Tania Boler open with an arts-based approach within teacher development, focusing on drama work in Ghana. In their discussion of Theatre for A Change, directed at training teachers to teach about HIV/AIDS, they explore the significance of gender and identity in such work. Fatuma Chege then describes the ways in which she used written memory work with beginning teachers, both male and female, in Kenya to encourage them to recall instances of gender violence in their own lives as starting points for looking at themselves now as teachers. Similarly, Gladys Teni-Atinga used memory work, along with focus groups and interviews, in her work with beginning teachers in Ghana. Her study raises new questions about interrogating institutional practices in teacher training institutions – admission procedures, examinations, record-keeping etc – positioning such an approach as an entry point to 'starting with ourselves'. Jackie Kirk describes a project with classroom assistants in West Africa, which highlights work in conflict zones and shows how school personnel other than teachers can be involved in participatory approaches to counter gender violence. Robina Mirembe describes a school-based AIDS education curriculum in a co-educational secondary school in Uganda. Her critical argument is the importance of confronting gender violence and aggression in schools in teaching effectively about HIV/AIDS, as gender inequalities and injustices underlie both phenomena. Fittingly, as the final chapter in the book, her account of the intervention reminds us of the significance of a rights-based curriculum in combating gender violence.

New directions in the study of gender violence in and around schools

We envisage this book at a crossroads of scholarship and activism in relation to the study of gender violence in and around schools. Drawing from the issues that emerge in Part 2 and the rich range of interventions described in Part 3, we hope that the book maps out an agenda for future work in this area. Although we make no claims to having provided a comprehensive or even representative account of the issue of gender violence in schools, it is important to acknowledge that there are gaps in the literature. For example, we found surprisingly few interventions that are driven by young people themselves. Seldom do we hear the voices of girls or boys commenting on their own lives and the actions they are taking in and around the classroom. When we do, the interventions are frequently small-scale and one-off. In a study of youth participation and sexual abuse in Swaziland, young people made the point that 'we are the ones most affected; we are the ones who need to be looking at solutions' (Mitchell and Mothobi-Tapela, 2004).

We also know very little about the abuse and harassment of *boys* and about how work on masculinities plays out within school settings in developing countries, as most of the work has been done outside of school. Yet engaging with the structures and processes of schooling and understanding the major role that schooling plays in perpetuating aggressive masculinities is crucial if gender violence is to be effectively countered.

Although much has been written in the policy literature about the way schools ought to function and be managed, we found surprisingly little work that actually documents how gender violence is being dealt with in schools, which suggests that little is being done. What types of school leadership are most effective in combating gender violence? What are the possibilities for teachers to take action and bring about change? When are we going to see in-depth studies of how teachers are implementing the various teacher-based programmes emerging on gender violence?

Method and methodology are critical issues and, although the studies described here draw on conventional surveys and ethnographies as well as innovative qualitative approaches such as memory work and visual arts-based approaches, work of this type indicates the need to deepen our understanding of child-focused research tools for investigating power imbalances, abusive normative practices and human rights violations. The area of research methodology itself is a burgeoning one and clearly central to new agendas for engaging in shifting the boundaries of knowledge within social science research (Leach, in press; Mitchell, in press). From the challenges of understanding what counts as informed consent and ensuring a protective environment for children to participate in both research and interventions, to the blurring of the boundaries between research and social change, gender violence is clearly a key area for deepening our understanding of methodologies within social science research.

Note
1 It also includes violence by teachers on other teachers, eg sexual harassment, but this is not fully addressed in the book.

2

Failing the future: development objectives, human rights obligations and gender violence in schools

Erika George

International development initiatives for advancing educational equality

I f the international development community's goal of ensuring education for all the world's children is to be reached by 2015, particular attention must be paid to girls in many countries of South Asia, West Asia, Sub-Saharan Africa and the Arab States, where gender discrimination denies girls equal access to education. The gender gap is greatest in these regions because traditional customs and practices relegate girls to subordinate status and cultural preferences for boys and family economic constraints may direct parents to favour educating their sons rather than daughters (UNESCO, 2003).

Appropriately, the international development community has urged governments to advance access to education for women and girls as a weapon to combat the attitudes and practices that encourage discrimination and inequality (UNICEF, 2005). Nevertheless, discrimination against girls continues to perpetuate the education gap. While much attention has been given to the numerous discriminatory barriers that block girls' access to school, less has been paid to the obstacles girls confront in schools, including sexual harassment and gender violence.

At the same time, we need to acknowledge that boys also experience gendered forms of violence in school and that this too has not received the attention it requires. However, as the chapters in this volume testify, empirical evidence suggests that girls remain much more likely to be routinely confronted with sexual violence and harassment in school, and that this contributes to their early drop-out and lower achievement in many countries. So while not denying the right of boys to non-discriminatory and good quality education, this chapter focuses on girls.

School-based gender violence is a global phenomenon that has remained largely unexplored, despite numerous international commitments to promote girls' education. This chapter positions recent international development policy objectives and priorities relating to gender equality and education alongside the international human rights legal framework. Failing to bridge the gap between development priorities and human rights principles, and ignoring the costs and consequences of school-based gender violence will mean the global failure to achieve gender equality in education by 2015 or beyond. The development and human rights frameworks should be brought together to combat gender violence in schools and provide meaningful equality in education.

Overall, the development community has established that positive effects of education for girls benefit the whole of society and justify equal school access for girls alongside boys (Dollar and Gatti, 1999; Lorgelly, 2000). Recognised long-term social benefits of girls' education include increased family income, delayed marriage, reduced fertility rates, reduced infant and maternal mortality rates, better nourished and healthier children and families, as well as greater opportunities and life choices for women (Hill and King, 1995). Evidence suggests that it is secondary and higher education that have the greatest payoff for women's empowerment and equality (Grown *et al*, 2005). Yet it is precisely at secondary level that parents in some countries become apprehensive about sending girls to school, because of the risk of unwanted contact with the opposite sex. And most sexual harassment and gender violence is reported by secondary school-aged girls at or after puberty (*ibid*).

Education for All: international ambitions

The 164 governments represented at the World Education for All Forum in Senegal in 2000 adopted the Dakar Framework for Action on Education for All (EFA), committing themselves to ensuring that all children, especially girls, have access to and complete a basic education cycle of good quality by 2015 (UNESCO, 2000a). They pledged to eliminate gender disparities in primary and secondary education by 2005, and to achieve gender equality in education by 2015, with an emphasis on ensuring girls' full and equal access to, and achievement in, basic education.

These EFA gender equality ambitions complement other recently announced global development goals, principally those contained in the United Nations Millennium Declaration, referred to as the Millennium Development Goals (MDGs). The second goal calls for the achievement of universal primary education by 2015. The third goal is to promote gender equality and empower women, and includes a target 'to eliminate gender disparity in primary and secondary education, preferably by 2005, and to all levels of education no later than 2015' (UNESCO, 2003).

Falling through the development framework

Significantly, none of the quantitative development indicators currently in use to measure the performance of EFA and MDG inspired policies addresses the problem of gender violence in schools or assesses how the quality of education for girls is affected by violence and harassment (George, 2005). For example, the commonly used primary enrolment and completion indicators only provide information about the numbers of children in school and offer no insight into why some children may not be enrolled or why school survival differs for different children. Nor can they offer insight into the scope and prevalence of gender violence in schools because many girls remain in school despite the abuse they experience. Moreover, the fact that a girl may learn that she is not equal to her male peers and might be discriminated against in various ways while in school is still an unidentified problem in the present development indices of success, despite the commitments to gender equality.

Human rights obligations: end violence to promote equality in education

Despite declarations of commitment to closing the gender gap in education, all the gender-based discrimination against girls, including violence, helps perpetuate the gap. Policy makers and all those concerned with educational quality and equality need to look beyond the development indicators to the international human rights legal obligations that countries have adopted.

The right to non-discriminatory education

International human rights treaties, to which most EFA and MDG participating countries have already acceded, recognise education as a fundamental right. Pursuant to international legal standards, governments are obligated to ensure that no child is denied an education on the basis of race, colour, sex, language, religion, national or social origin, property or birth. But if gender violence is not prevented or punished, it impairs girls' enjoyment of this fundamental human right to education on an equal basis with others.

The 1948 Universal Declaration of Human Rights (UDHR) provides that 'everyone has the right to education. Education shall be free, at least in the elementary and fundamental stages. Elementary education shall be compulsory.' Similarly, the 1967 International Covenant on Economic, Social and Cultural Rights (ICESCR) requires free and compulsory primary education.

The 1981 Convention on the Elimination of All Forms of Discrimination Against Women (CEDAW) also acknowledges the existence of a right to education and obliges countries to pledge to take all appropriate measures to eliminate discrimination against women so they have equal rights with men in the field of education.

The 1989 Convention on the Rights of the Child (CRC) guarantees 'the right of the child to education' as a fundamental human right. It calls upon states to endeavour to provide free and compulsory primary education to all, to make forms of secondary education available and accessible to every child, and to take measures to encourage regular attendance at school and reduce drop-out rates.

In addition to requiring the provision of primary education, these legal instruments all share broad prohibitions against discrimination, such that governments must ensure that women and girls enjoy education on equal terms with men and boys. Independent expert committees exist to evaluate countries' compliance with the human rights treaties and have well developed procedural mechanisms for reporting and monitoring violations. Mechanisms are needed which provide opportunities to bring the issue of gender violence in schools before the treaty committees responsible for monitoring women's rights, children's rights and economic, social and cultural rights; this would help raise awareness about the problem and help forge solutions.

Human rights methodology, with its emphasis on the collection of testimony, is also of value. When they conduct investigations into violations of rights, human rights monitors gather qualitative data about an individual's experience of violation through lengthy interviewing. From such documentation techniques, investigators can perceive patterns, identify underlying structural causes of violations and assess the corresponding obligations of duty bearers. This information is then used to reinforce government responsibility to protect human rights. There is no reason why these human rights norms, techniques and structures could not be deployed to combat gender violence in schools.

Sexual violence is discrimination

International human rights law also requires countries to ensure that women enjoy all basic human rights and fundamental freedoms on an equal basis with men. The United Nations CEDAW Committee, which is charged with interpreting and enforcing the terms of the women's human rights treaty, has noted that gender-based violence is a form of discrimination which seriously inhibits equality for women. Acts which inflict physical, mental or sexual harm or suffering, threats of such acts, coercion, or other deprivations of liberty violate international human rights law. Many instances of sexual violence and harassment reported by girls around the world rise to this level of violation.

Through their ratification of the CEDAW treaty, governments assume the obligation to pursue by all appropriate means and without delay a policy of eliminating all forms of discrimination against women and girls; this includes gender-based violence in schools. Governments can only meet this obligation by ensuring that public authorities and institutions across the country act in conformity with this obligation through adopting and enforcing legislation and taking other measures, including sanctions where appropriate, to prohibit all discrimination against women. It also requires that governments ensure effective protection through competent national tribunals and other public bodies.

Framing the way forward

The purpose of education as enshrined in the 1989 United Nations Convention on the Rights of the Child is to foster development of the child's personality, talent and mental and physical abilities to the fullest potential to prepare him or her for a responsible life in a free society, in the spirit of understanding, peace, tolerance, equality of the sexes and friendship among all peoples. It is true that the education gender gap is closing and that increasing numbers of girls are in school, but without addressing the underlying school environment, greater numbers of girls in school may simply mean more girls are subject to gender-based violence in a setting that has not been made welcoming for them.

While a number of countries have already closed the gender gap in access to schooling – at least statistically – they have not solved the problem that gender-based violence presents for equality in education. Sadly, most have not even identified it as an important issue. The contents of the 151 country reports submitted by governments as part of the EFA 2000 assessment in preparation for the Dakar World Education Forum (UNESCO, 2000b) revealed that the issue of sexual harassment as a barrier to the right to education re-mained unidentified and presumably unaddressed in countries' strategies to ensure educational equality. There is little evidence that the level of awareness has increased since then. Even where gender parity in school enrolments has been achieved, issues still remain around the extent to which this achieve-ment has actually contributed to gender equality and to the empowerment of women.

A capabilities approach

We need to go beyond enrolment numbers and EFA targets to situate school-based violence against girls in the larger context of the international develop-ment objectives and human rights obligations outlined here. There are many possible points of mutual reinforcement, synergies and commonalities of interest between development policy and human rights law. For instance, combining a development rationale with rights principles has the potential to bring an important instrumentalist dimension to achieving goals while com-plementing the principled or normative arguments advanced for the social and economic rights sought. The capabilities approach developed by Sen (1999) 'considers that the evaluation of equality, for example in education pro-vision, needs to be based on an understanding of human capabilities – that is, what it is that each individual has reason to value' and relies on 'positing a strategy based on an ethical notion of valuing freedoms and affirming rights as ethical obligations of each person to another' (Unterhalter, 2005: 28). A review of the capabilities endangered by the presence of sexual violence against girls in schools would therefore illustrate just how disabling certain school environments can be for girls. A capabilities approach reveals what is required for all children to enjoy equal education.

Directing attention towards girls' capabilities sharpens our understanding of the consequences when sexual violence in schools remains unchallenged, thereby bringing us closer to realising the true content of the right to educa-tion and to a better understanding of the state's obligation to ensure it. Thus situating the issue of gender violence within the framework of international human rights law informed by an appreciation of the substantive content of the education right to the development of basic human capabilities can signi-ficantly contribute to efforts to advance girls' education and confront sexual harassment and violence.

In practical terms, a focus on the *capabilities* that human rights are intended to protect would require policymakers to ask what girls can actually do with their schooling and whether the education they receive and the manner in which they receive it will promote positive freedom for them to enjoy well-being and live lives of dignity (Sen, 1999; Nussbaum 2003). According to this approach, evaluations of policy success would have to include measuring the personal capabilities developed through education. This would require a qualitative assessment of success to complement existing quantitative development indicators. The qualitative methodology of human rights monitoring and investigation could prove a useful guide here too for the developing community in its efforts to achieve gender equality in education.

Promising national interventions

The international human rights obligations voluntarily undertaken by each signatory government should be one of the key reference points taken into account in MDG and EFA planning and implementation. Yet present policy approaches vary between ignoring human rights altogether and treating rights solely in tokenistic fashion. For example, few of the EFA 2000 reports described education as a fundamental human right; still fewer made any mention of sexual violence or harassment in schools as a problem, let alone offered solutions. There were some notable exceptions; Egypt, for example, devoted a considerable portion of its report to the legal and political framework of education and the country's obligations under the international economic and social rights treaty. It also reviewed Egypt's positive experience with the approximately 280 community-based girls only schools (UNESCO, 2002b).[1]

Few of the EFA 2000 reports submitted by countries in the regions identified above as most in need of special attention, mostly in South and West Asia, Sub-Saharan Africa and the Arab States, explicitly acknowledged gender-based violence in their schools. However, Mozambique pledged to strengthen enforcement of existing policies barring sexual harassment and indicated that its Ministry of Education would conduct studies to investigate the gender constraints that make girls less likely than boys to remain in school (UNESCO, 2002b). More recently, the Ministry of Education in Malawi has revised its code of conduct for teachers and included an explicit statement that teacher misconduct includes 'behaving immorally with a pupil' (DFID, 2005).

Although Ministries of Education around the world have been slow to address gender violence systematically throughout their school systems, some non-governmental initiatives have emerged over the past few years to expose and counter it by encouraging children to analyse power in gender relations and their own behaviour in personal and institutional settings. For example, the *Tuseme* (Let's Speak Out) clubs, started by the Forum for African Women

Educationalists (FAWE), which has chapters in many African countries, offer peer networks where students can discuss issues of concern to them such as sexuality, health and HIV/AIDS prevention (Subrahmanian, 2005).

Some organisations also offer programmes of workshops and other activities for students, aimed at identifying destructive gender norms, developing alternatives to violence in resolving conflict and shaping positive self-images, sometimes in co-operation with government. In Bolivia, workshops dealing with violence and gender discrimination inside and outside schools have been carried out by UNICEF in co-operation with a government ministry (Mirsky, 2003). The Venezuelan Association for Alternative Sex Education has trained high school students by fostering dialogue through structured weekly training sessions. In Sri Lanka, UNICEF, in co-operation with the Ministry of Education, has hosted a series of seminars on concepts of equality with an emphasis on gender violence as a human rights violation (*ibid*).

In the Gambia, Kenya, Namibia, Rwanda, Senegal and Tanzania, FAWE has created 'Centre of Excellence' schools and provided a package of interventions to develop holistic initiatives to improve the quality of schooling from a gender perspective. FAWE works in these schools to achieve gender sensitisation of all stakeholders through in-service training on gender responsive pedagogy for teachers (Subrahmanian, 2005). In the United States, Mentors in Violence Prevention, a gender violence and bullying prevention programme, employs an innovative 'bystander' model that teaches students to take an active role in promoting a positive school climate by developing skills to confront violence and the resolve to speak out against rape, battering, sexual harassment and violence (Katz, 1995).

Although growing in popularity, such programmes are generally limited to small numbers of schools. Such individual efforts must be evaluated and, if found effective, expanded. There are few rigorous evaluations to determine which interventions have the greatest impact on increasing girls' participation in secondary education and more research is needed. At the same time, public and private co-operation is a central piece of the MDG project and eradicating gender violence will require the involvement of all sectors of society. In the meantime, it would appear that prevention programmes geared specifically to gender violence in schools seem to share a focus on developing the capabilities of students to construct and practise different options in response to incidents of harassment.

Conclusion

Eliminating gender disparities in primary and secondary education by 2005 was the first credibility test for commitment to both the EFA goals and the MDGs. The international community has failed this test. The next test comes in 2015 when the goal that must be reached is to achieve gender equality in education. To have any realistic hope of doing so, the right to education must be understood to consist of more than a seat in the classroom. It is vital for stakeholders to move beyond issues of access and to resist the temptation to use rights merely rhetorically. Girls can legitimately demand a reconceptualised set of social arrangements, norms, institutions and laws to support the creation of enabling environments that can best ensure their equal enjoyment of the right to education. One element of this must be the freedom to develop capabilities which will allow them to grow into women able to create lives of dignity for themselves. A gender-violent environment can play no part in an equal right to education.

The application of human rights-based approaches that are rooted in effectively protecting the capabilities of the holder of the rights demands governments and the development community to make a paradigm shift. There is a difference between talking about education objectives and speaking of realisation of the right to education (Alston, 2005). If development objectives can be made more human rights aware, then the human rights framework may be better employed to enhance the effectiveness of the EFA and MDG initiatives.

Development projects should further the realisation of human rights projects; human rights standards should guide all development; and development should contribute to the fostering capacities of duty bearers and rights holders. Institutional arrangements for monitoring processes and outcomes for establishing some form of accountability, such as the committees monitoring the international agreements, are indispensable in any human rights context and could prove equally relevant and necessary for increasing the awareness of gender-based violence in schools and the commitment to eradicating it.

Note

1 Although the single-sex schools strategy may alleviate parental anxieties about gender mixing and curb abuses by boys against girls, it may not offer a comprehensive solution to gender violence in schools more generally.

3

Gender violence in schools in the developing world

Fiona Leach

Overview

Until the mid 1990s, gender violence was not a recognised problem in schools in the developing world. Nor indeed were gender issues more broadly, until 1990, when the international community, at its World Conference on Education For All in Thailand, realised that it could not meet its commitment to achieving universal primary education without addressing the urgent issue of why, globally, more girls than boys were out of school. This brought the topic of girls' education to the fore, to be replaced later by a discourse around gender in education. Barriers to girls' participation were perceived at the time as largely external to the school, originating in adverse economic conditions and socio-cultural practices, such as poverty, early marriage of girls, preference for sons, and the use of girls for household labour. As most educational research consisted of quantitative surveys, there was also little appreciation of in-school factors that might deter a child from entering, or continuing in, school. About mid-way through the decade, however, concern over poor and sometimes declining standards of education led to a shift towards examining conditions in school which might undermine participation, and particularly that of girls.

Alongside the emerging concern over girls' under-representation in education in the early 1990s was a move towards understanding education as a human right, a theme explored by Erika George in her chapter, rather than as an economic and/or social investment. The issue of the sexual abuse of girls in schools emerged within this combined set of concerns. This was first covered by a brief report on sexual harassment in schools and universities in a number of African countries (African Rights, 1994). The issue was also raised in a study of girls' academic underachievement in Zimbabwe (Gordon, 1995) and in a World Bank report on girls' education in Sub-Saharan Africa (Odaja and Heneveld, 1995). An early intervention to protect schoolgirls from sexual exploitation in Tanzanian schools included some research into the problem (Mgalla *et al*, 1998). Little more, however, was known about the scale or nature of the problem until several small-scale studies explored the sexual abuse of girls in schools in Africa, eg Human Rights Watch (2001) in South Africa, Rossetti (2001) in Botswana, and Leach and Machakanja (2000) and Shumba (2001) in Zimbabwe. These studies covered secondary school age children, but recent research provides confirmation that sexual abuse is also prevalent among primary age children, eg Wible (2004) in Benin and Burton (2005) in Malawi.

Additional impetus to study gender violence in schools came during the 1990s as part of the response to the AIDS pandemic. As it tightened its grip on Africa, the notably gendered dimension of the disease was revealed. Statistics indicating that girls in the 15-25 age group are most vulnerable to HIV infection (www. unaids.org) has turned attention towards the school both as a site for teaching about HIV prevention and, contradictorily, as a site of sexual violence (Mirembe and Davies, 2001).

Over the last few years, knowledge of this issue within both the academic and development communities has expanded, at least in Sub-Saharan Africa, although research is still limited and usually small scale (see USAID's annotated bibliography of unsafe schools, 2003). Nevertheless, we now have better understanding of which groups of children are most at risk, why gender violence exists, and how it might be addressed. In particular, we have come to understand that girls are not always passive victims of violence, that the circumstances surrounding sexual abuse of schoolchildren are not always clearcut, and that girls are sometimes the perpetrators of gender violence, and boys sometimes the victims.

Defining the problem

Only among the less developed regions in Sub-Saharan Africa has violence in schools been consistently framed in overtly gendered or sexual terms.[1] It is interesting to speculate why. It may be partly due to the AIDS epidemic and also to more relaxed social attitudes towards sex outside marriage than in other parts of the developing world. That research studies on girls' education are funded by international development agencies anxious to close the gender gap, studies which sometimes involve outside researchers and consultants with a feminist orientation, may also have contributed to framing the problem in gender terms.

This is in sharp contrast to Asia and Latin America, where violence in schools is rarely perceived as being rooted in unequal gender relations, and sexual harassment is largely seen as confined to universities (Mirsky, 2003). In Asia, the little research that exists has focused on corporal punishment and has ignored its gender dimension (eg Kim *et al*, 2000; UNICEF, 2001); the chapter from Pakistan in this volume breaks new ground in this respect. In Latin America and the Caribbean, the problem has tended to be seen as gang violence, often linked to the trafficking of guns and drugs (Chevannes, 2004; Abramovy and Rua, 2005). Where violence in and around schools is fuelled by civil or armed conflict, its gendered dimension is often missed too, as the chapters from Nepal and West Africa in this volume show.

Even in the industrialised world, studies of violence in schools have not readily embraced a gender-sensitive framework, as the chapter from Russia reveals. In North America and Europe, student-on-student violence is usually categorised in gender-neutral terms as bullying, intimidation or assault (Stein, 2003). Where distinctions are made between violence perpetrated by or on girls and boys, this tends to be reported in terms of patterns of frequency only – eg boys bully more than girls; girls prefer to use psychological abuse.

This book takes the view that, regardless of terminology and conceptualisation, violence always has a gendered dimension. However, much confusion exists as to how to label it, as already indicated in chapter 1. In the African research, the focus has shifted over time from examining the well defined but narrow area of (sexual) abuse of girls in schools to encompassing school-based gender violence more generally; this includes the gendered dimensions of all forms of peer- and teacher-instigated violence, including corporal punishment (Mirsky, 2003; Dunne *et al*, 2006; Humphreys in this volume). We would expect this wider perspective to include violence targeted at boys, but it rarely does, despite a few surveys capturing some boys reporting being sexually abused (eg Burton, 2005, Rossetti, 2001).

Manifestations of gender violence in schools

It is useful to distinguish between explicit and implicit forms of gender violence in schools. *Explicit* gender violence is overtly sexual in nature and may involve aggressive or unsolicited sexual advances, other forms of sexual harassment which include touching, pinching, groping and verbal abuse – such as 'prostitute', 'slag', 'gay' – and acts of intimidation, assault, forced sex and rape. *Implicit* or symbolic gender violence covers actions which are less visibly and directly gendered, and emanate from everyday school practices which reinforce gender differentiation. These practices may in themselves be violent, like corporal punishment, or they may indirectly encourage violent acts.

Forms of gender violence are not fixed; they evolve to fit different times, circumstances and cultures. So, for example, acid attacks on women and girls in South Asia, eg for snubbing a boy, turning down an offer of marriage, or, as in Afghanistan recently, daring to be a teacher (Reuters, 2002), and jackrolling (gang rape) in South Africa are particularly horrific forms of violence against young women. Some attacks are directed at schoolchildren and some take place on school premises. Gender also interacts in different settings with other social markers such as class, race, caste, ethnicity and religion, to create complex patterns of discrimination. However, underlying context-specific manifestations of gender violence is a common cause: the relative powerlessness of women in patriarchal societies.

Few statistical studies exist to show the scale of the problem. Even where they do, there is confusion over terms, inadequate definition of what constitutes gender violence, sexual harassment etc, and an imprecise and unreliable research methodology – for example, one which ignores the possibility of boys over-reporting and girls under-reporting sexual activity (Leach, 2006). However, in Sub-Saharan Africa studies have now been carried out in at least eight countries, seven of which feature in the USAID 2003 annotated bibliography and the eighth, Benin, is covered by Wible (2004). These reveal a consistent pattern of sexual abuse and/or harassment of girls by male students and teachers. Both girls and boys repeatedly indicated that some teachers in their school abused their position of authority to demand sexual favours from girls, often in exchange for good grades, preferential treatment in class or money.[2] Despite the attention given to cases of teachers' sexual misconduct – and rightly so – the evidence points to older students being the main perpetrators of violence against girls.

Some studies report extremely high levels of sexual harassment and abuse. One by Rossetti (2001) surveyed 560 students in Botswana. It found that 67 per cent, including a few boys, reported being sexually harassed by teachers, and 20 per cent reported having been asked by teachers for sex. Of these, 42 per cent had accepted, mostly because they feared reprisals from the teacher. Other studies report much lower figures: Brown's (2002) survey of 466 primary and secondary students in Ghana, in which 13.5 per cent of the girls and 4.2 per cent of the boys – the ratio of girls to boys in the survey was 1:3 – said they had been a victim of sexual abuse at school. These differences may be due in part to the terminology used, sexual abuse being generally perceived as more serious than sexual harassment. But despite the disparities, when taken together with official figures of reported cases and frequent media coverage in many countries, these studies confirm that sexual harassment and abuse is an endemic problem in schools in much of Sub-Saharan Africa. In other regions of the world, there has been an almost total lack of either quantitative or qualitative research. However, emerging evidence from Asia, Latin America and the Caribbean, including reports submitted to the UN Study on Violence against Children (www.violencestudy.org), suggests that here too it is a common phenomenon.

Why is there gender violence in schools?

Violence in schools cannot be divorced from violence in the home, the community and the workplace. This violence originates in the imbalance in power between males and females, in the gendered hierarchy and separation of tasks and responsibilities, and in socially accepted views of what constitutes masculine and feminine behaviour. The school, alongside the family, is a prime site for the construction of gender identity and gender relations built on socially sanctioned inequalities. The structures and practices which fill the school day with explicit and implicit rules, norms and symbols serve to guide and regulate behaviour. In so doing, they reinforce the unequal gender relations already reproduced in the home, and perpetuate and institutionalise notions of male superiority and dominance (Dunne *et al*, 2006). Examples include: teacher tolerance of boys' domination of classroom space at the expense of girls' participation in lessons, the celebration of masculine competitiveness, the allocation of more public and higher status tasks and responsibilities to male students and teachers and private domestic-related tasks to female students and teachers, the acceptance of bullying and verbal abuse as a natural part of growing up, and teachers' unofficial use of free student labour, especially that of girls. These taken-for-granted, routine practices of schooling all too often teach children that masculinity is associated with aggression, while femininity requires obedience, acquiescence and making oneself attractive to boys (Leach and Machakanja, 2000; Dunne *et al*, 2006). In this way, male violence becomes accepted in adolescent relationships and thus perpetuated in adulthood.

This dominant version of gender relations promoted by the school is almost exclusively framed in terms of a compulsory heterosexuality (Mirembe and Davies, 2001). Males seeking to strengthen their status among their peers may interpret this as the need to show dominance over females, to demonstrate sexual prowess and to compete over girls. This encourages gratuitous acts of sexual harassment, such as boys cornering girls, touching and groping them, or shouting demeaning obscenities, and male teachers directing sexist or derogatory comments at female students or teachers, or making physical contact with girls during lessons, eg touching a girl's breasts while pretending to read her exercise book (Leach and Machakanja, 2000).

The peer culture plays an important role in the gender socialisation process, with both girls and boys policing the boundaries of acceptable gender behaviour. Anybody who is judged to have transgressed may become the target of violent acts, as the chapters here from the UK and USA also reveal. For example, a boy who is perceived to behave in a cowardly or effeminate way, or a girl who does not behave sufficiently modestly or who scorns a boy's advances may be punished by being bullied, victimised or ostracised. There are no in-depth studies of homophobic violence in schools in the developing world, although a recent report by Human Rights Watch and the International Gay and Lesbian Human Rights Commission (HRW and IGLHRC, 2003) highlights its prevalence in schools in several countries in Southern Africa.

Despite the importance attached to discipline by school authorities in the developing world, acts of gender violence often go unreported and unpunished. Students may not report incidents out of fear of victimisation, punishment or ridicule, or because violence is seen as an accepted and inevitable part of school life (Human Rights Watch, 2001; Leach *et al*, 2003; Dunne *et al*, 2006). Even if they do, teachers often consider such incidents as not worthy of reprimand. By tolerating or ignoring violence, however, school authorities are implicitly sanctioning and helping to perpetuate its practice.

In many parts of the world, there are poor levels of accountability in the educational system and a lack of good management and professional commitment, whether because of poor training, low salaries, poor support from the authorities, poverty or other factors. Evidence from Sub-Saharan Africa suggests that teachers who exploit the advantage of their sex and their authority by having sexual relations with students are rarely expelled from the teaching profession, even when they cause pregnancy; at most, an offending teacher will be transferred to another school (Leach *et al*, 2003; Dunne *et al*, 2006). High levels of bureaucracy, apathy among officials, parents' and students' ignorance of how to lodge a complaint, and reluctance to believe students who make allegations are contributory factors. To complicate matters, for economic or cultural reasons not all parents, teachers and girls disapprove of teachers or older men having sexual liaisons with schoolgirls (Leach *et al*, 2003).

Knowledge gaps

Despite the dearth of research beyond Sub-Saharan Africa, it is a mistake to assume that gender violence in schools is a problem specific to that region, or that girls are always the victims. Chapters in this volume, as well as evidence emerging from the country reports submitted to the UN Global Study of Violence Against Children, testify to the fact that gender violence on school premises, including sexual abuse, forced sex and rape, is a global phenomenon, even in the Middle East and South Asia, which have strong religious and cultural traditions of gender segregation. It exists despite – or perhaps because of – communities' efforts to keep males and females separate; it may take subtler forms and so be harder to observe. Research in these countries is urgently needed if children are to be protected from sexual exploitation. Even in Sub-Saharan Africa, where most of the existing research has been conducted, there is a need for more systematic large-scale studies which assess the prevalence of gender violence in schools and which advance our understanding of how and why it happens, and its impact on individuals and on learning outcomes.

Most of the available research documents the sexual abuse of girls but, as noted, there is emerging evidence that boys, female teachers and those who are lesbian or gay may also be targets. In particular, we cannot ignore the strong likelihood that the sexual abuse of boys, whether in heterosexual or homosexual encounters, occurs in school and that widespread homophobia exposes female, as well as male, students and teachers who do not project a socially acceptable heterosexual identity to violence. Boys are also more likely to be a target of sexual abuse in cultural settings where it is risky to molest girls and where any accusation of impropriety towards a woman or girl can bring swift retribution from the community, sometimes even causing riots and deaths.[3] We are also discovering that violence in schools is not an exclusively male preserve; girls may also be perpetrators, as several chapters in this volume testify. None of these dimensions of gender violence have been systematically researched in a school setting.

The research methodology of gathering sensitive data from children in the developing world is also poorly developed (Leach, 2006). Conceptualisation of gender violence remains muddled, resulting in sketchy understanding of what can be done about it. It is hoped that the case studies and interventions discussed in this collection will offer valuable insights and advance our understanding of the issues.

Conclusions

This chapter has provided a brief overview of the issues surrounding gender violence in schools: how the problem has come to international attention, how it manifests itself in different settings, who the perpetrators and the victims are, and why it appears to thrive in school environments. A link can be made between the sexual misconduct of certain teachers, peer violence among students and corporal punishment: one form of violence feeds on another, and through acts of aggression from students and teachers, including corporal punishment, violence becomes a means of formal and informal control and regulation in schools. The tacit acceptance and normalisation of aggressive male behaviour provides the conditions for antagonistic gender relations and further violence (Dunne *et al*, 2006). Sexual advances made by teachers to their students are particularly shocking because of the abuse of trust and power, but the negative impact such incidents have on victims and the dangerous role model they present to male students are also important considerations. A single case in a community may discourage parents from sending their daughters to school (Leach *et al*, 2003).

Concerted efforts are needed at national, international, local and school level to counteract gender violence in schools, involving legislation, policies, curriculum and leadership initiatives, teacher education and the professional development of head teachers. A school ethos that respects every individual's right to education in a safe and supportive environment is crucial. Education authorities need to take vigorous measures to stamp out all forms of violent behaviour, including excessive corporal punishment, and to actively promote constructive adolescent relationships. It is after all the school's mission to teach life skills as well as academic knowledge; this should include supporting adolescents in the development of meaningful and equitable social relations. We are failing our children if we cannot ensure that schools provide the safe haven to which they are entitled.

Notes

1 A few studies of corporal punishment in Africa exist (see the chapter by Sara Humphreys in this volume).

2 Sexual abuse of school children by male teachers is not a recent phenomenon, nor is it unique to Africa or the developing world. Media reports appear from time to time in many parts of the world, including the UK, where sexual relationships between teachers and their students have been illegal since 2000.

3 *The Daily Times* of Pakistan recently reported a Minister of State claiming that sexual abuse by clerics in Koranic schools was widespread (www.dailytimes.co.pk/default.asp?page=story_9-12-04_pg1_6).

PART 2
**CASE STUDIES FROM AROUND
THE WORLD**

4

Cyber-hierarchies:
a new arsenal of weapons for
gendered violence in schools

Shaheen Shariff and Rachel Gouin

Introduction

New technologies in the last five years have created enormous policy dilemmas for schools in North America. Cyber-bullying, for example, is an insidious and covert form of emerging social cruelty among adolescents. Cyber-space magnifies the harmful psychological effects of bullying among classmates, to include an infinite audience that preys on victims through online harassment and abuse. Its arsenal of weapons includes electronic mediums such as cell-phones, web-logs and websites, online chat rooms, MUD rooms (multi-user domains, where individuals take on different characters) and Xangas (online personal profiles where adolescents create lists of people they dislike).

Cyber-bullying is one form of cyber-violence, a term which we use to define a range of unacceptable and violent online behaviour. Other forms include but are not limited to: flaming (angry, rude, vulgar messages about a person sent to an online group or via email or other text messaging), online harassment (repeated offensive messages via email, chat rooms or web-logs), websites designed to harass specific students, defamation (harmful, untrue or cruel statements or photos about a person, or people, sent or posted online), cyber-stalking (harassment that includes threats of harm or excessive intimidation), masquerading (pretending to be someone else online and sending or posting material that makes the person you are pretending to be look bad), and ex-

clusion (cruelly excluding, ostracising, shunning, barring or ignoring someone from an online group).

This chapter explores forms of violence that can be perpetuated online, challenging the *real* versus *virtual* dichotomy. We consider the violence schoolgirls
may experience – and engage in – during social interactions in virtual space,
and discuss its repercussions in the physical school setting. Drawing on
human rights jurisprudence on sexual harassment, we contend that educational policy-makers and teachers can foster inclusive school environments
through education, critical assessment of systemic barriers and modelling
respectful discourse in physical school settings and virtual space.

Real or virtual violence?

Bullying in the physical school setting is tangible and easily identified as *real*
violence. But threats or harassment in cyber-space, and their impact, are less
tangible and therefore more difficult to establish as actually harmful.

Bullying and cyber-bullying have characteristics in common: both are unwanted, deliberate, persistent and relentless. Both create a power imbalance
between perpetrator and victim. Victims are blamed and isolated to justify
socially excluding them. This renders them vulnerable to continued abuse, re-
peating the cycle of violence. Research in Europe by Salmivalli *et al* (1996)
found that in cases of general bullying, 30 per cent of bystanders support perpetrators and that bystander participation increases as the bullying persists.
What begins in the physical school setting as friendly banter can transform
into verbal bullying that continues in cyber-space.

The difference in cyber-space is that hundreds of perpetrators can participate,
and class-mates who may not bully at school hide behind technology to inflict
relentless abuse. Power imbalances between victims and perpetrators are
intensified by the extent of the infinite audience available to aggressors. Moreover, most cyber-bullying is anonymous, as screen names shield perpetrator
identity. Racist, sexist or homophobic statements and compromising sexual
photographs can be altered and sent to limitless audiences. For example,
thirteen-year-old Taylor Hern was added to a 'list of Hos' (whores) on a peer's
Xanga. The perpetrator (Immsgirlsgot2hell) left Taylor a message: 'Go to my
Xanga, bitch' (Chu, 2005:42). Chu explains that incidents of online bullying are
like cockroaches in that for every one that is reported, many others go un-
recorded because they are difficult to track.

Cyber-bullying in virtual space has an impact on learning in the physical
school environment. Fear of unknown perpetrators among classmates and

bullying that continues at school can be psychologically devastating for victims and socially detrimental to all students, distracting them from their schoolwork. It creates unwelcome physical school environments where equal opportunities to learn are greatly reduced (Shariff, 2004).

Disturbingly, studies on cyber-bullying confirm it is a growing trend. For example, Li (2005) surveyed 177 middle school students in Alberta, Canada, and reported that 23 per cent were bullied by email, 35 per cent in chat rooms, 32 per cent by known school-mates and 41 per cent by anonymous perpetrators. Similarly, a survey of 3,700 American adolescents found that 18 per cent had experienced cyber-bullying (Chu, 2005).

There is no escape for victims, who feel trapped knowing that an infinite audience can view their humiliation. Ybarra and Mitchell (2004) of John Hopkins School of Public Health, in Baltimore, USA, found that 51 per cent of students bullied at school are more likely to harass others in online environments, as are young people who experience high levels of depression or trauma in real life. Such young people also seek out close online relations to fill voids in their lives, further increasing their vulnerability to online exploitation.

Gendered hierarchies in cyber-space

Although both genders engage in cyber-bullying, there are differences. Cyber-bullying involves substantial sexual harassment, usually by boys. Barak (2005) identifies online sexual harassment as including offensive sexual messages or remarks, gender humiliating comments, offensive nicknames and online identities (wetpussy and xlargetool, for instance), unwanted pornographic content and pop-up windows, uninvited communication of sexual desires or intentions, and sexual coercion. Adolescents are influenced by hormones and by socialisation. They also face intersecting and interlocking systemic barriers of oppression based on race, gender, sexual orientation, (dis)abilities, cultural hegemony, androcentrism and Eurocentrism. While females are more likely targets of cyber-violence because of their location in the hierarchy of power, adolescent girls are also active instigators of cyber-bullying. Chu (2005) reports that out of 3,700 American adolescents, seven per cent of the girls confessed to online bullying compared to ten per cent of the boys.

Barak (2005) reports a study in which 19 per cent of American girls surveyed experienced at least one online sexual solicitation per year. Although homophobia directed at males is also prevalent on the internet (Harmon, 2004), the larger gender pattern of online violence against females cannot be overlooked. It is perpetrated downward along a power hierarchy, reinforcing societal gender inequalities. The psychological effects on victims are very real. Glaser and Kahn (2005) observe that online misogynist comments, unwanted sexual harassment and coercion were rated as more threatening than face-to-face threats or harassment. Herring (1999) points out that the internet is itself organised hierarchically, with certain operators and administrators – usually middle class, white, English-speaking males – empowered to make policy de-cisions that affect thousands of users. As internet regulation is largely male dominated, this presents a social and historical context in which the playing field is far from level, even when it might appear to be. Since women do not control the resources to ensure equal outcomes, it is hardly surprising that such outcomes are not achieved, despite the efforts of outspoken and persis-tent female participants (Herring, 1999).

Power is often used to limit female participation by presenting narrow, un-desirable choices: conform or be kicked out and vilified (Herring, 1999). The virtual world is eerily similar to the physical world, forcing reconsideration of the dichotomy. This division is further challenged when we consider cyber-violence and its real and powerful consequences in school environments. If, as Ybarra and Michell (2004) found, young people know who they are attack-ing (84% of those surveyed knew their targets), the physical school environ-ment becomes very frightening for victims who share classes, hallways and schoolyards with their aggressors. Yet schools have done little to tackle the issue of cyber-bullying. This may be due to a policy vacuum and the absence of clear direction from the courts.

The policy vacuum and confusing court decisions

So far courts have provided little guidance. In Quebec, Canada, a $160,000 law suit was filed in 2003 by Ghyzlain Raza, who was made famous when a video-tape showing him emulating Star Wars characters was posted on the internet; but this case was settled out of court. David Knight, an Ontario university student, filed action against his school board for failing to protect him when a website set up by his school-mates labelled him as a paedophile and homo-sexual.

American courts are largely out of touch with the real needs of threat assess-ment and what schools should do to stop cyber-violence. Judicial rulings on internet threats under constitutional, civil and criminal law suggest that US judges fail to recognise the vital difference between a threat and its perceived impact. They ignore the complex and multi-faceted factors, including power hierarchies, that influence social relationships in school contexts, whether physical or virtual. For example, a Wisconsin lower court dismissed charges in the case of A.S., a thirteen-year-old boy who threatened to shoot his assistant principal and rape his teacher, and to hang a police officer by her wrists, break her arms and legs, and then kill her. The court found A.S.'s comments to be 'an extreme level of adolescent trash talking, which produced no immediate disorder' (Redfield, 2003: 709). The Appeal Court however, reversed the decision, observing that the teacher and police officer were both frightened by the threats.

In another American case involving a teenage boy, a lower court ruled that a sexually charged essay about killing his female teacher with a machete did not constitute a true threat because the boy, Douglas D., had no record of violence. Earlier American decisions support this position, considering cyber-threats to be fictional and finding perpetrators innocent of wrongdoing. In *United States of America, Plaintiff v. Jake Baker* (Wallace,1999), James Baker posted a story to the newsgroup alt.sex.stories, graphically describing the rape and torture of a university classmate. He also communicated his plans via email to a friend for actually carrying out the rape. The district court disallowed the claim holding that, because no possibility of physical rape existed on the internet, there was no claim for harassment. In *The People vs. B.F. Jones* (cited in Wallace, 1999) a judge ruled as follows:

> It is not the policy of the law to punish those unsuccessful threats which it is not presumed would terrify ordinary persons excessively; and there is so much opportunity for magnifying undefined menaces that probably as much mischief would be caused by letting them be prosecuted as by refraining from it. (quoted in Wallace, 1999:228)

These cases confirm a judicial reluctance to open the floodgates to litigation involving cyber-space. Servance (2003) and Redfield (2003) both report that when asked to rule on cyber-bullying, American courts rely on three US landmark precedents dating back to 1969: *Tinker, Fraser* and *Hazelwood*.[1] They report that despite the ubiquitous character of the internet, courts consistently separate on-campus student expression from online (off-campus) threats and harassment. The *Tinker* standard established that unless student speech 'materially or substantially disrupts learning' it should be allowed. The court in *Fraser* held that the speech would have to interfere with the 'educational mission' of the school to justify intervention. Finally, the *Hazelwood* decision facilitates school intervention if the threats are made using school property. So if a student is suspected of sending harassing comments via email from a school computer, the school can monitor or discipline his/her actions. For example, in *Beussink v. Woodland R-IV School District*[2] a student created a website that harshly criticised his school in vulgar terms and linked it to the school's website. A classmate accessed the website from a school computer and reported him. The court supported the school's decision to suspend Beussink.[3]

Servance (2003) believes that by restricting the cyber-bullying analysis to traditional on-campus/off-campus considerations, the courts provide themselves with greater flexibility to manoeuvre the deference they give schools. This stance helps them avoid engaging in litigation relating to cyber-space. Thus, while courts have recognised the lack of borders in cyber-space,[4] many judges ignore this fact. In doing so, argues Servance, they perpetuate power hierarchies that begin in the physical world and become magnified in cyber-space.

The confusing messages and narrow judicial construction of on-campus and off-campus rights of student expression leaves a serious policy vacuum for schools. Not only are traditional responses to bullying ineffective, they are inapplicable to cyber-space because of its complexities.

The courts have not completely let women down, however. Because so much cyber-bullying is gender based, we found that although courts are reluctant to define cyber-threats as real violence, the jurisprudence on sexual harassment in Canada and the United States acknowledges its *effects* on women, and an institutional responsibility to address them. In this regard, established human rights law is instructive and highly relevant to developing policy standards for schools.

Consider a landmark Canadian decision involving sexual harassment by a co-worker. This case can be extended to the cyber-bullying context *Robichaud v. Canada* (Treasury Board).[5] The Supreme Court of Canada ruled that institutions are responsible for providing safe environments for employees even when the sexual harassment by a co-worker occurs outside the workplace. School officials often maintain they are not responsible for harassment among students that occurs outside school hours on home computers. Emphasising the effects of the harassment in the work environment, the high court confirmed that if a victim has to face perpetrator(s) within the institution, its leaders are responsible for correcting the problem through effective educational means.

Subsequently, in a controversial landmark decision in 1998 in *Davis v. Munroe*[6], the American Supreme Court broke their tradition of avoiding opening the floodgates. Grade 5 student Lashonda Davis was sexually harassed persistently. The teachers and principal were informed but did nothing. Lashonda's grades dropped and her health deteriorated. The Supreme Court ruled that the school created a 'deliberately dangerous environment' that was preventing 'equal opportunities for learning'. It can be argued that cyber-bullying creates a similarly dangerous environment for victims in the physical school setting, especially because they do not usually know the identities of their perpetrators. This uncertainty creates fear and distraction, preventing victims from equal opportunities to learn.

The effect of electronic verbal harassment is evidenced by the suicide of Canadian teenager, Dawn Marie Wesley. Hearing a classmate say the words 'You're f.....g dead!' on the phone convinced her that real harm would come to her. Her perpetrator was convicted of criminal harassment. The court ruled that harm *perceived* by the victim amounts to *actual* harm (Shariff, 2004).

A wall of defence

Victims allege that schools put up a wall of defence or deny responsibility when approached for support. Shariff's (2004) review of emerging litigation disclosed that school administrators often assumed that victims invited the abuse, that parents exaggerated the problem, and that written anti-bullying policies were sufficient to protect victims.

Although many schools implement inclusive and well-intentioned educational policies to address bullying, research suggests that some perpetuate hierarchies of power (Giroux, 2003). Glover *et al* (1998) discovered that teachers respond to physical bullying but tacitly condone verbal harassment – even though 90 per cent of children they interviewed experienced verbal bullying. This may be influenced by fear of litigation and ignorance about the complexities of cyber-bullying. Such fear is driven by confusion about the legal boundaries of their responsibilities to students, which are becoming increasingly blurred as technology and diversity change the landscape of North American schools. When school administrators are confronted with un-precedented problems, some react like the courts. They ignore the root causes and redefine the problem to fit traditional policy approaches. When this does not work, it is easier to blame victims for inviting the problem, do nothing and hope the problem disappears.

Moreover, developmental psychology perspectives dominate scholarship on bullying (Craig and Hymel, 2005) and, although these perspectives are important to understand young people's behaviours, we need to remember children do not operate in a vacuum. They attend educational institutions where systemic power pervades every aspect of school life, marginalising some students. Hence there is a crucial need to re-conceptualise research and educational practice away from fixing the kids to fixing the system. It is important to take a critical look at what schools are doing to protect and educate students in every aspect of school life, physical *and* virtual. Cyber-bullying ought to be considered within the larger context of adult and media-perpetuated violence and the lived realities of young people who turn to online abuse. This means discarding current zero-tolerance policies on violence in schools. Giroux (2003) suggests such policies ignore root problems, overlook systemic barriers that marginalise students and perpetuate a cycle of cyber-victimisation. They sustain Eurocentric and androcentric hegemony and ignore intersecting and interlocking influences of race, gender, sexual orientation and (dis)ability. They rarely produce effective results and they criminalise young people, unnecessarily burdening the criminal justice system (*ibid*).

While parents undeniably have an obligation to monitor their children's activities on the internet, schools have a pivotal educational role in societal progress. Educators, like parents, must adapt to a rapidly evolving technological society and guide children to become civic-minded citizens. The fact that schools use technology to deliver curriculum and assign homework makes it imperative that it is not misused. It is essential that schools and courts recognise and establish standards with respect to internet and cell phone use, and define acceptable boundaries for students' social relationships in cyberspace. The valuable role of educators in fostering inclusive school environments and socially responsible discourse must be acknowledged, encouraged and supported through scholarship, legal and policy guidelines, teacher preparation programmes and professional development.

Conclusion and implications

We have drawn attention to challenges facing schools as a result of new technologies. Our preliminary findings reveal that cyber-bullying is prevalent among adolescents. Of significant concern is the high level of gendered cyberharassment. And the research suggests that schools are reluctant to carry out their responsibilities to protect and educate students in socially responsible and inclusive electronic discourse. It is imperative that schools re-conceptualise bullying and work towards creating equal opportunities for students to learn – a guaranteed constitutional right – in all educational settings, physical and virtual.

The law is unclear regarding unprecedented issues of bullying in cyber-space, but existing jurisprudence on sexual harassment is applicable to institutional responsibilities. Sexual harassment cases support the argument for institutional responsibility, whether harassment occurs in or outside the learning environment, and that perceived threats amount to real harm. These and similar court rulings begin to establish relevant standards for schools, providing guidelines which must be incorporated into teacher preparation and professional development programmes.[7]

Schools make use of technology and are responsible for protecting students who use it. If virtual realities are difficult to deal with in schools, then actual hierarchies of power in the classroom ought to be tackled to reduce cyber-violence. The guidelines we introduce here begin the process. To succeed, schools need to lower their walls of defence, remove blanket zero-tolerance policies and meet the challenges of cyber-bullying through non-arbitrary and inclusive educational practices.

Notes

1 *Tinker v. Des Moines Independent Community School District*, 393 U.S. 503 (1969); *Bethel School District No. 403 et al. v. Fraser, a minor, et al.*, 478 U.S. 675 (1986); *Hazelwood School District v. Kuhlmeier.* 484 U.S. 260 (1988).

2 *Beussink,* 30 F. Supp. 2d. at 1177 – 78. 1180.

3 See also *New Jersey v. T.L.O.*, 469 U.S. 325 (1985) as cited in the Students Guide to Internet Law (last viewed October 2004) at http://splc.org/legalresearch.asp?id=22.

4 In *Reno v. ACLU,* 521 .S. 844, 851 (1997) the court noted 'Cyberspace – located in no particular geographical location but available to anyone, anywhere in the world, with access to the internet'. See also Erik G. Swenson, Comment. Redefining Community Standards in Light of the Geographic Limitlessness of the Internet: A Critique of *United States v. Thomas*, 83 Minn. L. Rev. 855, 876-78 (1998).

5 *Robichaud v. Canada (Treasury Board)* [1987] 2 SCR.

6 *Davis v. Munroe*, 526 U.S. 629 (1999).

7 Shariff is currently the Principal Investigator on a research project funded by the Social Sciences and Humanities Research Council to study emerging academic scholarship on internet harassment. In the meantime, professional development and teacher preparation courses ought to introduce an improved understanding of substantive human rights principles and help educators recognise the congruence of such principles with educational theories of social justice, leadership and ethics of care (Shariff, 2004).

5

Gendered harassment in North America: recognising homophobia and heterosexism among students

Elizabeth Meyer

What is gendered harassment?

Gendered harassment describes any behaviour that serves to police and reinforce the traditional gender roles of heterosexual masculinity and femininity, such as bullying, name-calling, social ostracism and acts of violence. It takes various forms: homophobic harassment, heterosexual harassment and harassment for gender non-conformity. All constitute gendered harassment because the motives behind them are linked to the norm setting and public performance of traditional (heterosexual) gender roles (Larkin, 1994; Smith, 1998; Renold, 2004). Physical harassment is the most obvious form acknowledged and addressed in schools, but verbal harassment is more prevalent and often ignored even though it has been found to be equally damaging to students (Hoover and Juul, 1993; Bochenek and Brown, 2001; Williams *et al*, 2005). While I do not wish to ignore the painful experiences that victims of physical harassment and violence endure, this chapter focuses on how to understand and reduce the emotional violence caused by the much more insidious and often ignored issue of verbal and psychological gendered harassment.

I began investigating this problem as a result of my experiences as a high school teacher in the USA. I observed the hostile climate that existed for gay, lesbian, bisexual and transgender (glbt) students and learned that this prevailed across the country (Kosciw, 2001; California Safe Schools Coalition,

43

2004). As I investigated further, I learned that, although glbt youth are commonly targeted for harassment, they are not the only ones suffering because of the homophobic and heterosexist climate of the school. Nor is the problem limited to the United States; studies conducted in the UK (Duncan, 1999; Renold, 2004), Australia (Martino and Pallotta-Chiarolli, 2003) and Canada[1] (Smith, 1998; Williams *et al*, 2005) show that such a climate is widespread throughout western industrialised nations. Any student whose behaviour is perceived to be different in some way can be isolated and harassed using anti-gay insults, and any student who wishes to assert and defend his/her place in the social order of the school must engage in heterosexualised behaviours that include the forms of gendered harassment outlined below (Smith, 1998; Duncan, 1999; Renold, 2004). Homophobia is also a global issue, and its impact on the lives of individuals living in countries where homosexuality is still considered criminal are more obvious than in North America, where it has gone underground. It still has negative impacts on the lives of students; they are just more insidious and harder to identify.

In Kosciw's nationwide survey of glbt high school students in the USA, 91 per cent reported frequently hearing homophobic remarks in school (Kosciw, 2001). What is disturbing is not only this prevalence, but the lack of intervention by educators to tackle the problem (Kosciw, 2001; California Safe Schools Coalition, 2004). Educators are not stopping such harassment, and this teaches students that schools as institutions, and their home communities, condone it. By showing students that homophobic and heterosexual harassment is tolerated, schools support the discriminatory attitudes that cause it to happen in the first place. As democratic institutions in a diverse and changing world, schools must teach to transform such damaging behaviours and work to reduce their impact on students. In so doing, we will be able to more effectively work to reduce prejudice and violence in schools.

It is useful to distinguish between homophobic harassment, harassment for gender non-conformity and heterosexual harassment. Clearly understanding these behaviours is an essential first step to creating more effective interventions in schools. This chapter draws mainly on North American studies and ends with specific suggestions for how schools can reduce the incidence of gendered harassment.

Homophobic harassment
Homophobic harassment is any sort of behaviour that reinforces negative attitudes towards gay, lesbian and bisexual people. The most common form is verbal in nature and includes the use of anti-gay language as an insult (for

example, 'that's so gay', 'don't be such a fag') and anti-gay jokes and behaviours that make fun of gays and lesbians (such as affecting the speech and walk of a stereotypically effeminate gay man to get a laugh). The prevalence of such activity in schools allows homophobic attitudes to develop and grow. As George Smith observes in his article on Canadian schools, *The Ideology of 'FAG'*:

> The local practices of the ideology of 'fag' are never penalised or publicly condemned. Explicitly homophobic ridicule in sports contexts goes un-remarked. Effective toleration of the ideology of 'fag' among students and teachers condemns gay students to the isolation of 'passing' or ostracism and sometimes to a life of hell in school. (1998: 332)

In Kosciw's study, 84 per cent of glbt youth reported being verbally harassed in school and 64.3 per cent reported feeling unsafe (Kosciw, 2001). Students reported less harassment and increased feelings of safety when a teacher intervened 'sometimes or often' to stop name-calling (California Safe Schools Coalition, 2004).

In addition to the risks faced by glbt youth in schools in a homophobic climate, students perceived to be different or gender non-conforming are also frequent targets. Harassment of those acting outside the narrow boundaries that define gender norms is often linked with homophobia, but it is important to investigate this area separately so as not to further confuse existing misconceptions of gender expression and sexual orientation.

Harassment for gender non-conformity

Harassment for gender non-conforming behaviours is under-researched. But it is important to understand it. According to the California Safe Schools study, 27 per cent of all students in California schools reported being harassed for gender non-conformity (2004). Thanks to the prevailing stereotypes in society of gay men and lesbians who defy traditional gender norms, anyone whose behaviour transgresses popular notions of masculinity and femininity are often perceived to be gay themselves. This is a dangerous assumption as it mistakenly conflates the concepts of sexual orientation and gender identity. There is not enough room here fully to explore the notions of sex, gender identity and sexual orientation, but each of these identities is distinct and may be expressed in a variety of ways.[2] For example, although many biological females (sex) identify themselves as heterosexual (sexual orientation) women (gender identity), it does not mean that this is the only possible combination of identities. By perpetuating these misconceptions, schools reinforce traditional notions of heterosexual masculinity and femininity that reduce educational opportunities and school safety for all students.

Research has demonstrated that the more rigid the adherence to traditional sex roles, the more negative are the attitudes and violent behaviours towards homosexuals (Bufkin, 1999; Whitley, 2001). The negative threat of being *perceived* as a sissy or a tomboy, particularly after puberty, and the homophobic backlash, limits the students' participation in school life. Martino and Pallotta-Chiarolli (2003: 52) describe an interview with a student who was harassed for his interest in art: 'On his way to school one morning a group of boys at the back of the bus from one of the local high schools started calling him names. Initially, he was targeted as an 'art boy' because he was carrying an art file. But the harassment escalated and they began calling him 'fag boy''. Here the students used an anti-gay slur to harass a student for his gender non-conforming behaviour.

North American society's ongoing misogyny and negative attitudes towards femininity makes gender performance harder on boys than girls. North American schools generally place higher value on strength, competitiveness, aggressiveness and being tough: qualities widely seen as masculine. Whereas being creative, caring, good at school and quiet are often considered feminine qualities and are viewed by many as signs of weakness – particularly in boys. It is not surprising then that bullying studies report that

> typical victims are described as physically weak, and they tended to be timid, anxious, sensitive and shy … In contrast, bullies were physically strong, aggressive, and impulsive, and had a strong need to dominate others.

> It seems difficult to effectively intervene to stop bullying when the qualities that bullies embody are the ones that are most valued by many and demonstrate a form of power that is generally esteemed in a male-centered, or patriarchal, society. The pressure on boys to conform to traditional notions of masculinity is great and the risk of being perceived as gay is an effective threat in policing the boundaries of acceptable behaviour. (Hoover and Juul, 1993: 26)

In order to assert their masculinity, many boys act out heterosexualised behaviours as this is seen as the best way to avoid being called gay. One gay student told me:

> You know when all the guys would be making girl jokes, you'd have to go along with them, as much as you tried not to, you still had to chuckle here and there to not raise suspicion … very frequently, jokingly, some students would say to other students – when they didn't necessarily conform to all the jokes and the way of thinking of women students – they'd say, 'what, you're not gay, are you?'. (Smith, 1998: 324)

This example provides an opportunity to discuss the third area of gendered harassment: heterosexual harassment.

Heterosexual harassment

As with the other two forms, verbal harassment is the most common form of sexual harassment reported by students. Male students often assert their masculinity by degrading their female peers with terms such as 'bitch', 'baby', 'chick', and 'fucking broad' (Larkin 1994: 268). Males also perform their masculinity by sexually objectifying their female peers and discussing the sexual acts they would like to engage in – or have already engaged in (Larkin, 1994; Stein, 1995; Duncan, 1999). Such discourse is seldom stopped by teachers, and some even participate in it. Students report that male teachers might 'laugh along with the guys' (Larkin, 1994) or add to the comments and even blame the victim (Stein, 1995).

Although sexual harassment is by definition sexual in nature, I identify it as a form of gendered harassment in light of theoretical understanding of its roots: the public performance of traditional heterosexual gender roles. It is important to acknowledge that men too can be victims of sexual harassment, mostly from other men and usually homophobic. Young women may also be implicated in such behaviours, most commonly directing verbal insults towards other females when competing for boyfriends, or between friendship groups (Duncan, 1999).

Sexual harassment describes how patriarchy works: how men continue to assert their power over women. Though this is a useful place to begin, we need to stretch our understanding to include how highly valued forms of traditionally masculine behaviours are allowed to be performed and privileged over the devalued forms of traditional notions of femininity. Traditional gender roles are established within a heterosexual matrix (Butler, 1990) that allows for only a single dominant form of compulsory heterosexuality (Rich, 1993). As long as these attitudes and behaviours go unchallenged, schools will continue to be sites where young people are harassed out of an education. To stop this, we must learn effective strategies for intervention that will help educators create schools where such discriminatory attitudes and behaviours are replaced by inclusive notions of respect, equality and understanding.

Successful strategies for intervention

While physical acts of violence are difficult for schools to ignore, daily acts of psychological violence persist and affect students' lives in ways that many teachers and administrators fail to acknowledge. The entire culture of the school is implicated, so if these behaviours are to change, the culture must shift. This means that all stakeholders in the community must be involved in the process: students, families, teachers, administrators and school board personnel. The tone must be set by the leadership, but everyone has to be engaged in changing the culture of the institution. In an attempt to identify what steps can be taken at each level, recommendations **are** provided for: 1) administrators and school boards, 2) teachers and support staff, 3) students and 4) parents and community members.

Administrators and school boards

At the school leadership level, changes are needed in three areas to create a positive and supportive school environment: in policy, in education, and in resources and support. Without institutional support, the isolated efforts of overworked teachers, frustrated parents and targeted young people will have only a small, short-term impact on the experiences of the students. What is required is systemic change.

Policy: A whole school policy that outlines clear, definite guidelines on actions against bullying, including response protocols and implementation strategies, is essential (Sharp and Smith 1991). The language must be clear and consistent. Specific protection against harassment, violence and discrimination based on sexual orientation and gender expression (Goldstein *et al*, 2005) must be stated.

Education: A policy cannot be effective unless those expected to enforce it know their obligations, and community members are informed of the changes. The new policy should be discussed in staff meetings, a law expert should present a workshop on definitions of harassment and the school's duty in preventing it, study circles of staff should examine the policy and discuss implementation strategies, information needs to be published in school newsletters and brochures distributed that give information about the new policy.

Resources and support: The school district needs to allocate resources – time, money and materials – to ensure that the school climate changes. Instead of hiring a one-off invited speaker, some school boards have created full-time positions to ensure that expertise and knowledge is readily available to support efforts in the schools. On the Toronto District School Board, several posts were created that were integral to the success of their programmes: human sexuality programme workers, equity department instructional leaders and student programme workers (Goldstein *et al*, 2005: 28). The institutional support offered by these various initiatives gives credibility and value to the daily efforts of individuals on the front line.

Teachers and support staff

Teachers and support staff such as bus drivers, cafeteria personnel and lunch-room monitors have most opportunity to observe and intervene in incidents of gendered harassment in schools. The teachers and support staff will need to develop their understanding of the policy, the tools for successful intervention, and curricular materials and programmes to support a more inclusive school climate. Accordingly, teachers and support staff will need to attend workshops and courses, and take some responsibility for their own professional development, while also participating in the educational opportunities provided by the school administration. Many resources are available, some of which are listed at the end of this chapter. Curricular interventions can address some of the underlying issues of gendered harassment, for example:

- A campaign against name-calling that includes education about what words mean and why certain insults are inappropriate and discriminatory
- Inclusion in the curriculum of contributions by gays, lesbians, bisexuals and transgendered people to history, art, science, literature, politics, and sport
- Providing inclusive and diverse information about sex, gender and sexual orientation in biology, health and sex education classes
- Conducting critical media literacy activities that analyse gender stereotypes and heterosexism in popular culture.

Although teachers and support staff have a significant impact on school climate, a true shift in culture and behaviour cannot take place without the participation of the student body.

Students

Students are the largest percentage of a school community and they set the trend for what is valued in school. Without the support and investment of student leaders, student-only spaces like locker areas, washrooms, and areas in playgrounds and athletics fields will still be sites for incidents of harassment. Schools that successfully engage student leaders such as athletics team captains, student council members and peer mediators, can have broader and deeper influence on the lives of all students in a school. This can be done through summer leadership retreats, student discussion groups or weekend workshops that educate students about gendered harassment and solicit their help and support in challenging it and other forms of bias in the school. And all students should be informed of the school's policies on harassment and discrimination. A code of conduct should be posted in each classroom, students should sign a behaviour contract, and home-room discussions should be held about the policy, what it means and how it might affect them.

Families and community members

Finally, the input and influence of families and community members is important. Parents' associations and other community groups should be encouraged to become actively involved in developing the school policy on gendered harassment and the educational strategies required. By developing partnerships with the community early on, schools can anticipate any resistance or potential backlash and work through them before they grow into negative publicity for the school. By building strong ties with parent groups and other community organisations, schools can create a lasting network that will potentially expand their efforts to reduce gender bias in the community at large.

Conclusion

Bullying and sexual harassment intervention programmes are becoming more common in North American schools, but many leave the attitudes and prejudices that reinforce the behaviours they are seeking to change intact. Although this chapter relates to North American schools, the theories of how masculinity and femininity are expressed in schools are relevant in a variety of cultural contexts. Western industrialised nations have the resources and political climate to support educational interventions like those recommended here, and other like-minded educators and activists may wish to consider the implications of homophobia and heterosexism in their own contexts. By examining these related issues together and explicitly addressing the underlying homophobia and heterosexism, we will be able to create more integrated approaches to addressing violence in schools and help educators understand how to change the culture of their schools by transforming sexist and homophobic practices, policies and curricula.

Notes

1 My current dissertation research is investigating this problem in secondary schools in Quebec and exploring how educators respond to acts of sexual and homophobic harassment.

2 See Butler (1990) for a more in-depth explanation of these concepts and their differences.

6

Girls' violence and aggression against other girls: femininity and bullying in UK schools

Neil Duncan

Background

In recent years, public concern – and research – about violence in British schools has tended to concentrate on bullying. Much of this research is arguably gender-blind: even where it differentiates between boys' and girls' experiences of bullying, it does so in an over-simplified way, as 'boys bully physically, girls bully verbally' (Bjorkqvist *et al*, 1991). Whilst there is some evidence that this actually is a general pattern (Crick and Grotpeter, 1995), there are many examples of alternative patterns, as boys and girls are not monolithic groups. Within the gender boundaries are a variety of individuals whose attitudes and behaviours are informed by factors such as personality, age, culture and much else.

In addition to these complexities, which have not been explored in any depth in bullying theory, lies the problem of intra and inter-gender bullying. This chapter explores some examples of girl-on-girl violence in school bullying, but it does so in the context of male presence and male influence. Pioneering male researchers of bullying have tended to overlook girls' violence in favour of male aggression, due to lack of interest or evidence (Olweus, 1993 *inter alia*). In contrast female researchers, particularly earlier feminists looking at the harassment of schoolgirls, have played down the agency in girls' aggression and violence in a defensive way, with some denial of individual girls' responsibility for their behaviour (Jones, 1985).

Work by Owens *et al* (2000) shows the importance of feminine forms of aggression in girls of school age. This is mainly verbal and emotional, described in the literature as 'relational' or 'indirect' aggression. In a similar way, the more destructive aspects of girls' friendships have been popularised by books that reach beyond the academic domain (Simmons, 2002; Blanco, 2003). Traditional bullying research tends to treat this form of bullying as less significant since it involves less physical violence. However, Owens *et al* (ibid) have demonstrated that the effects of destructive behaviours, such as spreading rumours and social exclusion from friendship groups, are considered by the targets to be just as serious as physical attack.

Recent research

More recent research by feminists from outside the field of bullying has shown that females have a long history of violence against one another (Chesney-Lind and Shelden, 2004). In most cases, this behaviour is described as exceptional and is separated from mainstream concerns by its pathologisation of individual girls, and its masculinisation or institutionalisation (Heidensohn, 1985). Other evidence, however, indicates that violence between females has been far more part of everyday life than the studies suggest. Work in the UK by Burman *et al* (2000) shows that many girls inhabit a community and a culture in which physical violence is common, and not seen as masculinised or pathologised. This vitally important study paints a detailed picture of the girls' construction of violence, and their navigation through it, as highly normalised and integral to social relations.

In most studies of violence and aggression that have a gendered sensibility, there is a tendency to focus on either boys or girls rather than to examine the interplay between them. My own study on sexual bullying (Duncan, 1999) sought to address that omission by examining the conflicts between pupils that had a gender component, collecting data from both boys and girls that explored girl-on-girl, boy-on-boy, girl-on-boy and boy-on-girl aggression. Findings from that study indicated that a great deal of what passes for ordinary bullying is underscored by a sexual motive, specifically a struggle for a desired sexual identity. Later work (Duncan, 2002; Duncan, in press) concentrates more specifically on the unique features of girls' relationships with other girls in high school, albeit set within a male-dominated society.

Girls, popularity and bullying

In the seven schools that collaborated with my studies in the north-west and midland conurbations of England, I interviewed two sets of young women aged 15. Individual interviews were carried out with girls who had been victims of violence from other girls, and I held group interviews with un-involved girls, to ascertain the tenor of the school culture vis-à-vis female bullying. These young women were not known to be directly implicated in violence, either as perpetrators or victims, or even in the non-physical forms of bullying. Instead, they were selected by their schools' pastoral staff as being well-adjusted, intelligent mainstream pupils who were street-wise and knew what was going on in their school community. They were recruited in small friendship groups to increase their confidence in speaking about issues relevant to girls' friendships and fallings out.

The group interviews followed two prompts: a *vignette* about a girl transfer-ring schools because she had fallen out with her friends, and a set of cards listing items associated with making a girl popular or unpopular. These were discussed and ranked to form a Q sort, which later underwent factor analysis (McKeown and Thomas, 1988). The girls quickly conflated the concept of be-ing popular with being socially powerful and aggressive, and linked the characteristics of a popular girl with the ability to be successful with boys.

The three items most strongly associated with popularity were: being popular with boys, being loud and being fashionable. The three most strongly asso-ciated with being unpopular were being a lesbian, having special needs and being quiet. The rationale for these choices was discussed at length in the interviews, and was clearly centred on pleasing, or appealing to, boys. The second tier of choices for popularity related more obviously to social and physical power, and included: being tough, coming from a family with a tough reputation and getting involved in fights with other girls.

Interestingly, the Q-items chosen as neutral – so not influencing popularity or power significantly – included the two descriptors of race. During the dis-cussions, these items were regularly queried by girls who could not see why they were included in the study or how they could affect popularity (Duncan, 2004). Whilst this study does not claim generalisability, this finding seems at odds with other studies where female aggression has been identified as racialised (Jiwani, 2005), indicating the need for further study.

The girls spoke eloquently about the compulsory competitive heterosexuality that prevailed in their high schools. They described a subculture where popu-larity was synonymous with social power, which was founded upon two com-petences: management of an exclusive group of girls who spent much of their school time organising and controlling the social affairs of other girls, and the ability and willingness to attack girls physically when it served their political interests. Such a complex set of alliances that restricts alternatives, backed up with physical coercion, is referred to as hegemony.

The fact that girls beating other girls was considered fairly rare did not diminish the girls' fear of physical violence:

ND*:   Is there a lot of fights between girls?

Lucy: A few...

ND: How often, every day, week, month?

Grace: Every month...

MA: So when was the last fight between girls?

Lucy: About a couple of weeks ago?

Mandy: Yeah, a couple of weeks ago. There was a fight with two lads and two girls at the same time.

The very rarity of the beatings points to their effectiveness in controlling the girls' social life, as they internalised those controls to self-police their activities.

A consistent finding throughout my research is that girls and boys will give different initial explanations for conflict. When asked what boys fight about, both boys and girls tend to give varied responses, such as who supports which football team, who is better at particular skills, or who is the better fighter (Duncan, 1999). When the question is changed to what girls fight about, the answer is almost invariably 'boys'. It seems that in schools in England at least, the most contested social capital amongst high school girls is being desired by males. Girls' preoccupation with pleasing boys is a critical problem for feminists and their allies that goes far beyond the issue of girl-on-girl school violence.

Identity and aggressive competitiveness

There appear to be two distinct categories of target for girls' violence. The first is *the other*, depicted as all that a popular girl should not be: fat, lesbian, disabled, unattractive, unfashionable and friendless. One victim was Laura Rhodes (BBC, 2004), who was tormented for supposedly being a lesbian and eventually overdosed in a suicide pact with her friend. The second category is *the traitor*, a popular or potentially popular girl who has somehow transgressed the controlling clique's codes, perhaps by becoming too popular her-

*   Initials stand for adult interviewers, either myself or one of the female collaborators present at every interview

self, as did Hayley Yarwood. She was 'humiliated and beaten by two other girls' for being too beautiful and successful (*Manchester Evening News*, 2001). Bright's (2005) academic paper on one family's experience captures the paradoxical power and subtlety of the destruction of an erstwhile friend's self-esteem.

The girls who do not wish to be constantly engaged in competition to win a desired male face the threat of exclusion and 'othering' by the vociferous and powerful majority, who quickly seize on their difference and use it to strengthen their own positions. It is only by creating the Other that one can create the Self, and frigidity, unattractiveness (however locally defined) and lesbianism are the negative side of dominant heteronormativity.

The canon of abusive names used by girls against girls testifies to the sexualised nature of the value system: slag, whore, bitch, lezzie, tart and so on. Many sexually derogatory terms may have originated from, and still be used by, boys as a controlling strategy, but they are certainly common currency for girls too. Apart from the obvious disputes over girls stealing other girls' boyfriends, the interviews revealed a much more pervasive and complex set of practices. The most popular girls could prevent relationships from forming between other young people if they thought they could be indirectly damaging, or if the girls simply wanted to emphasise their power over the peer group:

Claire:	...if (a popular boy) likes a girl, (the popular girl) turns round and says you can't go out with her, she's ugly, or something like that...
Donna:	...the boy'll back down...
Claire:	... the boy'll back down...
Emma:	Or, because if they *do* go out, the popular girls will pick on that girl and make sure they get stick for it.
ND:	Even though that boy and girl are 'in lurve'?
Fiona, Emma, Claire: Yeah!	
Donna:	They won't leave them alone.
ND:	And the boys'll go along with that...(responding to unheard comment) ... because they are a bunch of...?
Emma:	Yeah! Cos they are scared that they'll...
ND:	Because the boys are...?
Emma:	They are...they're scared...

ND: Really, they are scared of the most popular girls?

Emma, Claire, Beth: Yeah!

This scenario echoed a case study in Duncan (1999), in which a popular boy had spurned the advances of a popular girl, but was attracted to another girl from outside the popular clique. That girl was threatened and then beaten up for the temerity of succeeding where the popular girl had failed. According to the girls, some boys were unaware of these protocols but others were actively engaged in manipulating them for their own entertainment and aggrandisement.

Feminine aggressive dominance

The outcomes of physical conflict for the losers were profound. As well as being beaten up and having their relationships ruined, they often felt so humiliated and so afraid of the continued gloating and harassment that they considered changing school. Group interviews with uninvolved girls confirmed that transferring to another school was considered an extreme measure, as it held the threat of starting anew and the risk of not being accepted into an existing social network. The interviewees were clear that the social factors were more important than disruption to academic progress.

A significant difference between how boys and girls managed violence was that girls tended to do a lot more preparatory talking. A girl fight or attack was usually well advertised. Allegiances were confirmed and altered by the girls in the social group and close friends of the protagonists canvassed for support. Though boys also spread rumours that a fight would be taking place, girls appeared to organise their fights to maximise social power across the group. Boys' conflicts could be described as episodic but girls' conflicts were chronic:

Carrie: Yeah, lads'll not talk about it and just fight – then it's finished, but girls string it out...

Beth: ... and it goes on for a long time ... the argument does.

Carrie: Every time they see her, they'll say something.

Whereas the vast number of boys were neutral bystanders, girls who took no part in the actual fight still tended to be emotionally involved and would talk heatedly about the event long before, and long after, it had taken place.

A good deal of feminist literature on girls' friendships notes the intimacy that girls have compared with the more disconnected and independent boys. Though this is a generalisation, since there are many boys who have, or would like to have, close relationships, as well as girls who are less reliant on strong feminine bonds, it is a perception commonly expressed in interviews with young people. As a result, girls are expected to belong to a friendship group. However, these can develop individuals who have exceptionally strong skills in managing relationships, not only between themselves and other girls but more remotely between two or more other girls. Girls' groups are often managed in a more anti-social and destructive way than boys' groups. (Hey, 1997)

The intimacy of such groups often generated powerful feelings that could not be contained peaceably within the group but spilt out. Usually one girl would be expelled from the group and thus socially excluded.

Abbie: ...and they all look up to this one leader of the group, like, say if one girl falls out with another girl, then they all fall out with that one girl, or most of them do, and they all go to the one most popular girl. Then, say if some of the girls really like the other one, they'll still stick with the other most popular girl because they know that they'll get picked on by their group.

Beth: But sometimes if they fall out, they'll try and stick with the others but then if the popular one finds out they'll try and stop them, so the popular one will fall out with them too.

In some cases the excluded girl tried to regain her place by contesting the leading girl's dominance or setting up a rival clique in which the social capital was intimate secret knowledge of the girls in her original group. Physical violence, or certainly the threat of it, was a common outcome, but the derogation of reputation as a loser of physical fights meant loss of popularity too. The pain of this was perpetuated by name-calling long after the event. Rather bizarrely in this case, the common abusive term for a male homosexual was applied to weaker girls:

MP: (Referring to a Q-card item) So would a girl that gets involved in fights with other girls be popular? (...)

Nikki: It depends if they won or not, if they won the battle...

MP: I see ... if they won they'd be popular and if they lost...

Nikki: If they lost they'd call you a poof and that...

ND: What? They'd call you a poof?

Nikki: A poof, a wimp...

ND: They'd call a *girl* a poof?

Nikki: Yeah, a girl, a boy, anyone...

In solo interviews with the casualties of this aggression, truancy, family disruption, self-harm and eating disorders emerged as associated difficulties. But these mostly went unnoticed because most pupils fleeing harassment avoided making complaints as they did not believe the school system would support them. Those who felt compelled to leave preferred to keep a low profile on entry to their new school.

Television and feminine aggression

There is considerable evidence that female aggression is not a new problem, nor that it has worsened in the recent past (Steffensmeier, *et al*, 2005). Its higher profile might be due to the increase in television programmes that promote an aggressively competitive female sexuality, such as *Wife Swap* or *The Jerry Springer Show*, where females are manipulated to express sexualised aggression. So are males, but as they have long been seen as competitive and predatory, the representations of aggressive female sexuality are more noteworthy.

Significantly, Syvertsen's (2001) study of dating game show participants in several countries found that women were usually the ones who set up people, male and female, to go on TV and compete for a date:

> ...production staff indicate that it is quite common that mothers apply on behalf of their sons, and sisters, aunts, grandmothers and even ex-wives play a part in encouraging their relatives to go through with a 'blind date'. (p324)

Clear parallels exist between these televised examples of female practices and the modes and drivers of girl-on-girl violence in high schools. Whether one precedes or reflects the other is impossible to say, but their co-existence might well reinforce the legitimacy of both.

Conclusion

This chapter has explored some of the issues relevant to girls' bullying in schools. The way the phenomenon is constructed will greatly influence professionals' responses to it: if the traditional over-simplification of 'boys hit, girls talk' goes unchallenged, the problem cannot be solved. Professionals and others concerned about safe schooling need to focus on the cultural background of the pupils at local level and engage with their concerns. Pupils need support to develop awareness of the cycle of oppressive sexism that underlies so much peer conflict in schools and to opt for pro-social ways of acquiring self-esteem.

Ironically, televised spats between women because of sexual rivalry and competing forms of femininity offer opportunities for dialogue with pupils. Using the same basic techniques of data collection described above, Q sorts and discussion groups can be modified to provide a safe, moderated forum in Personal Social and Health Education lessons for discussing the dominant and competing forms of femininity and masculinity.

7

Corporal punishment as gendered practice

Sara Humphreys

Introduction

Corporal punishment[1] is still an integral, albeit contested, feature of school life in many countries. Much has been written about it worldwide – though more in the home than in school – highlighting its detrimental physical, psychological and emotional effects (Newell 1989; Holdstock, 1990; UNICEF, 2001). And there is mounting evidence suggesting that while corporal punishment might sometimes succeed as a short-term deterrent, it does little to induce more long-term behavioural reform and frequently leads to escalations of violence (Holdstock, 1990; Hart, 2005). As the old adage goes, violence breeds violence. In schools excessive corporal punishment has been linked to student truancy and drop-out (Human Rights Watch (HRW), 1999; Kuleana, 1999; UNICEF, 2001).

Although it has proven both fairly harmful and ineffective, the practice persists in schools in many countries even where it has been banned, including South Africa (Morrell, 2001), China (Kim *et al*, 2000) and Zambia (Soneson, 2005). Moreover, in countries where corporal punishment is still sanctioned, widespread abuse has been documented, which can result in serious physical injury and even maiming or death. See, for example, Chianu (2000) in Nigeria, HRW (1999) in Kenya, or Kuleana, (1999) in Tanzania.

Links have been made between corporal punishment and sexuality. First, and most obviously, caning has been associated with sexual gratification (Holdstock, 1990), as evidenced in pornography (Gibson, 1978, cited in Newell, 1989). Second, in recent studies of children and violence in Africa, disciplining of older girls – generally verbally more than physically – is used to regulate their perceived sexual activities (Soneson and Smith, 2005; Naker, 2005). In addition, male teachers have been accused of beating or threatening to beat female students for rejecting their sexual advances (Kuleana, 1999; Dunne *et al*, 2005; Naker, 2005) or of hitting older boys because they are viewed as rivals for the attention of older girls (Pattman and Chege, 2003; Naker, 2005). Naker's Uganda study also suggests that older female students may be punished in ways that leave no lasting physical marks, so that their value in terms of bride-price is not diminished.

Despite such explicit connections with sexuality, corporal punishment has usually been interpreted and contested within gender-neutral discourses of culture, including religion, or human rights. The recent UNESCO publication (Hart, 2005) reviewing studies and practices of corporal punishment world-wide scarcely mentions gender, except to state that both at home and at school boys are generally physically punished more often than girls. Further, although a number of the predominantly quantitative studies on corporal punishment differentiate between the female and male respondents, they rarely specify the gender of the teacher. More importantly, they have not considered corporal punishment as a gendered practice, nor made the connection between it and gendered institutional identities. Female and male teachers and students generally relate to and experience corporal punishment differently and may be punished for different offences. As the instances of policing female sexuality suggest, this is gendered practice. And corporal punishment is central to the way teachers, male and female, act out masculine authority. I contend therefore that a gender perspective is vital when devising effective strategies to eradicate corporal punishment.

In his 1998 study of sixteen government schools in the Durban area of South Africa, Robert Morrell (2001) is unusual in specifically analysing corporal punishment within a theory of gender relations, exploring the connection between school beatings and local but racially divergent constructions of masculinity. He concluded that constructions of masculinity are significant in perpetuating the practice of corporal punishment and that this in turn is likely to promote some of the qualities of these masculinities. This chapter builds on his insights but explores further the complex interplay of physical punishment with both masculinities and femininities and the implications for attempts at its elimination.

Corporal punishment as gendered practice

The following exploration of corporal punishment as gendered practice draws primarily on an ethnographic study of four junior secondary schools in the south-eastern part of Botswana (two rural, one peri-urban and one urban) with additional references to other studies in Sub-Saharan Africa.

The study was carried out in two periods of field work in 2000 and 2001 (Humphreys, 2005). Data comprised 63 lesson observations from eight classes, 35 semi-structured interviews with the twelve participating teachers (six female, six male) and four head teachers (three male, one female) as well as 23 same-gender focus groups with students from the classes observed[2] (eleven female, twelve male). Although the research focus was mainly on gender relations and classroom discourse, issues surrounding the threat or practice of corporal punishment and, to a lesser extent, verbal reprimands emerged as crucial determinants of classroom behaviour and as inhibitors of learning.

In Botswana corporal punishment is still legal. It can be ordered as a punishment by the judiciary in both customary and magistrates' courts (www.gov.bw, n.d.) and it can be applied in schools, following certain procedures. The Education Act regulations (1978) are different for primary and secondary schools and for girls and boys. These differences offer insights into corporal punishment as gendered practice. In both primary and secondary schools caning can be carried out by the head teacher or 'a teacher or boarding master or matron or parent to whom authority to administer corporal punishment has been delegated', but 'no male teacher except the headmaster [sic] shall inflict corporal punishment upon a female pupil'. In primary schools girls – unlike boys – may not be beaten on the buttocks but only on the backs of the calves or the palm of the hand.

In forbidding male teachers to hit female students, the Botswana regulations would seem to be underpinned by a notion of gender based on perceived biological difference, according to which *all* boys are conceived as physically stronger than *all* girls, irrespective of age, and all male teachers as physically superior to female teachers. Alternatively, or perhaps additionally, there is implicit recognition that corporal punishment is 'sexually dangerous' (Gibson 1978, cited in Newell, 1989) within a framework of heterosexuality and that the act of beating girls might tempt predatory male teachers – but not the head master [sic], who is presumed to be beyond such temptation – to use corporal punishment as a pretext for sexual harassment or abuse. This fear was substantiated by two groups of female students in the study: one group reported that a male teacher fondled their buttocks before beating them and the other complained of a male teacher pinching their breasts as punishment. Research in Tanzania (Kuleana, 1999) and Zimbabwe (Leach and Machakanja, 2000) has reported similar findings.

Teachers' views on corporal punishment

All the teachers I talked to about corporal punishment, formally or informally, endorsed its use to some degree, although all the male teachers interviewed were more in favour than the female teachers and more convinced of its effectiveness. This was probably because male teachers generally encountered greater compliance whereas, according to a number of students and teachers, some male students, particularly older ones, refused to be beaten by some female teachers. This was also found in Dunne *et al*'s (2005) study in Botswana and Ghana and Morrell's (2001) in South Africa.

The teachers generally agreed that there were gender differences in the way that female and male teachers disciplined students and that they meted out punishment differently to girls and to boys. When asked about disciplining in general, the teachers adopted the discourse of equal opportunities, saying that they tried to treat girls and boys the same and that this was how it should be. But once the discussion moved on to more specific questions about discipline, teachers acknowledged that boys were punished more heavily than girls. As one female teacher put it: 'We tend to lessen the punishment with the girls but with the boys you just do whatever you want to do. You just hammer them.' She and several other teachers readily accepted, however, that this inconsistency was unfair and that it caused resentment among some boys, as noted in other studies in Botswana (Pattman and Chege, 2003; Dunne *et al*, 2005).

Most teachers justified disciplining boys more harshly. They argued that boys' behaviour was generally worse than that of girls and therefore boys got punished more often and with greater physical force. However, several teachers acknowledged that sometimes they automatically assumed that a boy was to blame for an offence since this was usually the case. Their other main justification was that boys were inherently more 'playful', 'stubborn' or 'troublesome'. They ascribed these characteristics to socialisation in the home, where male authority was more valued, and to culture, which they saw as immutable and based on biological difference: 'It's their nature,' or 'That's how boys are'. A couple of teachers blamed adolescence and the need for boys to prove their manhood by rebelling against authority and enduring pain (Morrell, 2001; Pattman and Chege, 2003). Some female teachers therefore reportedly took male students to male teachers to be beaten – as also noted by

Dunne *et al* (2005). In a personal communication, Dunne suggested that female teachers were thus safeguarding their femininity.

Most teachers agreed that female teachers used verbal reprimands more than male teachers, again in line with Dunne *et al*. Unlike the female teachers, some of the male teachers considered the reprimands to be 'abusive', 'rude' and 'unacceptable' and occasionally blamed female teachers for provoking boys by using such language. The explanation, according to several teachers (both female and male) was located firmly in biology. As one male teacher put it: 'Females are naturally like that. They are very good at talking – at using such words – such abusive words. Generally, females can talk too much.' A group of female students from the same school expressed the same view. Female physical inferiority was also offered as an explanation for higher levels of verbal reprimands: 'Women are not strong enough on corporal punishment,' one male teacher said. Another explained: 'Because they [boys] fear me as a male I can threaten them 'I will kick you' but the female teachers can not. And I can cause more pain with lashes.'

What is interesting in this discourse of punishment is the implicit recognition by both the women and the men that corporal punishment is the norm, whose success, they believed, depended to a large extent on 'masculine' physical strength, against which verbal reprimands (and other punishments) must be measured. Verbal reprimands, the 'feminine' way of disciplining, are second best, used when corporal punishment, the masculine way, has failed or when female teachers feel unable to administer it. This implied discourse ran counter to the official discourse of counselling[3] first and beating as a last resort.

Students' views on corporal punishment

Most students did not oppose corporal punishment *per se* but objected to its abuse or its perceived inequitable application. The exception was in the most rural school, where more students were against caning and one group of boys was adamant that it should be abolished whatever the circumstances, perhaps because of the high levels of abuse that had been recorded in the school. As in some of the other studies in Sub-Saharan Africa (eg HRW, 1999; Kuleana, 1999), the students' main objections to corporal punishment were that it was allegedly often administered for what they considered to be trivial or non-deliberate offences and, secondly, that it was carried out in ways that were prohibited.

Most of the girls interviewed did not endorse physical punishment, on account of the propensity for its abuse and its general inability to correct behaviour. The boys, however, generally found it acceptable provided that it was administered fairly and for what they considered to be 'reasonable' offences, which they felt was often not the case. In particular, several groups complained that teachers often assumed automatically that boys were guilty and punished them. This gender discrimination, the boys claimed, was the main reason why they misbehaved with female teachers. The general perception in almost all the male group interviews was that boys were beaten more often and more harshly, sometimes 'without good reason' whereas teachers were more lenient towards the girls.

Explanations for gender-differentiated student attitudes towards corporal punishment were based on essentialised gender stereotypes held by both female and male students – and teachers – for example, girls' natural shyness and fear, and concern for their physical appearance as opposed to boys' toughness and bravery in standing up to teachers' injustices.

> Most girls are not as brave as boys. They are scared of being beaten and if we work with boys, they may say: 'We won't work. After all a stick is not a death penalty'. *Female student at peri-urban school*

> Girls are afraid of being beaten and they don't want their beauty to be messed around with. Guys they just say: 'After all the stick does not kill'. [Laughter] *Male student at peri-urban school*

> Some boys it's not that they are not afraid of the stick. They just want to prove the point that they are brave. *Male student at peri-urban school*

Thus corporal punishment also invited 'competition in machismo' (Connell, 1989) among some boys. This same competition extended itself to male teachers as some of the rural boys thought male teachers in the school wanted to hit boys because they wanted 'to fight other men', a case of older men putting young pretenders in their place. Male on male corporal punishment has been interpreted in studies elsewhere as part of the toughening up process, a necessary rite of passage from male adolescence to manhood (Morrell, 2001; UNICEF, 2001; Pattman and Chege, 2003), thus underlining its importance in the construction of dominant school masculinities.

The frequently mentioned resistance of some male students to being beaten by female teachers in particular can be read as a questioning of the legitimacy of women to discipline young adult men (Morrell, *ibid*), as well as an objection to unfair punishment. In the most rural school, one group of boys explained that female teachers also struggled to impose their authority because they were considered to be 'minors' in the village and young female teachers in particular were therefore viewed as their 'age mates'.

There was far less agreement, however, on the gender differences between teachers in terms of who was keener to use the stick, although, like the teachers, most agreed that the men could beat harder since they were physically stronger, and that female teachers were more likely to use verbal reprimands or abuse.

Attitudes to teacher-student gender relations in relation to disciplining were complex. When asked to list qualities of a good teacher, many students inclined towards stereotypically feminine qualities of patience, kindness and understanding, preferring someone 'who didn't use the stick'. Yet at the same time, they emphasised that boys only respected male teachers, primarily because they feared them on account of their perceived physical superiority, demonstrable above all in their application of corporal punishment. As one boy put it: 'They [some male students] don't respect female teachers because they don't have strong muscles to beat them so they respect those with strong muscles'. When this apparent contradiction was pointed out, the students in that group maintained that a balance was possible. In essence, they wanted teachers to be both 'strict' and 'understanding,' able to discipline (male) students who misbehaved while remaining sensitive to student needs. However, interviews and classroom observations indicated that it was more difficult for female teachers to strike this balance when many students, especially boys, clearly had a deficit view of female teachers from the outset. This was exacerbated when male students felt the need to assert their own masculinity by challenging female authority – sometimes with justification.

Addressing these complexities, a group of girls in the urban school argued that although the male teachers 'are the ones that like beating', they did not need to prove their authority or force respect by applying corporal punishment, because boys usually feared them and so behaved better. On the other hand, the girls argued that female teachers felt pressured by boys to prove their authority, yet when they did so, especially if they were inconsistent, as a number of male students implied, they paradoxically lost the very institutional authority they were trying to establish. Male teachers, it seemed, could 'gain respect' and maintain control and authority by *not* exerting physical power. However, I argue that the basis for that authority resided in the belief held by both male and female students that men had both greater capacity and legitimacy to exercise that power if necessary since it conformed to dominant understandings of masculine superiority.

The gendered effects of corporal punishment

The examples described here illustrate how teacher-student interactions surrounding the practice of corporal punishment were informed by stereotypical beliefs about gender, institutional and other identities. These oppositional gender binaries were further entrenched through these interactions.

The antagonistic and hierarchical gendered institutional identities were not only negotiated, contested and constructed by the teacher and students directly involved in a particular disciplinary incident but also by the gender, institutional and age-related dynamics of classmates and school members who witnessed it. Thus, as noted in other studies (eg Dunne *et al*, 2005; Soneson and Smith, 2005), humiliating punishment and verbal abuse in front of peers was often considered worse than a beating as it could be a greater threat to their status.

The more obvious effects of corporal punishment included increased student anxiety, fear or resentment in class. Girls, in particular, remained silent, and were mistakenly dubbed 'lazy' or 'shy' by some teachers, and so did some boys. Other boys absconded or refused to co-operate in female teachers' classes, eg by talking off topic, cracking jokes, playing with matches, disobeying orders. Other studies have also found that excessive physical punishment, generally of boys, can prompt truancy (Dunne *et al*, 2005) and/or feelings of aggression (Naker, 2005).

More positively, there were girls and boys who rejected corporal punishment outright as a way to change behaviour. Several boys readily admitted to feeling afraid and recognised the negative effect of corporal punishment on their ability to concentrate. Similarly some girls ignored harassment by male students or teachers and spoke up in class. Such contestations of the gender hierarchy constitute important indications of the potential for change.

Ways forward

I maintain that corporal punishment is not simply a human rights issue, concerned with adults safeguarding children's rights: it is a gendered practice and inseparable from issues concerning gendered institutional identities. So before we can eliminate it, we need to understand it in relation to dominant female and male teacher and student identities and power relations in all their complexity. These operate within the accepted gender hierarchy in schools, which they in turn help to sustain, where aggressive, competitive masculinities are valued most. This has implications for the generic strategies proposed to eliminate corporal punishment and for the non-violent alternatives promoted (see, for example, Hart, 2005, and the Save the Children studies cited in this chapter). These include: ensuring democratic decision-making in schools and involving students in establishing rules and regulations, such as through student councils and class charters; encouraging positive reinforcement to guide students towards self-discipline; educating teachers on non-violent approaches to disciplining students; encouraging restorative justice practices; and conducting public awareness campaigns.

All are useful strategies. But they have been couched in genderless human rights terms whereas they need to start from a gender perspective. Further, the precise forms they take should be context specific and negotiated among local actors. Students and teachers, and members of the wider community, need first to be given opportunities to reflect on their own gendered identities in relation to beating students, perhaps through discussion groups, or drama and role-play. Such activities should not focus on corporal punishment in isolation since it is interlinked with a whole system of physical and symbolic gender violence which exists not only between students and teachers but also among students, institutionalised through the prefect system and occurring informally through bullying and harassment. Although there is clearly a need to outlaw corporal punishment and to monitor it more closely where it is still permitted, the success of any attempt to eliminate the practice is likely to depend on a fundamental reconceptualisation of what it means to be a female or male teacher or student, and on working towards broadening the range of masculine and feminine identities available in schools.

Notes

1 'Corporal punishment' is defined differently in the various studies mentioned in this chapter, sometimes including physical labour or enduring physical discomfort, such as being made to stand out in the sun or to assume degrading postures.

2 Some interviews were conducted in English, the medium of instruction, and some in Setswana with an interpreter.

3 Although 'counselling' in practice sometimes consisted of verbal abuse.

4 The first two quotations have been translated from Setswana.

8

'The usual evil': gender violence in Russian schools

Olga Zdravomyslova and Irina Gorshkova

S ince the late 1980s, new concepts and issues have begun to influence Russian life. While some have been easily accepted, others have not been accepted as subjects for reflection, writing or discussion. Gender is one such issue. It has become particularly obvious in recent years that Russian society is extremely wary of the findings of studies in gender even when they are conducted by Russian researchers – a peculiar reflection of the spirit of the current Putin era, with its drive to marry the value of individual success in private life with a neo-conservative ideology in the public sphere. Russia is increasingly rejecting feminism; the bestseller of 2005 was Aleksandr Nikonov's book *The End of Feminism: What is the Difference between a Woman and a Human Being?* Presented at the Moscow International Book Exhibition, the book was met with lively public interest.

At the same time female researchers and activists from women's organisations and the media have continued to introduce gender issues into the public discourse. The public is slow to embrace this, and there are periodic departures and failures because the decades of silence mean there is almost no language for discussing gender issues, and a strong prejudice against public discussions. So gender violence is difficult to investigate and is largely closed to debate.

The beginning of research into school violence in Russia

Violence is widely perceived by Russians as cruel and brutal oppression, characterised by physical and moral abuse. It is usually associated with criminal offences or arbitrary practices by authorities. It is within this frame-work that the concept of violence is used by liberal public figures and human rights activists. The common perception and usage of the word 'violence' certainly influences public opinion on gender violence. Analysis of this phenomenon has won it the right to exist only in sociological studies of the Russian family and in the activities of crisis centres.

A few years ago shocking figures on domestic violence were published for the first time, identifying it as one of the most acute problems in Russian families today (Gorshkova and Shurygina, 2004). There are reasons to believe that, in the 1990s, Russian citizens started to feel less safe in the family. This affected women, children and teenagers above all (Yenikopov, 2003; Zdravomyslova, 2003). Worrying questions such as: What is happening in the family? How and why is cruelty generated in relationships among closely connected people? started to emerge in Russian society. In the 1990s, the problem of domestic violence was finally recognised and efforts were made to investigate and discuss it. But the research remains marginal and is seldom the subject of wide public debate.

Gender-based violence is difficult to recognise: the words 'power' and 'violence' are rarely used to describe family relationships: in marriage, between parents and children, relatives, acquaintances, etc. This is certainly true of gender violence in school, which is virtually unexplored. Only a few questionnaire surveys have been carried out, together with a few interviews with the staff of crisis centres and with experts – who point out that the problem of school violence generally is becoming acute (Mertsalova, 2004; Safonova, 2005). The findings of research conducted in the Perm Region by the Center of Civil Education and Human Rights in 2004 at all levels of schooling, for example, suggest that one out of five teachers is aware of incidents of violence by teachers against pupils, and only 39 per cent of schoolchildren reported that they had never experienced violence from teaching staff (*Tsentr grazh-danskogo obrazovaniia i prav cheloveka*, 2005).

A well known survey conducted in 2000-2001 in schools of the Murmansk Region (D'yachenko, 2002) revealed a clear tendency: the number of girls bullied by boys is two to three times higher than the proportion of boys bullied by boys. Although both figures tend to drop towards high school (senior secondary school), the situation does not change radically. Already in primary school children say that 'when boys bully girls, they show in this way their force and power,' while girls bully boys to 'take revenge' on them for these acts. Remarkably, teachers usually turn a blind eye to these blatant incidents.

Researchers describe gender violence in school as stemming from authoritarian family upbringing and from experiences of domestic violence, whether between parents or experienced personally, which are projected onto relationships with classmates. Thus, even the small-scale and fragmentary evidence to date has revealed that gender violence is widespread and deeply entrenched in Russian schools. Some argue that a hidden civil war between boys and girls exists in school groups (D'yachenko, 2002).

Gender violence in Russian schools: findings of a qualitative study

Gender violence in schools is a practice that includes the following: firstly, powerful peer pressure among pupils, and, secondly, powerful teacher pressure on pupils, which *compels* boys and girls to follow certain models of being a 'real man' and a 'real woman' and to construct particular views of adolescent masculinity and femininity. From this point of view, gender violence is a component of bullying, an important part of boys learning to be men, as well as girls learning to be nice, obedient and attractive to men.

As a way to respond to the perceived gaps in this area, we conducted our own research in October and November 2005, based on focus-group discussions, interviews and essay writing, to try to uncover the situation in schools. We proceeded from the assumption that within all qualitative research there is the need to define a problem which is hidden but deeply traumatising. We decided to work with first year university students, who would still have memories of school life but had already left it behind and might be expected to have recovered from any traumatising experiences at school. We also thought they might offer their views more freely than if they were still in school. In total, 40 first-year students aged between 18 and 20 from several Moscow-based institutions of higher learning took part. They were asked to describe the psychological, physical and sexual pressures in pupil-pupil and teacher-pupil relationships that they recalled from their own school experiences. As we show, their stories suggest that school violence is observed, experienced, directed at and suffered by pupils throughout their school years both from other pupils and from teachers.

Violence in pupil-pupil relationships

A few typical patterns could be identified from the stories told by our respondents.

Violence against outsiders or outcasts

This refers to situations where the entire class or most of the pupils join forces against one person. As one student described it: 'They find losers to pick on and start bullying them all the time, they are driven into the corner, ignored and left out'. Often this is viewed as something 'quite natural'. Boys, we were told, run higher risks of finding themselves in this role. Moreover, the accounts of boys who were picked on as outsiders reveal that the humiliation of a boy is characterised by physical bullying more usually than with girls. Many of these young outsiders eventually break down and move to another school.

The following extracts from essays and interviews are telling:

> A quite humble girl from a low-income family was always jeered at by our classmates, who were children of well-off parents. Caustic jokes were aimed at her looks and attire. Each day was a torture for her. Finally, in the 7th Grade she moved to another school. (female student)

> When I was in the 5th Grade, everyone was bullying me, because I was a small fat boy, and my spectacles were big. I was very upset. (male student)

> A boy from our class was the youngest child in a large family and had developmental delay. Everyone was humiliating him, making unpleasant jokes of every kind, aimed at him and his family. (female student)

According to the students, the main reasons for being singled out as an outsider include:

– unorthodox appearance – being overweight was the most widespread problem for both sexes, and being short was a problem for boys

– insufficient support from the family – eg coming from a single parent or large family, or having disabled parents, or parents on a low-income

– clothes which indicate the family's low-income status

– physical or mental disability

– unsociability, aloofness, or quiet behaviour

– ethnic origin – belonging to non-Slavic ethnic groups, such as Caucasian or Jewish

– good academic performance – very able pupils were called names or their personal belongings such as pens, pencils and pencil-cases were damaged

Violence by a group or a leader against the rest of the class

In secondary schools a leader or a group – usually of poorly performing pupils – often emerges among boys, who try to impose their ways on the rest of the class, primarily building power relations within the group. As one boy explained in an interview:

> In high school a group of big shots segregated itself from the class – two boys and three girls. The rest of the class tried to stay closer to them and copy everything they did. Once they hurt someone, the entire class started to bully that student.

Although girls are sometimes part of powerful forces in the class, as this extract shows, they usually find themselves among those who are oppressed. This ultimately compels them to accept the balance of power being established.

Violence used in interpersonal relationships

Such situations emerge in various combinations: among boys, among girls and between a boy and a girl, as the following essay extracts illustrate:

> Two boys quarrelled all the time: one of them was bright; another boy was strong. The strong boy always harassed the bright one; the bright boy lost his nerve and they had fights – to be more precise, the strong boy beat the bright one. (male student)

> I was beaten by a girl for having repositioned her bag. It was a hurtful experience and a morally distressing one because that incident was consequently long remembered by all the classmates. (female student)

Pupils: growing up and gender violence

The stories supplied by our respondents confirm the findings of other Russian studies which revealed changes in gender violence in relationships between schoolchildren as they move from primary to secondary and high schools and into adulthood. During the first three grades of primary school, physical violence (kicking, punching and pulling braids), name-calling (offensive nicknames and rude language) and actions against personal property (damage to belongings, stealing, extortion of money and playing with other pupils' possessions without permission) are prevalent. It happens both within homogeneous groups (more often among boys) and between groups (more often against girls). Some girls do get into fights with boys on an equal footing and even initiate fights but this is rather exceptional. Girls are more often targets of attacks and use force in response. For example, an adolescent girl recounted in her essay an incident of a boy being beaten by a group, after he had long been attacking the girls, one at a time, with impunity.

In secondary schools, displays of force and actions against personal property remain the main forms of bullying, supplemented by verbal abuse with sexist overtones. Although an intensive sorting out of relationships takes place in homogeneous groups, in particular, building up a hierarchy within groups of boys, the animosity displayed by boys towards girls persists. It suggests that in the struggle for a place in the general hierarchy, some boys try to assert themselves through humiliating girls – displaying their power over them. Meanwhile, the readiness of girls to offer physical resistance to boys is lower than in primary school.

In high school girls become targets of sexualised bullying. Many adolescent girls associate the final years in school with obscene verbal abuse, sexual innuendo, questions, jokes and unsolicited physical contact. As one girl put it: 'Some boys do not keep their hands to themselves; their arms become too 'long''. Meanwhile, the adolescent boys start to classify girls according to how easy they are. And they almost never question the legitimacy of their harassment.

> Once during a lesson a male student started to openly harass a girl, trying to sexually touch and kiss her. He responded to her resistance with verbal abuses and threats. No-one came to her help – everyone was afraid of the guy. Even the teacher pretended he did not see anything. (female student in a focus group discussion)

Certainly the most typical incidents are sexual assaults by adolescent boys, though it does not preclude the opposite scenario – when girls rule the roost in the classroom and impose their ways, putting boys in a subordinate position. Girls who dominate in the class usually gossip and spread rumours – 'smear campaigns' – against boys as well as girls.

In the high schools, respondents reported some decline in the general aggressiveness. This seems linked to the fact that pupils are busy preparing to continue their education in institutions of higher learning; quite often classes are re-organised depending on the focus of further education. However, boys might continue to directly abuse their physical power. Boys' rudeness towards girls is widespread, linked to their inability to find correct ways to show their attraction to girls.

Teachers' power and gender violence
Soviet schools employed an authoritarian style in both teaching and relationships between teacher and pupils. The teaching staff was predominantly female, the profession becoming heavily feminised during the Soviet years,

and this persists today. Thus, when children and teenagers develop their patterns of behaviour within a hierarchy during their school years, the main figure of power is usually a woman. Male teachers are often pushed out to the periphery of the school hierarchy to teach secondary disciplines like Physical Education or Handicrafts and rarely high status subjects such as History and Mathematics. So one aspect of gender in teacher-pupil relations makes itself known from the moment girls and boys cross the school threshold.

Our research suggests that many teachers do not appear to have clear ideas about the boundaries of where educational influence ends and violence begins. Psychological pressure on the entire class is widespread as tension builds up and so is rough treatment of pupils who do not learn fast enough. For example angry teachers were said to call pupils 'stupid', 'slowpoke', 'idiot', 'moron', 'booby', 'swine', 'muddle-head', 'fool' and so on. Psychological pressure was often accompanied by physical violence and by actions against personal property, particularly in primary school. Teachers used their pointers as tools of punishment and intimidation, to strike children on the hands, head and body. Teachers might also destroy pupils' school accessories if they did not comply with school regulations. There were stories about angry teachers throwing objects at pupils such as pieces of chalk, wet blackboard cloths, bunches of keys, shoes, bars for handicraft lessons. Respondents cited incidents where teachers used physical force, clipping pupils on the back of the head, pushing them and sometimes banging their heads against the blackboard or school desk, grasping them by the hands, scratching their faces and so on.

In the accounts about primary school, boys mostly feature as the victims, as they are perceived as less disciplined and less diligent than girls. This is one possible reason why the female teachers are more aggressive to the boys. Another is the belief held by teachers – men as well as women – that boys need to be toughened up, to be educated as real men. It may be assumed that feeling their power over pupils, they treat boys roughly, as they resent men's dominance in society. As boys grow older, the use of physical force against them by woman teachers declines sharply. In secondary and high schools, any physical force used against boys is by male teachers. However, women teachers may employ covert forms of oppression such as biased low grades, nagging, etc. Boys who are subjected to repression by women may in turn show hostility to girls in the class, redressing the violence against them by female teachers. So a vicious circle of gender violence is created. We consider this phenomenon as one of the roots of gender violence in school. Girls are targets of violence by teachers too. Typically they put pressure on vulnerable pupils – such as girls from poor backgrounds or girls with little family support. Criticising a girl's appearance is a common form of humiliation.

In stories about teacher violence, students recalled that teachers of subjects such as Physical Education, Life Safety Fundamentals and Handicrafts were most likely to perpetrate violence. In the overwhelming majority of cases these courses are taught by men, sometimes with no professional educational background. Physical Education teachers often indulge in insulting behaviour: they humiliate and mock pupils, distort their names, use obscene language, make derogatory comments about the students' actions and appearance, particularly girls. Boys recalled male teachers drinking alcohol, using obscene language, and, in the case of Handicrafts teachers, using force. Not infrequently there were conflicts between students and Life Safety Fundamentals teachers, who are generally former career servicemen. Such teachers find it particularly difficult to relate to their students. One can assume that boys will develop sceptical and even hostile attitudes towards the army and the military through confrontations with these teachers.

Girls find themselves vulnerable to sexual harassment by almost any male teacher, who may make rude jokes or sexual innuendoes, and conduct inappropriate discussions of sex topics in lesson time. Some respondents remembered there being rumours about girls being seduced by male teachers. Incidents of sexual pressure on boys were cited far less frequently. Some interview extracts:

> Class tutor badly yelled at us. At first everyone was getting scared. She screamed at me, too. And I was shocked by that. And later I ceased to pay attention to it, just carried on with what I was doing before. (female student)

> You report to the principal, but anyway it would be the student who would suffer. The teacher would not be sacked anyway, while pupils still have to attend his classes. (male student)

> What's the use of complaining? If you may be found guilty?! At first it pains and hurts you. Then I shrugged it off altogether; I just didn't care. (male student)

We conclude that children learn at school to take little notice of the violence of teachers and classmates. The respondents were often philosophically indulgent, explaining away the teachers' aggression by identifying the causes: their lack of qualifications, their inability to have dialogue with pupils, and their disregard for the children's own psychological state.

Towards new research and public debate

Already the key findings of this research suggest that one of the most damaging lessons children and teenagers learn in school is that, after the painful experiences and fears they go through, they gradually get used to violence and become less sensitised to it. At the same time they come to believe that any form of violence goes unpunished if it is instigated by someone who has strength and power. This implies that when forming their first friendships and romances, children become accustomed to the fact that violence is incorporated into such relationships, just as it is into relationships with adult women and men – the teachers. Thus does gender violence become a widespread and common evil that is *allowed and acceptable* in relationships with people they are in close contact with, particularly with those who are weaker and more dependent – usually women and children.

There is no denying that Russia saw some progress in gender education in the 1990s. But it seems to have affected schools only negligibly (Zdravomyslova and Kigai, 2005). Public opinion clearly does not link the fact that schools have failed to address gender issues to the rise in school and family violence. Therefore, the immediate project must be to make public the findings of this research and make them the subject of public debate. This is especially important for post-Soviet Russian schools which are going through the reform process. The goal must be to make school a safe and pupil-friendly place of learning, a place where boys and girls can develop constructive relations in preparation for adult life.

9

Violence against girls in the education system of Pakistan

Nazish Brohi and Anbreen Ajaib

Introduction

Violence against girls in the education system in Pakistan is part of an overarching constellation of violence facing women in this society. Statistics indicate that primary education enrolments in Pakistan have risen considerably, but much more so for boys than for girls (USAID, 1999). After Afghanistan, Pakistan has the widest gender gap in primary education enrolments in South and West Asia (74 girls to every 100 boys in school according to UNESCO, 2003) and dropout rates are much higher among girls than boys. Lloyd and Grant's survey of 8000 adolescents (2004) revealed that, whereas 70 per cent of boys in the 15-19 age group had completed primary school, only 40 per cent of girls had. The interface of violent forces and structural constraints peaks at the secondary school level. Before the age of twelve, the primary site for violence, discrimination and exploitation of girls is the family but then this changes drastically. The onset of puberty and fertility also has implications for sexual activity. Community members take on collective responsibility to curb this and to keep intact the community's honour, which is vested in the sexual purity of girls.

Pakistan has no laws specifically criminalising sexual harassment. The onus of responsibility is on the woman or girl. At times, her mere existence is considered a provocation and any sexual act, with or without her consent, carries a suffocating stigma. Presumption of female guilt and culpability is coupled with the community's assumption of responsibility to preserve girls' purity and its employment of repressive methods for its preservation. At secondary school level, the sites and actors controlling a woman's agency increase, multiplying into violent forces which subjugate girls both internally and externally.

81

Family and community aggravate the problem for girls by perpetuating a culture that sanctifies silence about violence against women. The culture shields honour killings, allowing them to be used to initiate and settle conflicts, tolerates domestic violence as normal and perpetuates gender bias in thoughts and attitudes. It accepts discrimination against girls and women at the familial, social and political level and has laws that work against the interests of women. Although women's bodies are regarded as the holders of a community's virtue, and in this sense are treated as a public site subservient to the community, acts of violence perpetuated on them such as domestic abuse are seen as a private matter. This is true even when the violence has been triggered in the interest of the community, such as in honour killings.

Traditionally in Pakistan, interaction with, and exposure of, girls and women is kept limited, supposedly in everyone's best interest. Schools are the chink in the armour. In areas of tribal control, girls have been attacked or kidnapped from school premises or from outside schools to settle scores of tribal enmity. Girls have been kidnapped for revenge or ransom even from urban areas such as Karachi. In Layyah, Punjab, a rejected suitor recently threw acid on a girl returning from school. In Hyderabad, a male student sexually harassed an eighteen-year-old girl, who reported it, and fights ensued for three days among male students, resulting in the death of the harasser. Her parents withdrew the girl from the college. In Quetta, a girl was assaulted and molested by her teacher, who had called her in after school hours for extra lessons.

Although such overt acts of violence are isolated, at least according to media coverage and the observations of social analysts, their effect on families and communities is far-reaching. In Hyderabad, girls did not attend college for several weeks after the incident, and many transferred to other institutions. In Layyah, some parents who had rejected marriage proposals for their daughters withdrew them from schools, fearing similar repercussions. In Quetta, some girls said they would prefer education at a religious institution, since the teachers would be pious and God fearing and the environment safer; the school experienced an immediate 23 per cent drop in the number of girls attending after the incident. Even in areas where no such cases of physical violence have been reported, the threat, or perceived threat, of violence is totally disproportionate to the actual risk of violent acts occurring.

Violence against girls in the educational system

Although education is universally framed as an agent of change, in Pakistan the system is designed to prevent critical thought, inhibit questioning and promote acceptance.

Legally, onlookers of crime who make the crime possible and abet it are considered accomplices. The education system of Pakistan could accordingly be viewed as an accomplice to gender-based discrimination and violence. But while schools aid and abet, other key perpetrators prepare the ground. Any effort to examine only violence in schools in the Pakistani context would be isolationist and exclude the fundamental problem: that there is no institutionalised form of violence in Pakistani schools whose roots can be traced exclusively to the schooling system itself. Schools are merely an extension of larger, systemic power imbalances that result in violence against girls and women.

The government has made numerous pledges in international covenants, national plans of action and education policies to increase educational access. As most primary schools in Pakistan are segregated, Pakistan has established more girls' primary schools staffed by female teachers, so as to meet this commitment and overcome the reservations of families where interaction between the sexes is restricted. There are far fewer secondary schools and most are mixed-sex and, in cities, privately run, so the incidence of violence is likely to be higher. Moreover, as there are few government secondary schools for girls, they can be a long way from villages, and this requires girls to travel and increases their vulnerability to violence.

A plethora of research studies testify to many education systems, not only in Pakistan, that reinforce gender stereotypes to prepare girls to be perfect homemakers and boys to be the breadwinners. These stereotypes are inculcated through the roles played by teachers in school, and through storybooks, textbooks and extra-curricular activities. The messages perpetuate and entrench gender discrimination and the suppression of girls; the forcible maintenance of such parameters are in themselves acts of psychological violence. The education system and other institutions reinforce the dominant paradigm which exploits women, creating a vicious circle that locks girls and women in their place at the bottom of the social, economic, political and cultural ladder.

The study

The research briefly reported here was conducted for the NGO Actionaid in 2004 in two cities, four towns and ten villages covering all four provinces of the country. It involved around 300 school-going girls aged between five and eighteen, together with ten groups of parents and opinion makers such as village elders and school teachers. Data were gathered through semi-structured interviews and focus group discussions.

The findings show that sexual harassment is most commonly experienced at secondary level, when girls are aged between twelve and eighteen. This appears consistent with figures in the broader social context of Pakistan, as discussed.

The girls who took part in the study were uncomfortable about highlighting the issue of sexual harassment as they felt they were better off than if they were kept outside the school system. At times they were almost protective about their schools, offering excuses for others' transgressions, fearing that focusing on them would prompt their families to remove them. Schools, too, promote the idea of 'good' girls, who turn the other cheek, remain passive in the face of aggression, comply with familial obligations with obedience and do not expose their dirty linen in public.

Forms of sexual harassment

Secondary schools give predatory males from the outside world opportunities to interact with girls, and this presents a threat to girls' perceived purity. The threat comes from several sources: from male students and teachers in the school; from males encountered on the way to and from the school; from exposure to different lifestyles and thoughts; and from the ideas imparted by the educational system. Girls and their relatives participating in the study expressed some of these perceived dangers:

> My uncle has told my father to not let me attend computer classes because I will be able to send messages to computers of other men. (female student)

> Our local cleric told me that my daughter would not only learn western knowledge, but also their lax ethics if I let her continue at school. (father)

> The head of our clan is right when he says primary schooling is good enough for girls. They know how to read and count and about the country we live in. Studying further has no use since my daughter will never work; it will only make boys notice her. (father)

> You think I will stand and watch as all these young men let their daughters go to class to become like the women on television? As an elder, I have a responsibility. They will shame our zaat (caste). (father)

> My neighbour told me my sister was followed home from school by a boy from the other village. How can I let her study further? I have to take care of her. (brother of a fourteen-year-old girl)

All such reservations expressed by parents and relatives rest on a common base: the threat of romantic or sexual activity. As a consequence, many girls are either not allowed to gain a secondary education or are kept under strict vigilance, being morally policed while they continue their studies.

The girls identified sexual harassment on the way to and from school, as well as in school, as a common, pervasive and threatening occurrence. The aggressors were all male, either older students loitering outside the school and male passers-by on the road, or, in school, other students and school staff. Verbal and physical harassment ranged from singing sexually explicit songs, throwing chits and love letters, making sexual comments about the male or female anatomy, or making lewd suggestions and offers, to brushing, stroking and pressing up against female students. Boys used special terms to describe acts they considered harmless fun: calling out remarks, making suggestions, offering invitations, making bets for daring acts, and staring at girls and women. It was an accepted social outing for boys, the very fact of its discourse indicating its pervasiveness.

One student said the school guard would unbutton his pants and hold his exposed penis as he opened the school door for girls. Another said boys had broken the safety locks on the doors of all the girls' toilets, and would run in while they were inside and pull open the door. In Toba Tek Singh, a girl decided to stop going to school because of continuous harassment by the bus driver, and in Kasur, a mother forbade her daughter ever to mention to anyone that she was chased by two boys on her way home. A student in Peshawar described how a group of older boys standing outside her school rushed towards her, one of them pinching her very hard while the others ran round her. Another girl told the researcher how the bus conductor would stand with his groin level with her face while she was sitting, and would thrust forward every time the bus lurched. In Islamabad, three girls in different classes found the same teacher brushing or pressing up against them repeatedly and sliding his hand down their arms on various pretexts.

Violence against women and girls continues to be regarded as a personal issue to be addressed in the home, even though its impact in school is evident. The schools' response was to brush aside any obligation on their part. For example, one school principal said:

> We cannot be responsible for what's happening on the road, nor can we take the class to every girl's house so she doesn't have to come on the road. So why should I ask if students have to face that, if I can't do anything about it? If it happens in our school, then we will deal with it strictly. But you know these girls watch everything on television, and try to act it out sometimes. So then this happens. I don't know what the world is coming to.

Girls spoke about humiliating comments from teachers directed towards the female sex, contemptuous of their understanding and mental skills. In a feudal area in Upper Sindh, students said that teachers often responded to girls' questions with answers such as: 'Just listen to what you are told, and don't confuse yourself with questions. It is not as if you will have to apply this at college or work since you will never get that far.' Or: 'You want to work for fun whereas men have families to support, but you want their jobs.' They said they were consequently reluctant to ask questions and seek clarifications on anything they did not understand. They believed that rote memorisation was the safest method of learning in school: it pleased the teachers and got them good results.

The girls also identified occasional corporal punishment, although none of them said it was frequent or serious enough to deter them from coming to school. This was in contrast to boys: other studies by UNICEF (UNICEF, 2001) and Sahil (a local NGO) have noted brutal physical punishment and shaming in front of their peers, causing many to drop out.

Support systems for girls facing sexual harassment

No proper support system exists for girls facing sexual harassment. Almost every woman and girl faces harassment at different levels and intensities; very few lodge a formal complaint. Pakistan has no laws expressly forbidding sexual harassment. The only law remotely applicable is the almost unknown clause in the Pakistan Penal Code, which is vaguely worded: 'Whosoever insults the modesty of a woman ...'. Even if the matter is taken to the police, it is difficult to prove. And the police are unsympathetic and indifferent; often it is insinuated that provocation was the cause of the harassment.

Girls who experience sexual harassment rarely receive support; they are expected to keep quiet or sit at home. None of the girls who had experienced sexual harassment had made a formal complaint and few had discussed it with their mothers. If a girl did, she would be vowed to silence, or removed from school, or closely monitored if this was convenient – for example, brothers would drop their sisters off at school and pick them up. So most girls preferred to keep silent. As a fourteen-year-old girl said: 'I keep quiet, because otherwise I have to choose between saying it happened and continuing to go to school. It won't be possible to do both.'

A seventeen-year-old said: 'They can never find out. I know who that boy is, and he does the same thing every day. They will not believe I am not happy about it.' And a twelve-year-old: 'My brother will hit me.'

It is widely believed that sexual harassment does not happen to girls who act modestly and are properly covered and virtually invisible. The onus of responsibility is therefore on the female to deflect attention; any lapse is seen as deliberate provocation. Since the man is victim to his sexual urges, it is the female's responsibility to not incite or create any attraction that may lead to harassment. This is the logic behind the veil, the *burqa*, the *chador* and the restricted public spaces for women.

Effects of sexual harassment on girls

Sexual harassment and the fear or threat of possible sexual harassment curtails girls' mobility and infringes their bodily integrity. It also exerts a heavy psychological and emotional toll. Where female sexual victimisation equals familial and communal dishonour, it also affects families and communities. The most feasible option for the family is to minimise the possibilities of its occurrence – by keeping adolescent girls out of schools. As one father declared when referring to the benefits of schooling: 'What is more important in society? My honour or her knowing where Yunaan (Greece) is?' Where girls and women are the object of collective honour, they are also repositories of culture and identity. Accessing the educational system leaves them susceptible to a host of perceived polluting influences which may threaten this culture and identity. Much of the resistance to girls' schooling stems from this belief.

Religious clerics in Pakistan have taken to denouncing girls' education in their sermons, as endangering ideology, culture and identity. This has led to a new trend of rising violence against girls. In Karak recently, a cleric stood outside a school, publicly denouncing all girls entering the premises as *fahaash* (vulgar, of loose character). In February 2004, six girls' schools were torched in the Diamer District in the Northern Areas. Another was blown up with a hand grenade. In Chilas, a school was razed to the ground in the same year. The local authorities and police have placed the blame on orthodox mullahs.[1] In Karachi, student members of the religious political parties stormed the visual arts department of the University of Karachi and destroyed music CDs and videos produced by students as part of their dissertations, branding them un-Islamic and citing the university's ban on vulgarity. The student body of the religious alliance *Mutahida Majlis-e-Amal* (Alliance for Collective Action) blackened women's faces on billboards all over Peshawar, claiming that advertisements using women's faces were vulgar and obscene. This creates a hostile culture, where women's and girls' power in their intimate sphere is corroded and their sense of self confidence and esteem is threatened. They become guilty of provocation by virtue of being female.

How to move forward

Actionaid has shared the research findings with various stakeholders. The study yielded some interesting lessons. Firstly, community-based organisations and NGOs did not emerge as the most appropriate partners for interventions to counteract violence against girls in school. This was primarily because they invest substantial energy and resources in convincing people to send girls to school and improving school infrastructure, enrolment and access; they are therefore stakeholders for whom it would be counter-productive to highlight flaws in the schooling system. Further work on violence against girls through the school system would necessitate the initiating agency taking them into their confidence. This concern was not explicitly stated but was the undercurrent picked up during the research.

This study indicates that girls seemed to accept violence inflicted on them in school and on the way to and from it as an extension of what they face within their families, and therefore as nothing to complain about. The educational system in Pakistan does not promote violence that stands alone; its roots can be traced to the society. The school is merely a mirror of this society's values. All efforts for redress must therefore be multi-dimensional, encompassing the social realities of girls in Pakistan.

Single sex schools are sometimes presented as a solution to the problem. The findings of this study suggest that they may well reduce the possibility of direct acts of overt violence in the immediate future, but that in the longer term they could have the opposite effect, projecting females as the Other, with whom boys have little contact. This might render girls objects of curiosity and experimentation, almost dehumanising them. The extreme position is where most boys study in *madressahs*, the consequences of which were globally evident in the Taliban's[2] approach to women in Afghanistan. Recent scoping studies in the districts of Kasur and Toba Tek Singh were emphatic that co-education would reduce what is known locally as sex-suspense, namely the assumption that if boys and men study alongside girls, they will view them as more than simply sex objects, which will, in turn, make the environment safer for girls.

It would also not suffice to dissuade the clergy from targeting schools. They must be encouraged or obliged to change their ideology to encompass all the rights of girls and women, including the right to education. Making teachers more child-friendly is not enough; their opinion of girls and women and their status in society needs to change so that they treat them as independent human beings. Men and boys will never stop harassing girls on the way to school until they cease to view any female walking on the road – to school, to work, or to their home or just strolling – as a moving target. Sexual harassment is a manifestation of the power imbalances that exist in gendered relations and are the root cause of violence against women. Social hierarchies must be dismantled and changed. Schools will not be safe for girls unless the larger society becomes safe for them.

Notes

1 Mullahs themselves have been accused of sexually abusing children in religious schools (www.dailytimes.com.pk/default.asp?page=story_9-12-2004_pg1_6 and http://news.bbc.co.uk/2/hi/south_asia/4084951.stm)

2 Plural of *Talib*, meaning student of a seminary (and the name adopted by the extremist religious group in Afghanistan)

10

Schools in Nepal: zones of peace or sites of gendered conflict?

Kay Standing, Sara Parker and Laxmi Dhital

Introduction

This chapter examines gender violence in and around schools in the context of the ongoing people's war in Nepal. Drawing on a British Council-funded research project exploring gendered experiences of schooling in urban and rural areas of Nepal, it examines the gendered impact of civil conflict on schools and school children. In Nepal, schools have been positioned as ideological, and sometimes actual, battlegrounds in the conflict. This has gendered implications for girls and boys, as their experiences of the violence differ. Very little information is available about gender-based violence against girls in Nepal (Watchlist, 2005). However, our research highlights, in particular, the *fear* of gender violence within the context of increasing levels of insecurity associated with the school and its environment, while emphasising the need for further research. The chapter also foregrounds the conflict resolution efforts to focus on gendered conflict around, as well as in, schools, in light of the important role of the school in the community. It ends with the suggestion that, by implementing and extending the 'Schools as Zones of Peace' initiative and by engaging in further research, steps can be taken to reduce the impact of the conflict not only on children but also on the communities in which they live.

Context

Nepal is the poorest country in South Asia, ranked by the World Bank as the 12th poorest in the world and 140th on the Human Development Index

(UNDP, 2004). Its rich cultural and ethnic diversity makes it difficult to generalise about gendered experiences, although the country remains dominated by the Hindu caste system and many discriminatory attitudes and practices against the lower castes persist (DfID, 2003). Nepal is one of the few countries where female life expectancy is lower than male (UNDP, 2004). Women and children living in remote areas are considered to be the most marginalised and excluded.

Since February 1996, the Communist Party of Nepal, the *Maobadi* (Maoist), has been waging what they call a 'people's war' to overthrow Nepal's constitutional monarchy. The conflict has escalated since 2001 and the Maoists now control large areas of the countryside. International concerns are growing about human rights abuses by both government forces and the Maoists. According to Amnesty International (2004), Nepal has the highest number of disappearances in the world and it is estimated that 12,000 people have been killed (Amnesty International, 2005). While some believe that the Government's initial failure to enter into dialogue with the Maoists is responsible for the insurgency, others feel that the inherent inequality of the elitist educational and political system and domination by the Hindu population and ideology lie at its roots (Gellner, 2002; Karki and Seddon, 2003).

It is difficult to estimate the physical impact of the conflict upon children accurately. But data suggest that, unlike in some countries, the death toll among children has been relatively small (419 out of the 12,000 reported deaths). However, a further 454 children have been injured and over 230 arrested by the security forces; additionally, over 8,000 children are estimated to have lost their parents in the conflict, leaving them without the security of a family household. Table 1 demonstrates that boys are over twice as likely as girls to lose their lives or be injured as a result of the conflict.

Table 1 Impact of the conflict on children in Nepal

Feb 1996 – Sept 2005	TOTAL	Boys	Girls
Children who have lost their lives	419	295	124
Children who have been physically injured	454	272	128
Children and teachers abducted	29,244		

Source: Adapted from Child Workers in Nepal (CWIN) 2005

The school is positioned by the government as a key arena in which to promote a unifying vision of the Nepali nation state (Caddell, 2005). Despite the inclusion of girls' education in each of its national plans, girls' participation in formal and non-formal education is low. Although the Maoists actively encourage the schooling of girls (Hart, 2001: 14) and the insurgency presents the possibility of developing different and more emancipatory discourses of education (Thapa, 2002) including the wide-scale participation of women, in reality the education of women and girls has been disrupted and violence against them has increased as a result of the conflict (Shakya, 2003).

The research project

The British Council-funded gender and development project (Thapa, 2004) explored gendered experiences in eleven public secondary schools in and around the Kathmandu valley during 2004. Classroom observation took place in Grade IX classes with 280 students (119 male and 161 female) aged 15-17; interviews were held with teachers, parents and community members, NGO activists and academics, and focus group discussions were held with groups of 4-6 children (48 boys and 46 girls). The students kept diaries of their school and home routines, and school record forms were used to gain information on enrolment, promotion, drop-out rates and repetition by gender and caste over a school year. The project found that, despite government plans, little had changed from earlier studies (eg Sibbons, 1998). Pedagogy remained teacher-centred and gender discrimination was rife in both the curriculum and organisation of the school. Schools were cited as being unsafe places; poor toilet facilities mitigated against girls' participation and teaching styles discouraged girls from participating in class activities. And the double burden of household duties hindered their studies. The research also found that boys tended to be transferred to what are perceived to be better schools in the private and boarding sectors.

Issues around the impact of the conflict on schools emerged from this project, so further research was conducted in semi-urban and rural parts of Kavre district in December 2005. NGO activists, teachers and children were interviewed, and a number of reports examining the impact of the conflict in Nepal were consulted.

We draw here on this small-scale research, together with published reports from agencies such as Amnesty International and Watchlist, to briefly describe the gendered impact of the conflict on schools and schoolchildren in Nepal.

93

The impact of the conflict on schools

The research revealed that schools were being used as political and at times actual battlegrounds, although the impact varies depending upon factors such as geographical location, level of conflict and local support for the Maoists, and the level of security force involvement in the area. Diagram 1 demonstrates in its upper section how the Maoists view schools as a site of recruitment, propaganda and potential source of income, which the security forces then use as a justification to attack schools. The lower section highlights the multi-faceted nature of the impact upon the school, affecting teachers and students in both similar and dissimilar ways.

Diagram 1 Impact of the conflict on schools

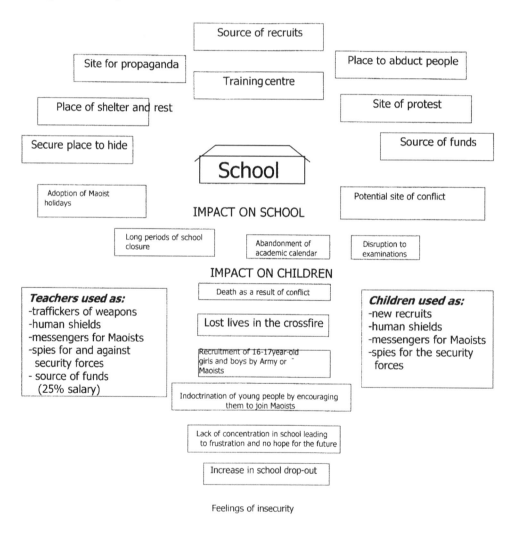

Gendered impact on children

As in any conflict, violence and the fear of violence have gendered implications. Girls as well as boys have been abducted and recruited as soldiers by both sides in the Nepal conflict. Rape and sexual abuse of women and girls by both Maoist and government forces have been reported. This inevitably affects girls' perceptions of safety, and fear of sexual violence is high. This prevents women and girls going into the jungle to cut grass and stops girls travelling to school in rural areas (*Nepal News*, 2004). Because of the fear of conflict, many young men have also fled or been displaced from rural areas, whilst others have been killed in fighting, leaving the double burden of agricultural and household work to women and girls, which affects girls' ability to participate in schooling and also women's safety (Shakya, 2003).

Diagram 2 illustrates the ways in which the conflict was found to affect children, in terms of both actual experiences of violence and fear of violence, in gendered ways.

Diagram 2 Gendered impact on children

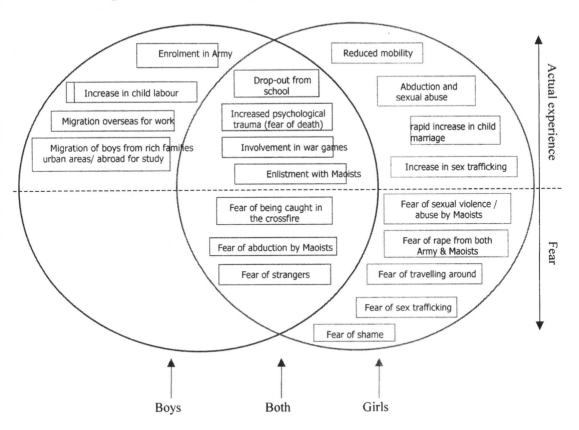

Child soldiers

Schools have been used as a recruitment arena by both sides. Maoists have kidnapped large numbers of teachers and students for what they call re-education (*Nepal News*, 2004), and children, including girls, are used in combat situations to provide ammunition or care for the wounded (Amnesty International, 2005). There are reports that the Maoists used the 2003 ceasefire to recruit 15 to 18-year-old secondary school children as child soldiers (Caddell 2005; Amnesty International, 2004). Both the government and the Maoists have denied recruiting and using child soldiers. However, our research confirmed the reports that this was widespread and that children were also used as spies, messengers and couriers. The duties of boys and girls may differ but a quote from our research reveals how boys, like girls, may also be recruited with promises of not having to fight:

> Due to compulsion, three ladies from our village have joined army. 90 per cent boys of our village have joined army (security forces) because it is easy to get job. The army soldiers come to our village to try to persuade us to join army. They lure us by saying as: 'You don't have to do hard duty and don't have to go in the battle field. You only have to take care of the injured soldiers.' (Boys' focus group)

Another informant reported being approached by Maoists who wanted to recruit him to the People's Army:

> I was also forced to go with them and they had given me a bag to carry. It was about 30 kg. I carried it for two hours, at that time I was about 13 years old. I cried due to the weight of the bag. The skin on my back was removed. I didn't know what materials were in the bag but after some time they opened bag in front of me and it was full of bombs. Like this we have to carry their bags and if we refuse to do so then we are beaten. (Boy, Class 9)

In some areas it has been reported that parents are sending girls rather than boys (who are considered more valuable) to the Maoists in order to fulfil the one-child-per-household quota demanded by the latter (Watchlist, 2005). Girls are likely to be placed in the political wing, with the job of 'motivator', going from house to house to try to gain support for the Maoists, but there is also evidence of girls being members of the military wing and receiving firearms training (Watchlist, 2005).

Gender-based violence

There is very little documented information about gender-based violence against children in Nepal. However anecdotal reports, local news stories and reports from international human rights groups and NGOs, such as Amnesty International and Save the Children Norway, indicate that sexual violence against girls by both the Maoist and security forces exists and is increasing (Watchlist, 2005). Shakya (2003) reports strong evidence of rape and sexual exploitation of women both by the police and within the Maoist movement, although the extent of sexual violence is difficult to ascertain given that many incidents are kept secret for cultural and religious reasons, fear of repercussions and shame (Amnesty International, 2005). There are reports of the girls being used as temporary wives by male militia:

> Sometimes we have to fulfil the sexual desire of our own level's activists and the militia. This is against the party rule and moral duty, but this is the fact of many women like me in the party.... Most of the women like us are the temporary wives of male militia. Sometimes ... the militia forces us to have sex with them. Sometimes we are forced to satisfy about a dozen each night. When I had gone to another region for party work, I had to have sex with seven militia and this was the worst day of my life. (19-year-old woman, cited in Watchlist, 2005: 38-9)

Watchlist (2005) has documented several incidents of rape, sexual assault and murder of school-going girls, including the torture and rape of a 16-year-old girl from Class 8 by two police officers dressed in civilian clothes and pretending to be Maoists. The local residents were threatened that their village would be bombed if they spoke out about the incident and were forbidden to take the girl to the city for medical treatment.

Our own research indicates that gender-based violence is also used as a political weapon against communities. One girl in Class 9 stated that: 'We know several cases that the Army raped and killed girls. Finally they blame the murder case to Maoists'.

NGOs such as Save The Children Norway (2005) are calling for more research to break the silence around this issue.

Fear of violence

Key to our findings was girls' fear of violence. Girls spoke of a double burden of fear: although both girls and boys were afraid of being caught in crossfire, abduction and recruitment, girls additionally feared rape and sexual abuse:

> Once, my sister's friend was coming to our home. The armies arrested her and accused her of being a Maoist, which was not true. After keeping her three to four hours in the army post they freed her because of the help from local villagers. Such cases are very common these days. Girls

feel very insecure and a lot of girls have left school because of rape case, kidnapping case and abducting cases. (Girl, Class 9)

We found that many parents refused to send daughters to school, fearing them to be at risk of abuse, and girls themselves spoke of fears about their safety travelling to and from school and whilst in school:

We girls always feel insecure and go to school in a group as much as possible. Our parents are also worried about us. They always remind us that they cannot give us security so we have to take precautions against the possible bad events. If we get some information about the Maoist or Army activities, we do not go to school that day. So irregularity in school is common for us. We also do not walk alone and do not come out in the night to save us from the possible bad events. (Girl, Class 10)

On the way to school, Maoists have bombs. Because of the fear of bombs, we have to go another way and sometimes we return home. We don't tell our parents because they would be afraid and not send us to school. (Girls' focus group)

Our research found that threats of violence came from both sides:

Armies used to tease girls instead of doing their work and giving people security. Once I was coming back home from outside I met armies on the way and they teased me a lot. They looked at me very suspiciously. While I was going they called me and asked for my ID card. By mistake I had not kept the card with me. They discussed arresting me. I became afraid, but in the meantime one of my relatives arrived and he saved me. If my relative had not helped me I am sure I would have been punished badly but without any cause. (Girl, Class 10)

This fear of violence contributes to the already high drop-out rates in schools. Rana-Deuba (2005) found that in a study of 227 families, 203 children had dropped out of school citing the conflict as the main reason; of these, 55 per cent were male and 45 per cent female. Our research found that, whilst girls are being withdrawn from school completely, boys are being sent to private schools in urban areas. The same fear is contributing to children migrating from rural areas, again with gendered impacts. Whereas boys tend to migrate to India or the Gulf countries as labourers, many girls fleeing the conflict end up in commercial sex work. Watchlist (2005) reports that fear of being recruited into the Maoist Army has led to a new surge of prostitution in the Kathmandu Valley; girls are being forced to have unprotected sex, thus increasing the spread of HIV/AIDS. There is anecdotal evidence of an increase in child marriages as a way of protecting girls from the conflict.

Conclusion: Schools as Zones of Peace

The conflict in Nepal has had different implications for girls and boys. Both suffer actual and psychological violence, but girls have the double burden of experiencing actual violence and fearing sexual violence. There is little information available about the extent of sexual violence in Nepal and more research needs to be done to uncover this hidden issue. In the current climate little action is taken against the perpetrators and communities are threatened with retaliation should they report instances by, or to, the security forces. Therefore steps need to be taken to enforce laws against sexual violence and to provide services for survivors. The psychological effects of the conflict on children need to be addressed; our research found only one international NGO providing counselling for children.

The most promising proposal is the National Coalition for Children as Zones of Peace (CZOP) a national movement spearheaded by Save the Children Norway – Nepal (SCNN). CZOP advocates children's basic right to survival, education, development and protection during conflict, and that schools should be zones of peace. SCNN along with other partners urges state and non-state parties to acknowledge and protect children's basic human rights. Schools are seen as important spaces where children can feel free from violence, gender-based or otherwise. This initiative has gained the support of five major political parties (CWIN, 2003) but lack of a functioning democracy and the return to full-scale conflict in January 2006 hinders any progress being made (IRIN, 2005).

> The government is responsible for solving the problem and the Maoists too. We can support only one – either the government or the Maoists. The schools in the urban area are comparatively peaceful but the rural schools are suffering from both sides day to day. The schools should be considered as the Zone of Peace. But in fact, if the government is unable to solve problem, how can we solve it? We just request peace on both sides. (Mixed children's focus group)

With no resolution of the political conflict in sight there is little hope of schools, or the wider community, seeing any zones of peace emerge. Schools remain sites of conflict and zones of fear for children, fear which is gendered in nature.

PART 3
STRATEGIES FOR CHANGE

11

'Speaking for ourselves': visual arts-based and participatory methodologies for working with young people

Claudia Mitchell, Shannon Walsh and
Relebohile Moletsane

Introduction

An emerging feature of work aimed at confronting and combating gender violence in and around schools is a recognition of the importance of the participation of children and young people, as well as those who work with them, in mapping out the issues and, more significantly, as protagonists in taking action. We are particularly interested in the ways in which visual arts-based methodologies, such as photography, performance, video documentary, drawing and other participatory approaches can be central to this process, either as stand-alone tools, or along with memory work, diary writing, focus group discussions and so on. We have been exploring the use of these methodologies in a variety of contexts in South Africa, Swaziland, Rwanda and Canada.

In prevention and education work related to HIV and AIDS, and particularly in the context of gender and violence, we see visual arts-based methodologies as significant in allowing participants to engage with themes and concerns that are not easy to put into words but which, once expressed visually or artistically, can pave the way for further reflection and for taking action. Such engagement is often taken up in feminist visual studies more generally. Not only do images have the power to disrupt and 'excavate' silences (Brink, 1998, cited by Stein, 1999), they also create imaginative spaces for change. Both are vital in addressing gender violence in cultural contexts where talking about sexuality is taboo and where unwanted or difficult to negotiate sexual advances are taken as normative. This may be true for many girls and young women but it is the school context which is particularly challenging because of the normative practices and gender regimes (Connell, 1987) within the institutional structures of school, with its frequent interplay of power, authority, pleasing the teacher and sexualisation (McWilliam and Jones, 1996).

What happens when children and young people participate in using visual forms, and how does this work support confronting and combating gender violence in and around the classroom? In this chapter we focus on three visual modes, starting with what we regard as the simplest in terms of method and materials, and then moving to photo-voice and collaborative video. At one level the work described might be thought of as 'seeing through the eyes of young people', focusing on what children and young people chose to represent visually in relation to 'feeling safe' or 'feeling not so safe'. At another level it is an example of what Schratz and Walker (1995) describe as 'research as social change'.

Art-making, sexuality and gender violence

The use of drawings and other artistic forms to study emotional development, trauma and fears has a rich history in psychology, particularly in relation to childhood sexuality. Using drawings in participatory research with children and young people is a well established methodology. As a recent Population Council study of participatory methodologies for working with young adolescents points out, drawings offer children an opportunity to express themselves regardless of their linguistic ability. They point out that using drawings within visual methodologies is economical as all it requires is paper and writing instruments, and it is highly generative (Chong *et al*, 2005). Drawings have been used with children to study issues ranging from children's perceptions of teachers (Weber and Mitchell, 1995), to their perceptions of illness (Williams, 1998), to their experiences on the street (Swart, 1988) and violence in refugee situations (Clatcherty, 2005).

In our work on gender violence, we have offered prompts ranging from 'draw feeling safe and not so safe' to 'draw violence' or 'draw gender violence' (see also Mak in this volume), to various mapping activities, such as 'draw the school and mark on places where you feel safe and not so safe', or, as a group activity: 'in your group, draw a full size outline on chart paper of one person. Now each of you can mark an X for places where you have been hurt'. One young girl in Rwanda drew an X on her head and another on her vaginal area, with the straightforward caption: 'I was raped'.

The opportunity to draw violence gave young people a way to express what they were seeing or feeling and to show what was difficult to put into words. The body maps, for example, provided a simple and relatively non-threatening way to initiate discussion: 'Who hurt you? What happened then?" As another girl from Rwanda put it: '*Ce problème est si grave de façon que les filles ne savent pas se défendre; elles préfèrent de garder par cœur*' (Mitchell and Kanyangara, 2006). As we discovered in an analysis of police records in several districts in Rwanda, the data on gender violence is already there:

> She says she was called into the house, undressed and raped and that it was her first time and that when she tried to cry out she was threatened of being beaten, and his wife caught them in action.

> She says she was given a lift on a wheelbarrow. Thereafter she was taken to the banana plantation, undressed and raped.

> She says she was told to have sex by the man, then the man inserted his bird (sexual organ) in her.

> She says they were coming from fetching water at 8:00pm. She was asked to give to him. She refused and he kicked her down, covered her mouth and raped her.

> She says she was taken into a house and was forced into sex with fingers.

> She says that she found inside the house the boy asking for his friend's trousers and he raped her.

> (cited in Mitchell and Kanyangara, 2006)

Sadly, such data does not always have the impact it should have on policy makers. Drawings as visual representations are perhaps harder to ignore, so can also be used as tools of advocacy. The drawings done by young people in one South African district became part of a video screened in school and community settings (Mak in this volume), and now form part of a training programme for teachers and school management teams on the issue of safe schools.

Photo-voice

Following the extensive work by Wendy Ewald (2000), James Hubbard (1994) and others working to give voice to children and young people through photography, we have been especially interested in the notion of artful engagement disrupting the silences around gender violence. The work we report on here comes out of fieldwork in Swaziland where we have been working with young people on issues of sexual violence in and around schools. In a region with a high incidence of HIV and AIDS, where young women are three to four more times likely than men to become infected with the virus, and where there has been silence around sexual violence and abuse, it is interesting to see how young people might participate fully as agents in the change process.

To test out approaches to tapping into the voices of students on the subject of sexual violence and safety in their school, we asked a group of Seventh Grade students in a school close to Mbabane to photograph 'safe places' and 'not so safe places' in their school. In single sex groups of four they took their pictures in about 45 minutes. After a brief introduction to the issue of sexual abuse and the technology of the cameras, 30 pupils (15 boys and 15 girls) set off to photo-graph safe spaces and unsafe spaces. Elsewhere we describe the range of pic-tures taken and, in particular, the gendered differences (Mitchell and Mothobi-Tapela, 2004; Mitchell *et al*, 2005a). We were, for example, interested in the fact that both boys and girls identified the toilets as danger zones. Both boys and girls took photographs to show how unsanitary the toilets were. The girls highlighted the fact that there were no doors on the toilets so there was no privacy, and that the toilets were a long way from the teaching block. 'You can be raped in the toilets' wrote one of the girls on the back of a photograph she took. Some of the girls actually staged rape scenes in the bushes around the school for the purposes of the photographs (Figure 1).

Figure 1

The process of making matters public is itself an important feature of arts-based work. Although we did not have an opportunity to mount an exhibition of the photographs in the school, we were able to organise the viewing process in such a way that interested teachers listened in and looked at the informal displays of photographs spread out on the playground. Like us, they were fascinated by the images that the learners had taken and several commented, for example, that they hadn't thought about the significance of the danger of the toilets. Brookes (2003) in her work in South Africa has noted that when schools develop a policy of monitoring toilets, the incidence of sexual violence goes down. While the act of display was only a tiny part of our project, it is possible to see the impact of the visual on both the learners and teachers. Moving beyond the local, showing these images of toilets in other settings – at a regional UNICEF workshop on girls' education, at an international workshop on Gender and Human Security, and at a conference on gender equity in South Africa – we found that the image of the toilet has provoked a great deal of discussion amongst participants. UNICEF, whose focus on the physical environment of schools has been important, has set up new alliances between the Child Protection Unit and those working on water and sanitation.

Collaborative video

Video has been extensively used as a tool for social change, inquiry and representation and is particularly suited to work with young people. Video is all around us, and young people often have a strong grasp of the language of visual media. Video captures an articulation of meaning that many young people understand fluently from watching and critiquing television, films, music videos, etc. The participants develop their existing skills in understanding filmic language, and video gives them a way to 'get out there' and have their work shown and possibly even affect the perceptions and understandings of others. Video affords participants the opportunity to see their lives and stories unfold before their eyes. Collaborative documentary video draws on important scholarship within feminist visual studies (eg Citron, 1999; Knight, 2001) and has also long been used by visual anthropologists and sociologists. Jay Ruby (2000), for example, discusses how reflexivity, autobiography and self-awareness can figure as central issues in critical anthropology, and this should be kept in mind when working with video on a sensitive issue like gender violence. Sarah Pink (2001) argues that ethnographic video can break down traditional hierarchies between visual and textual data. She maintains that these hierarchies are irrelevant to a reflexive approach to research that acknowledges the details, subjectivities, power-dynamics and politics at play in any ethnographic project.

In one collaborative video project in South Africa, young women were given the equipment and skills to make short videos, and participated in a facilitated discussion. The content of the video had to deal with something they felt was important in their own lives[1]. The young women (16-18 years old), all living in the vicinity of Cape Town, discussed ideas and issues together, using visual practices to explore emerging concepts. As issues surfaced, they narrowed their concepts to key priorities through a voting process, and storyboarded the ideas into a visual format. The workshop overall was highly collaborative and all the girls were included in the creation and articulation of ideas. The process of storyboarding challenged them to make sometimes abstract concepts more tangible and realisable, which additionally pushed them to challenge their own meaning-making and delve deeper into what they were trying to say. Talking through the idea in the small group and coming to consensus collectively also allowed the young women to begin to see problems and struggles between other women in the group as linked, instead of as just affecting their own life. This kind of symbiosis was critical in the Cape Town workshop. It integrated young women from different race and class backgrounds – from lower-middle-class coloured, upper-middle-class white and black township backgrounds – in one project.

Figure 2

The girls in this group discussed in depth the issues they faced in their lives, continually coming back to how they felt adults – parents and teachers – marginalised their voices. They identified several concerns they felt were important, but finally, achieving consensus through voting, chose to focus almost entirely on violence against women – on safety and rape. They felt that all else in their lives tied into the one major issue of safety and violence.

Using a mix of documentary and fictional styles, they developed, storyboarded and filmed a seven-minute video about their feelings and concerns about sexual violence. The collaborative video format allowed the girls, who were from different racial and economic backgrounds, to work together in a non-hierarchical way to create their end product. They entitled their video *Street Fear*, in acknowledgement of their shared feeling that the street was an unsafe and scary place for girls.

Street Fear begins with a young woman being treated like a 'dog', to be hollered at and harassed on the street. The girls had talked about this during the discussion group. It unfolds like this:

> We see Ann, a pretty black girl, strutting down the street in the sun. Two older guys lean against a car by the side of the road. As she passes them, they start hooting and hollering at her. She glances at them, out of the corner of her eye, but keeps walking.
>
> SCREEN TEXT: 'What I was really thinking...'
>
> The image shifts to black and white, and Ann imagines what she would have liked to do. She turns around and walks back to the two guys leaning against their car. When she reaches them she starts to gesture madly, telling them off, venting everything in her mind. We see Ann from the men's point-of-view. Finally, she punches out towards them, and we see she has a tattoo on her knuckles which reads S-T-O-P T-H-A-T'

In another scene, we see Karen in close-up. She is breathing heavily, her eyes darting back and forth. She is sweating. Finally she looks at the camera and shouts 'Fear!'

A major portion of *Street Fear* is dominated by interviews the girls did with each other about how they feel in their communities. Their questions explored what it was like to feel afraid. One girl from the township of Khayelitsha asks another girl from her community: 'What is it like where you live?'

> A: It's rough, tough, very messed up....
>
> Q: And how does it make you feel?
>
> A: How does it make me feel? I feel terrible. [in isiXhosa] I get so angry I feel like I want strangle someone or something! [laughs] I've said too much!

The girls discussed how important they felt it was to include the languages of all the participants in the video, so the final work includes English, Afrikaans and isiXhosa. A unity formed between the girls in the process of discussing and making this short work. They talked about how even though there were many differences between them, they shared a common experience of sexual harassment and violence. Through this unity they began to communicate as allies, learning and sharing together. Video proved to be a creative and collaborative way in which such work can be instigated without much intervention from facilitators.

Discussion

When drawings, photo-voice, collaborative video, video screenings, drama and other communicative arts are central to the process of addressing gender violence in and around schools, the loud silences about gender violence are shattered, and in the absence of language, participants begin to engage with the issues. As pedagogical tools, art forms are engaging and personally relevant, offering participants the opportunity to become cultural producers in relation to matters that affect them. As we note elsewhere on the contribution of photo-voice to addressing HIV and AIDS, it gives a face to the issues (Mitchell *et al*, 2005b). Beyond their use as tools of research and pedagogy, we see them as also vital tools of advocacy which can inform policy making (Roberts, 2004).

We must also recognise the limitations of these approaches when they form only part of the research mode or are a one-off activity with little space for longer term interventions. In one rural secondary school in KwaZulu-Natal, for example, where we worked with learners in small groups to produce short documentaries about issues of importance to them, a group of boys produced a documentary ostensibly to counteract rape. But the video appeared to glorify rape, and it positioned sexuality as either abstinence or rape, and nothing else. So without follow-up, video intervention could do more harm than good. With follow-up, however, it clearly maps out an intervention which would include the kind of movie therapy work suggested by Seshadr and Chandran (this volume) which probes the gender regimes of schools and particularly raises the possibility of alternative forms of masculinity (and femininity). And now that these boys have some skills of film-making, it could well lead to a video collaboration which would indeed interrogate dominant images of masculinity and gender violence, and which could be used as a youth-focused/youth-led intervention with other young people. Such a video could become its own tool of advocacy.

However, these approaches all have their strengths and limitations of cost and resources – drawing may require only paper and pencil; video production requires extensive equipment – as well as mode of representation. And they interrogate gender violence itself in quite different ways. With video, for example, there may be different opportunities and challenges to engage in self-reflexivity, but it can create a strong sense of collective response that includes both producers and viewers – although this could overshadow the individual. Photos, drawings and video, because they are potentially so powerful, work best when there is a recognition of ethical issues inherent in working with young people (Mitchell *et al*, in press) and when the idea of reflection and self-study is placed at the centre of the work. This is vital when working with young people but also, as we see in the work of Stackpool-Moore and Boler in their Theatre for Change project with beginning teachers (this volume), in relation to arts-based interventions with those who work with young people.

Note
1 *'Girls Speak Out!'* was a collaborative video project with girls in Canada, South Africa and in the US, led by Shannon Walsh, Farah Malik and Jackie Kirk and supported by a Seed Grant from the Association for Women's Rights in Development (AWID)

12

Unwanted images: tackling gender-based violence in South African schools through youth artwork

Monica Mak

Introduction

> Before her 18th birthday, one in three South African girls will be sexually assaulted (ANC Women's Caucus, 1998)

> In South Africa, schools are becoming the primary centres for rapists to target young women (Mlamleli *et al*, 2001)

These are some of the troubling facts featured in *Unwanted Images: Gender-Based Violence in the New South Africa* (2001), a nine-minute educational documentary video that explores such occurrences through drawings about gender violence in South African schools.[1] The artwork was done by pupils aged 11-16 at violence awareness workshops held in primary and secondary schools in the country's Free State province. Although the data were gathered prior to the film's release in 2001, these facts are as relevant today as they were then.

Throughout the course of the video, the drawings, accompanied by statistics and voiceover narration, illustrate how gender violence, be it rape, femicide, sexual harassment or homophobic violence, affects young South African children, teens and young adults, who are its witnesses, its victims and at times its perpetrators on the school premises. While the narrative mainly draws attention to the various forms of school-based sexual violence, the concluding scene urges educators to develop school policies and guidelines for curbing and eliminating sexual violence. In its various manifestations, gender-based violence remains rampant in the hallways, empty classrooms and toilets of South African junior and senior primary and secondary schools, as well as on the roads leading to school.

This chapter seeks to analyse three aspects of the *Unwanted Images* video. First, I deconstruct the creativity-based, multi-youth-authored participatory video-making approach used to create the video, in relation to two specific objectives. One objective was to make children's drawings the main attraction of the video narrative. An underlying motive was to allow youth a discursive space in which they could express, via artwork, their direct and indirect experience of gender violence within the school environment. The other objective was to rely on the artwork to turn *Unwanted Images* into a trigger video for instigating discussion among educators around viable methods and practices for combating school-based sexual violence. Some of the events at which *Unwanted Images* has been used as an educational tool are discussed and, finally, I focus on two questions that probe the video's role in advancing visual methodology.

Contextualising gender-based violence in South African schools

Incidents of gender violence in South African schools are microcosms of the sexual violence, especially against women, that prevails in South African society at large. Mathews *et al* (2004) point out that South Africa has the highest rate of reported sexual violence against women in the world and estimates that a young woman (14 years and older) is killed by her male partner every 6 hours. The South African Police Service noted that 51,249 cases of rape were reported in 1999 (cited in Human Rights Watch, 2001: 21). And in a study of 1500 students from Grade Eight to Twelve at schools in Soweto, Eldorado Park and Lenasia, Tabane (1999) found that almost half the boys said they had friends who were sexually violent and that three in ten males said they could be violent towards a girl.

There are numerous complex reasons why sexual violence against young women remains so pervasive in South Africa. The HIV/AIDS pandemic is one aspect. South Africa has the largest number of people living with HIV/AIDS of any country in the world. Jewkes *et al* (2004) reveal that a significant proportion of adolescent girls have sexual relations with older men in exchange for money to pay for tuition fees and other items. There is obviously risk of contracting HIV, since the man usually controls sexual relationships and may refuse to use condoms – and may be violent. Researchers at Human Rights Watch (2001) surmise that the 'virgin myth' (the false notion that sexual intercourse with a virgin can cure men of AIDS) increases young girls' vulnerability to sexual assault. School-based violence is a by-product of the climate of brutal oppression that engulfed the South African education system during apartheid although schools cannot be held entirely responsible for the country's history of oppressive gendered practices. Since the mid-1990s, educators have been working with schools to develop pedagogical materials and programmes to help pupils understand the attitudes and structures promoting gender violence in the post-apartheid period. *Unwanted Images* is the product of one such initiative.

Contextualising *Unwanted Images*

As a short educational documentary, *Unwanted Images* promotes awareness of gender-based violence among youth in and around South African schools. The video represents one of many concrete responses to the South African Gender Equity Task Team (GETT) Report:

> Education must play a dual role in relation to discrimination and gendered or sex based harassment and violence. Firstly, it must prevent such activities from occurring in education institutions. Secondly, it must mobilise the medium of education – including the curriculum – to develop in students the knowledge, skills and life orientation to ensure that they repudiate discrimination and gendered violence and become advocates against it. (Wolpe *et al*, 1997: 225)

Throughout South Africa's Gauteng, Mpumalanga and Free State provinces, teachers, school management teams and school governing bodies have employed *Unwanted Images* as a discussion piece or ice-breaker in awareness workshops addressing the various school-related forms of gender violence. These include pupil-on-pupil sexual assault, teacher-to-pupil sexual harassment and bullying prompted by homophobia. They have also used the video as a catalyst for inspiring workshop participants to come up with the three Ss – suggestions, strategies and/or solutions in relation to the problem.

Providing an artistic, discursive space for youth

During the production of *Unwanted Images*, we needed to provide youth with a space in which they could use art to express their own views on gender violence in and around schools.[2] We wanted to challenge one prevailing misconception of educational videos: the notion that, when committed to social reform, they are an exclusive platform for grown-ups' perspectives toward any given social issue and must exclude young individuals' points of view.

Our rationale was that the dominant presence of young people's voices would enable them to express for themselves what they felt were the major strands of school-based gender violence. We questioned the idea that learning via educational video refers only to the top-down dissemination of bland, factual instructional information from the sender (adult educational media designers) to the passive receiver (the youth). By employing the perspectives of young people to shape the video narrative, we wanted to offer an alternative to this linear approach, one that educational theorist Brian Goldfarb dubs 'a unidirectional, instructional broadcast model' (2002: 16). We also felt that other South African youth would be drawn to the video, once they saw that it features the artwork of actual learners in their age group. We believed the illustrations of gender violence by these young South Africans would validate the video's commitment to promoting the concerns of young people, via art.

Our video-making approach earns its *creativity-based* label from the intentional incorporation of young South Africans' drawings into the video narrative. It was a simple, albeit highly effective, way to present their perspectives in a visually stimulating manner that was as substantial and interesting to adult educators as to other teenagers. Our approach derives its *multi-youth-authored* designation from the multitude of young voices, conveyed through their drawings, that drives the narrative forward. Accordingly, although the concluding minute of this nine-minute video contains real-life footage of three boys drawing a picture of peace at a table, most of the time the video relies on children's drawings which draw attention to school-based sexual violence. These drawings reveal three different yet equally disturbing forms of gender-based violence:

Jackrolling (Fig.1)

Jackrolling, which consists of the abduction and gang rape of young girls, has been a common form of sexual violence committed by male school students in South Africa. In a survey of male youth aged 10-18 at 25 schools in Johannesburg, Human Rights Watch (2001) reports that young people of 15 to 19 were most likely to say it was 'good' or 'just a game.' The video draws attention to this disturbing phenomenon because still it has not been adequately addressed by school authorities.

Sexual harassment or rape of schoolgirls by male teachers or principals (Fig.2)

The video reveals that male teachers too can be culpable of sexual harassment. In fact, in a 1997-1998 study conducted at a school outside Cape Town, female learners complained about male teachers who spoke in a derogatory manner about the female body and punished girls by

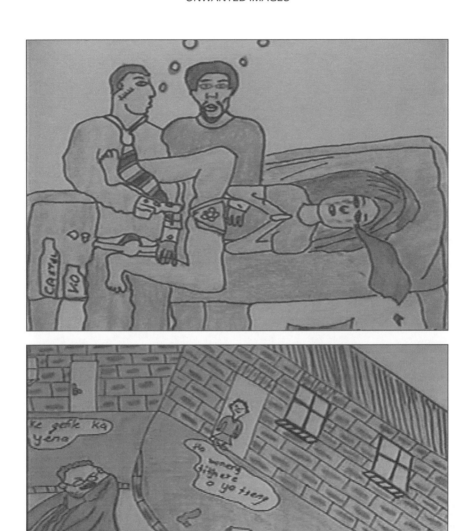

Figure 1 and 2

Figure 3

pinching their thighs or armpits. Our video illustrates that teacher-on-learner aggression can take even more sexually violent and traumatising forms, such as molestation or rape.

Bullying of learners instigated by homophobia (Fig.3)
The video alludes to the ostracism and physical assault of male learners suspected by their peers or teachers of being gay. Smith (2000) points out that the South African Bill of Rights to protect individuals against discrimination based on sexual orientation does not ensure, in practice, a change in societal attitudes toward homosexuality. As an ongoing problem, homophobia in secondary schools has led many gay and lesbian youth to drop out of school or, in some extreme cases, commit suicide.

Although Figures 1 to 3 are accurate reflections of these three forms of sexual violence, one picture epitomises them all. The illustration (Fig. 4) used on the front cover of this book depicts a young girl covering her eyes and pointing to her side (towards where the violent act is occurring). It encompasses and captures the horror of any form of gender-based violence, which no child should ever have to face. It implicitly alerts us to the fact that sexual violence in school grounds makes it difficult for female – and male – learners to concentrate on their schoolwork, to grow intellectually, and, ultimately, to receive a fair and good education.

Figure 4

Serving as a catalyst for social change

Our second objective was to make *Unwanted Images* into a trigger video to instigate discussion among spectators, particularly educators, on how to combat school-based sexual violence. We recognised that, if we were to make the production process as youth-participatory and multi-youth-authored as possible, we needed to include the perspectives of many young people via their illustrations of gender violence. But the notion of participatory educational video does not only mean bestowing decision-making powers on the individuals behind the lens. We echo Goldfarb's perspective on the *other* meaning of participatory video: 'Video can be said to have been made to function 'interactively,' if we are to understand interactivity [i.e. participation] to mean an engagement of the user in the production of knowledge and meaning, and not simply in the mechanics of making 'choices'' (2002: 16).

Like Goldfarb, we realised that *participatory* in youth-participatory video does not refer solely to individuals' involvement with the video narrative during the production process. It also pertains to the video's ability, in this instance prompted by young people's artwork, to function as an audio-visual catalyst. According to Nair and White (2003), this catalyst triggers or inspires viewers/ users to share their perspectives in post-screening discussions. Although youth participation was limited to providing the artwork for the video, this engagement afforded them the opportunity to discuss the three Ss – suggestions, strategies, and solutions – in relation to eliminating gender violence in South African schools. Paulo Freire (1972) equates *conscientisation* with an individual's act of developing consciousness imbued with the power to trans-form reality. I would argue that the fundamental purpose of Unwanted Images is not necessarily to provide the three Ss; its primary importance is rather in its role as a stimulant to help individuals achieve conscientisation. As an audio-visual stimulant, it facilitates viewers' interest in the issue of gender-based violence and compels them to think of ways to address this problem.

Consequently, our efforts to attract viewers to the subject required appealing to their emotional connection with it. In an attempt to move or rivet our audience, we instilled the following traits into the narrative:

(1) *vitality*: A potential problem with integrating still imagery into an animate medium like video is that it risks appearing aesthetically one-dimensional and dull. We therefore relied on a roving camera style to bring movement to the children's drawings and so give depth and life to them.

(2) *dramatic re-enactments*: We followed certain illustrations with dramatic re-enactments that alluded to them. For instance, *Unwanted Images* features a 14-year-old pupil's drawing depicting a male teacher caning a boy (Fig.5). The image is doubly disturbing since corporal punishment is banned in South Africa, and the boy's

Figure 5

pants are down, exposing his genitalia. The audience can only see his bare buttocks, since his back is toward the camera but the artist positions the male teacher directly beside the boy, showing that he has full view of the boy's private parts. The fact that the boy's arms are strapped down and that a puddle of urine lies beneath him intensifies the sexually disturbing nature of the picture. To accentuate the power of this illustration, we followed it with a stylised dramatisation of a wooden rod swinging toward the camera in a caning motion. Generally, we used dramatic re-enactments very sparingly as we wished to avoid excessive melodrama.

(3) *representational soundscapes*: We deliberately employed music that captured the moods conveyed by the children's drawings. One is sorrow, since gender violence continues to affect the youth of South Africa; the second is hope for its eradication through educational reform. So, in the first half of the film, we hear the mournful wailing of *Blow the Wind – Pie Jesu*, a score by Jocelyn Pook, and then we hear the gentle optimism of *Thula Sizwe Khay'Elisha* (Hush, the nation, we will have a new home), a post-apartheid freedom song by the Soweto String Quartet.

Surveying the impact of *Unwanted Images*

Since its release in 2001, *Unwanted Images* has been enthusiastically received by a variety of audiences, including educators, workshop participants, film festival patrons, education scholars and university and senior high school students, throughout South Africa and Canada. The film has served different functions for the different audiences.

It has served as an audio-visual complement to *Opening Our Eyes: Addressing Gender-Based Violence in South African Schools* (Mlamleli *et al*, 2001).[3] This educational module was created to help South African educators conduct gender violence awareness workshops and training in schools throughout the country. The video was also screened as part of the Men's Forum in the 16 Days Campaign of No Violence Against Women and Children, in Pretoria in December 2000. Over the past five years it has been screened at numerous education conferences across Canada, the US, the UK and, of course, South Africa. It won Best Student Documentary Video in the Student Division of the Montreal Film and Video Festival.

Theorising the role of visual methodology

Unwanted Images's success in inspiring dialogue on the subject of gender-based violence and on possible ways to challenge it raises theoretical questions related to visual media:

- How do the magnified images of the children's drawings operate on the audience?
- What is the responsibility of the video's creators when they see for themselves the experiences of children illustrated in their drawings?

Magnifying children's imagery

While the children's drawings were originally done on standard 8 x 10 paper, digital video technology enabled us to expand them to various distribution sizes, such as the dimensions of an average television set, a wall-size projection and even a movie theatre screen. In each case, the effect of blowing up these inanimate images and animating them through movement, music, and narration strengthened their ability to touch viewers. So most viewers, be they South African gender equity officers or North American film festival patrons who know little about South Africa, cannot help feeling moved by the video.

Unwanted Images's use of visual artwork, videography and music in combination with pedagogical material – the facts and statistics about gender violence in South African schools – has meant it appeals to people's emotional core as much as their intellect. This accounts for the generally positive reaction it has received from audiences of diverse backgrounds and academic or professional affiliations (see Mitchell *et al*, 2004, for the different readings that South Africans and non-South Africans have offered at multiple screenings of *Unwanted Images*).

Problematising visual ethics

Our primary responsibility was to protect the identities of the creators of the drawings. Excluding the young artists' names from the tail credits was initially greeted with some criticism from our South African collaborator, a gender equity officer, and her test audience of educators and parents. For them, acknowledging people's authorship represents a highly politicised matter for black South Africans since it symbolises a reclamation of their visibility and worth as citizens in post-apartheid South Africa. But given the context of the video, we insisted that our duty was first and foremost to protect the young artists. Putting the artists' names alongside their drawings of a sexual assault involving real-life abusers could endanger their lives. Issues around the politics of innocence and representation in the context of gender and HIV and AIDS are discussed in Mitchell *et al* (2004).

Conclusion

Although *Unwanted Images* is now several years old, copies of the video continue to be requested by women's organisations, NGOs and education and peacekeeping libraries worldwide. Its popularity may point to the tragic fact that gender-based violence remains a pressing issue in South African schools. But its longevity may also mean that as an educational catalyst for sparking discussion on the topic of sexual violence, even in a non-South African context, it defies the passage of time and surmounts geographical boundaries, year after year. Perhaps the continuing demand for it attests to the effectiveness of our creativity-based, multi-youth-authored participatory video-making approach in rendering children's artwork timelessly powerful.

Notes

1 *Unwanted Images* was produced as part of the Canada-South Africa Education Management Program (CSAEMP), a CIDA-funded partnership involving McGill University, the National Department of Education in South Africa, and three provinces: Gauteng, Free State, and Mpumalanga. For information on how to obtain a copy of Unwanted Images, please contact Claudia Mitchell (claudia. mitchell@mcgill.ca) or Monica Mak (monica.mak@mcgill.ca). A facilitator's guide is also available (Kirk and Garrow, 2002).

2 During the making of *Unwanted Images*, I served as principal videographer, Claudia Mitchell was the producer and my fellow CSAEMP researchers and the Gender Focal Persons of the Free State, Gauteng and Mpumalanga contributed to all stages of production. So the pronoun 'we' employed throughout this chapter refers to all of us, since the video resulted from our collaborative efforts.

3 This module was also created within the work of CSAEMP.

13

Harassment and harmful body practices: broadening the focus of body image education for girls

June Larkin and Carla Rice

Introduction

Throughout Western countries, the problem of sexual harassment in schools has been well documented. In studies conducted in North American schools rates of sexual harassment have been higher for girls and the impact on girls' confidence and school performance is more pronounced (American Association of University Women, 1993). Although a number of studies have also found that sexual harassment can have a detrimental effect on body esteem (Levine and Piran, 2004), the impact of harassment on girls' body dissatisfaction has rarely been examined in the context of school settings or health curricula. This chapter addresses this gap.

We draw on our research with Grade Seven and Eight girls from four middle schools (the level between elementary and high school) in the province of Ontario in Canada. Through individual interviews, we documented the kinds of harassment directed at girls' bodies and the impact of this abuse on their body perceptions and practices. Many described food and body monitoring activities they adopted to deal with their negative body image and stave off further body-demeaning comments. Through harassment, girls got the message that their bodies were potential or actual problems and many experimented with harmful attempts at solutions, such as starving, bingeing, purging and other body altering practices. In reviewing the Ontario school health curriculum, we found the emphasis on healthy eating and healthy weight failed to capture the range of body modifying practices adopted by girls and the reasons for their negative body esteem. In this chapter we suggest ways in which the connection between harassment and girls' harmful body practices can be incorporated into body dissatisfaction and eating disorder prevention work in schools.

Context for harassment and harmful body practices

The effects of sexual harassment on girls' body and self esteem may be especially strong in economically privileged, media-driven parts of the world, where women are identified socially with their bodies. Growing up in a Western context, most learn to aspire to a certain ideal of the body beautiful. As a result, many come to judge themselves, and be judged by others, on how their appearances and differences measure up to beauty ideals and body norms. For a whole range of girls coming of age in image-oriented cultures, images of standard and perfect bodies are difficult, if not impossible, to attain. Lack of positive imagery about diverse bodies can make it hard for girls to develop or maintain a positive sense of body and self (Rice *et al*, 2005).

There is a dramatic increase in body dissatisfaction and disordered eating problems as girls go through puberty. Research conducted in Canada suggests that most adolescent girls worry about appearance, 60 per cent start dieting (McVey *et al*, 2002), and up to 30 per cent experiment with extreme eating problems such as anorexia (self-starvation) or bulimia (bingeing and purging) to keep their weight down (Jones *et al*, 2001). In our research with middle school girls, harassment emerged as a major cause of the negative body perceptions leading to body modification practices that had serious consequences for their physical and emotional health:

> I know a couple [girls] who got really bad eating disorders because people were calling them fat...

> If the comment is ... that you are a pig ... the girl will stop eating ... until she starves herself ... some girls take pills to make them throw up.

The association between being teased about their appearance and the occurrence of body image and eating disturbances is well documented (Barker and Galambos, 2003). Yet the gendered nature of teasing is not always acknowledged and the behaviour is seldom labelled as harassment, a term which better takes account of the intersection of the body with inequitable social systems.

Socio-cultural and feminist models point to the importance of moving from a narrow focus on individual girls' beliefs or behaviours to a consideration of broader contextual factors that shape their investment in harmful practices (Piran, 1999). This moves the discussion of girls' body struggles beyond the dominant culture-of-thinness analysis that fails to address 'the complexities of gendered, embodied experiences [and] the ways in which power is enacted in social relations' (Evans *et al*, 2004:125).

A global perspective on eating disorders highlights additional limitations of the pressure for thinness model, in that it fails to capture etiological factors, ranging from acculturation to racism that can affect the body regulation practices of girls (Nasser and Katzman, 1999). Girls we interviewed who had emigrated to Canada said they were socialised into accepting North American weight standards and eating patterns, norms they described as different from those of their culture of origin. Their adoption of these standards was more about fitting in than about being thin and beautiful. A young woman from Romania explained it like this:

> I'm sitting at the store and I'm thinking of a bag of chips ... and I think, 'Do I need this bag of chips...?'...the answer is always 'no.' I hate that ... I always look at the back to see...the grams of fat. Grams of fat add up to a pound and that's what I hate. In the country that I come from, fat is what guys want 'cause if you're fat you're rich. You can buy all the good food and good meat. And if you're a skinny little girl you're considered not good enough. That's one of the good things about my country Romania.

Thompson (1992) proposes that for many women eating problems may begin as ways of coping with 'various traumas including sexual abuse, racism, classism, heterosexism, and poverty' (p547). Our research found that girls' anxieties about weight were heightened by racist harassment, which drew on racist stereotypes about their bodies and applied pressure to conform to white Anglo-Saxon norms:

> ...sometimes, if they're skinnier than most ... they'll get teased more because they have a different background ... [people say], '...all Oriental people are anorexic.'

Concerns that the incidence of body image problems among women of colour has been seriously underestimated (Thompson, 1994) were supported in our research by the accounts of racist comments that influenced body modification practices of racialised minority girls. Many of these practices were unrelated to weight. Some students attempted physical alterations to conform to white ideals of beauty, in response to comments about their skin colour, hair texture, cultural dress and other stereotypical notions of racialised bodies:

> My friend heard racist comments so she would wear a lot of powder on her face to make her lighter.

Comments about girls' early or late breast development can also contribute to the rise in girls' body dissatisfaction around puberty and the extreme forms of body modification they begin to contemplate:

> My friend she's like, 'I'm going to get implants'... cause she got teased for being flat ... my friend sounded very serious.

Considering that the number of cosmetic operations on under 18 year-olds in Canada is about 2000 per year and rising (Rumak, 2001), the notion that cosmetic surgery is a reasonable solution to body harassment needs to be taken seriously. Such discussions have an important place in the body image component of health education programmes in middle schools. In the following section, we suggest ways to modify the curriculum to include looking at the effects of harassment on the body regulation practices of girls.

Missing the mark: messages in North American health curricula

The tendency to attribute eating problems and body dissatisfaction to an obsession with thinness is reflected in North American schools' health curricula focused on eating and weight management. The 'healthy eating, healthy weight' message that informs the Ontario health curriculum (Ministry of Education and Training, 1998) is consistent with the approach of most prevention programmes in taking body size as the key body image issue (Levine and Smolak, 2001). Throughout the Ontario curriculum, the primary focus for teachers is on helping students to make good food choices and maintain a healthy weight. Harassment and other environmental factors are not acknowledged as reasons why girls may develop body image problems. Instead, health is viewed as an individual responsibility independent of the external forces that influence girls' body practices and problems. In curricula that privilege personal responsibility, improving nutritional knowledge is the ultimate goal, an approach that has not proven to be effective (Larkin and Rice, 2005).

Our research suggests that a healthy eating, healthy weight approach to eating problem and body dissatisfaction prevention can increase girls' anxieties about their bodies by encouraging further self-monitoring. In studies on body image, it is not uncommon for girls within the normal weight range to be dissatisfied with their bodies and try to lose weight (Young-Hyman et al, 2003). Girls we interviewed told us they get negative comments about their weight regardless of their size. These external messages appear to have far more currency than standard measures of actual weight. As one girl explained: 'If someone keeps telling you you're too fat or too skinny...you're going to believe it after a while.' When girls have a distorted view of their physical size, pressure to maintain a healthy weight is unlikely to correct problem body perceptions or eating practices:

> My friend thinks she's got a big butt but she doesn't ... She calls herself fat and she's way skinnier than I am ... A lot of people believe what other people say...

In the context of harassing comments about size, the curriculum focus on healthy weight may actually exacerbate girls' anxieties as they struggle to attain an illusive body norm:

> I'd say almost every single girl gets comments that they're either too fat or too skinny. I don't think people understand what the normal weight is supposed to be.

A focus on food and weight in health curricula also fails to address body modification practices undertaken by young women unrelated to weight as well as the reasons they engage in these practices. We need health curricula that conceptualise body dissatisfaction within the wider spectrum of body image issues experienced by various girls.

Harassment and body image curriculum
Media literacy
In the Ontario health curriculum the concept of body image is introduced through critical media analysis (Ministry of Education and Training, 1998). Studying the media takes body image and eating problems beyond the individual by acknowledging the role of social institutions in constructing and regulating behaviour. This is an important step. However, media-generated images of thinness and beauty may be less significant in shaping body image than harassment and other body violations occurring in girls' everyday interactions at school (Piran, 1999). Through media literacy, girls may come to understand that images of beautiful, slender women are constructed through computer and photographic technology but they also know that these are the standards against which their bodies are judged. For the girls we interviewed, such judgement often took the form of verbal put-downs:

> A friend of mine ... she started to starve herself because somebody said [she] was fat but she's really not.

Using the media to introduce the concept of body image can be an effective starting point. Our concern is when the focus is on the media to the exclusion of other contextual factors, especially those operating within school settings. Media literacy that considers images in the context of sexism, racism and other inequities can make room for discussions of the myriad factors that influence body perceptions and practices. Students could be asked to identify the ways girls are made to feel inadequate for not measuring up to media images of beautiful women. Harassment may emerge as a key factor in this discussion.

Beyond the medical approach

The effects of undereating and overeating are highlighted in the Ontario curriculum but causes of problem eating are not adequately explored. When prevention programmes highlight the negative factors of individual behaviour such as bulimia and obesity, girls are unlikely to develop the positive attitudes and coping skills that can mitigate future eating disorders. Moreover, curricula that focus on extreme problems of anorexia and bulimia can operate to construct particular bodies as diseased. In our research, labels such as 'Queen Anorexia' were used to hassle girls considered to be *too* thin. In these situations, medical labels became weapons of harassment.

Rather than emphasising medical diagnoses of anorexia and bulimia, a better approach is to situate eating problems and body dissatisfaction on a continuum that recognises the range of body regulation practices many young people take up. In relatively wealthy cultures where the size and shape of a woman's body are of prime importance, it is not surprising that dieting and other body modification practices have become the norm for girls. Developing a chart or map of the various social factors that affect body esteem is one exercise that can help move the analysis of body regulating behaviour away from individual pathology (Rice and Russell, 2002). Body harassment could then be taken up in the context of sex roles, power relations and larger discussions of social inequalities.

Addressing multiple inequities

Clichés about various cultural traditions offering alternative standards of beauty have contributed to the perception that girls of colour are protected from pressures to achieve the dominant version of white, heterosexual feminine beauty. The focus on culture rather than power can ignore the external machinery of racism, a form of discrimination often expressed through racial teasing (Iyler and Haslam, 2003). Poran (2002) argues that, for women of colour, resiliency to body dissatisfaction and eating problems is more likely to be acquired through awareness of racism rather than cultural buffers. One strategy for taking up beauty as a raced experience is to draw attention to body harassment that can lead to skin bleaching, hair straightening, and other body regulation practices not focused on eating.

For the girls in our study, body-based harassment was also connected to economic status. This was determined in most cases by the presence or absence of brand labels on clothing, symbols of cultural capital in the West:

> ...they go.... 'where'd you get your clothes, Value Village or Biway?' ...you have to have Tommy Hilfiger, Calvin Klein, Adidas and all that stuff.

The disdain for those unable – or unwilling – to flaunt the cultural symbols of economic capital was expressed through terms such as 'pov' and 'Biway babe', labels that often led to exclusion from the popular groups in the school. As one student explained: 'I've heard girls say that other girls [are] saying...you're too poor to be my friend.'

The ways in which conceptions of normal bodies can adversely affect the body image of students with disabilities and physical differences are also missing from body image curricula (Rice *et al*, 2005). Such comments about appearance and ability can be particularly cruel:

> ... this guy teases this girl all the time ... she has a bad jaw, like it sticks out ... He calls her ugly ... she cries a lot ... when I tell him he's bugging her he says it's just fun. It's not fun for her, I know that.

Developing a more integrative analysis that considers gender in the context of race, class, disability and other forms of discrimination will help girls understand the larger forces that influence their body perceptions.

Mainstreaming body equity
We have adopted the term 'body equity' (Rice and Russell, 2002:15) to capture and convey an approach that promotes acceptance and inclusion of diverse bodies in schools. Emphasising body *equity* over body *image*, we use this framework to shift the focus from changing student body images to creating equitable school cultures.

We propose mainstreaming body equity throughout the elementary school curriculum. Mainstreaming body equity in schools implies that issues related to the body should be regarded as cross cutting all school subjects. In Maths and Science classes, teachers could introduce the concept of the norm by teaching students how norms have been determined mathematically. This could include exploring how nineteenth century statisticians first defined the normal body during the industrial revolution, when a particular body type was determined to be most efficient for a productive labour population (Davis, 1995). Teachers could follow this with discussion of the social pressures students may experience to fit a variety of norms eg the sizing and shape of clothes, the architecture of schools that excludes kids with mobility disabilities, and scissors that fit right-handers only. We could offer many more examples, but suffice it to say that a critique of body norms could be woven across the curriculum into every subject area.

School culture

To be truly effective, prevention programmes must extend beyond the classroom to include changes in the social environment. Raising awareness about socio-cultural factors of body-based harassment can increase girls' anxieties if there is no parallel effort to address these larger concerns. Since most school boards have anti-bullying or harassment policies, body-based harassment could be built into pre-existing policies. Enforcing harassment policies is another challenge. In one study in which weight-related teasing was found to be a problem in schools, students and staff claimed it happened too frequently to monitor (Bauer *et al*, 2004). The formation of student groups to discuss harassment and the impact on body image and school culture might provide educators with information that could help to shape curricula and strengthen school policies.

In general, school personnel need to be better educated about the connection between harassment, the school environment and negative body esteem, a view that requires a more holistic approach to body image education than the current focus on food choices and weight control. What would such a programme look like? Levine and Smolak (2001) offer the following description:

> Rather than constructing more curricula with a disease-specific focus, teachers need to be encouraged to work together and with other influential staff (eg school nurse, coaches, principals) to identify and eliminate ... the following: fat jokes; weight-loss contests and public weigh-ins; sexist posters; sexual harassment in the halls; the absence of women in power from the administration, from textbooks, and from motivational posters on the walls... (p250)

Situating body image education within a wider social equity framework will help to create a positive school environment by providing a space to discuss harassment and other factors that impact on students' well-being in schools.

Conclusion

In this chapter we have used data collected from middle-school girls to describe the connection between body esteem and harassment and the importance of acknowledging this connection in body image health curricula. Our suggestions for curriculum are designed to provoke discussion of harassment and other contextual factors that play a role in the development of body dissatisfaction and problem eating. In shifting focus from personal responsibility for healthy eating and body weight to an understanding of social forces that influence harmful body regulation practices, we see potential for an approach to body image education that will have a positive impact on the overall culture of schools.

This chapter is adapted from an article published in *Body Image* (2005), 2 (3), 219-232.

Acknowledgements
The authors acknowledge the contributions of Marlene Bennett, Stephanie Cheddie, Marion Kelterborn, and Muriel Vandepol, and the support of the Waterloo District School Board and the Waterloo Community Health Department.

14

Reframing Masculinities:
using films with adolescent boys

Shekhar Seshadri and Vinay Chandran

The problem of violence against women cannot be addressed without paying attention to men's roles in society. However, in South Asia the burden of social change until now has rested on girls and women alone. Forms of control, including restrictions on women's mobility, have been automatic responses to situations involving such violence. These controls and the discourse around violence have only reinforced the status quo regarding men's alleged biological predisposition to violence. Children and adolescents internalise such messages and in turn grow up to keep such social inequities alive. Boys and girls seldom encounter alternative, positive, constructs of masculine identity.

Gender violence and the emergence of discourses of masculinity

The roots of gender violence can be traced to the silence around problematic childhood or adult experiences. Child abuse, especially sexual abuse, within or outside the family is ignored; domestic violence is dismissed as a family issue and disability rights are violated. From such behaviour within families and homes, violence spills out into public spaces and the norms of violence are reinforced through socialisation.

The struggle in the women's movement has been to find effective ways of triggering long-term social change. Since sermonising and admonishing –

'Don't hit women!' – have proved ineffective, it is being realised that an expanded conceptual framework on gender violence is needed to deal with it. Some of the discourses of masculinity that have emerged in the latter part of the twentieth century have provided a framework, as they have focused on deconstructing power and patriarchy and forced a re-examination of men's roles in social change. This new emphasis on men and masculinities has also arisen through public health concerns, particularly as a result of the HIV/AIDS pandemic, which has centred attention on male responsibility and sexuality vis-à-vis their impact on making men, women and children more vulnerable to infection.

Reframing masculinities

Promoting alternative models of masculine behaviour has to start early. Yet there are few conversations within families or in educational systems that include young people in the construction of knowledge and relationships in society. Children in South Asia often say that they have never spoken with their parents about changes in their bodies, or about their ideas on education, work, sexual desires, relationships and other such critical aspects of their lives. To most adults, this lack of dialogue is seen as a cultural response that avoids the potential difficulty or embarrassment involved in initiating or sustaining meaningful conversations with children. The impact on children of this culture of silence on matters crucial to their physical, emotional and mental wellbeing, for example in situations involving domestic violence or abuse, is ignored or trivialised and the voices and narratives of male adolescents and youth are completely lost. Poudyal (2000) observes: '...Gender studies, in focusing on the toll that patriarchy takes on women, has paid little attention to the cost extracted from men...'

To understand the costs of such powerlessness, as well as the power perpetuated by patriarchal processes of socialisation, we have to encourage boys to talk about their experiences of gender and engage them in trying to understand how masculinity and violence are not givens but constructions. Programmes must work with adolescent boys so they can revisit the socialisation process, rethink the impact of such socialisation and be helped to reframe their ideas of what a man can be.

Linking education with counter-socialisation

Most children's education in South Asia, formal and informal, has focused on lecturing children about what they should do, not encouraging them to express their opinions about perceived needs. Kumar (1994) suggests that schools have to act as counter-socialisers to tackle gender bias and discrimination. Therefore, methodologies that can set up such counter-socialisation have to be explored.

Didactic methodologies are known to be ineffective, so to challenge socialisation and increase chances of knowledge transformation, experiential methods that are non-didactic and reflective have to be used. Children can then discover newer forms of expressing themselves without being bound by stereotypical social expectations of boys and girls. There needs to be continuing opportunities for dialogue and life-skills training on self-esteem, conflict resolution, decision-making and other concerns to help young people understand and negotiate social pressures and gender roles.

Movie therapy

Since conversations between children and adults are limited, children infer ideas about relationships and gender differences from their observations and from visual sources. But the visual medium can also be used to subvert stereotypical ideas. Images and films have great potential to spark conversations about alternative models of masculinity. The advent of cable TV in South Asia gives access to a wide variety of visual media with 50 channels of entertainment and information. Young children are becoming more visually literate and identify with characters in television serials and films. Films can serve as pedagogical tools and link classrooms with society (Aiex, 1999), not just be intermissions in learning. In terms of engaging with notions of masculinity, Poudyal (2000) suggests: 'Film will be most effective if aimed at school-aged boys who are still unsure what it means to be a man and are open to alternative ideas'. The effectiveness of film can be seen through workshops held with the aid of four films that were produced by Save the Children Fund (SCF) UK and UNICEF, India.

Four films and a project

The South Asian Masculinities Film Project was set up and supported by SCF and UNICEF in late 1998 and produced films from Bangladesh, India, Nepal and Pakistan to help raise awareness about violence against girls as well as about HIV and AIDS. There were three documentaries and one feature film. Through various real-life or fictional characters, the films raise concerns about gender, patriarchy, gender roles, social expectations and sex, and much else.

The Bangladeshi film, *Our Boys* (Hassin, 1999), is a documentary about the life of a young boy who is an artist and the lives of boys who belong to a college rock band. All the boys are from the newly emerging middle-class families of Dhaka. Unsure of their futures, they open their lives up to the director, talking about duties and obligations, women and desire, confusions and contra-dictions.

The Indian film, *When Four Friends Meet* (Roy, 1999), is a documentary in which four boys share their life stories on camera. Their secrets, their desires for sex and girls, their dreams and failures, frustrations and triumphs all find space on screen. The friends are residents of Jehangirpuri, a working-class colony in Delhi, and are trying to make their living in a rapidly changing environment. Girls seem to be very bold; stable jobs are not easy to come by; and sex is a strange mix of guilt and pleasure.

The Nepalese film, *Listen to the Wind* (Rhitar and Tsete, 1999), is a feature film about a young Sherpa boy (Dawa) in the mountains of Nepal. Dawa's best friend is an old nomad whose eyesight is deteriorating and who wishes to see the rare *Kalma Metok* flower before he dies. Dawa has problems at his new school: bullying classmates, diminishing chances of securing a much-needed scholarship and the threat of being expelled. The film portrays Dawa's dilem-mas as he tries to realise his old friend's advice to listen to the wind and find his own answers amidst chaos.

The Pakistani film, *Now That's More Like a Man* (Nabi and Zaidi, 1999), is a documentary showing several women giving form to men through their words and beliefs about what men were, are or should be. The video intersperses the women's comments with shots of a group of children shown playing endlessly, suggesting the constant interplay of gender through the games.

Using films with adolescents

These films were used in a series of workshops with both adults and adoles-cents and a report was produced (Seshadri and Poudyal, 2002). Five work-shops held in Bangalore were attended by 143 adults from fifteen educational institutions and non-governmental organisations (NGOs) working with chil-dren. These workshops were designed to assess whether the films were useful for raising issues about gender, masculinity and other concerns with children. All the participants were enthusiastic about using them with children.

The films were screened at two more workshops in Bangalore, for 121 children aged 10 to 16. To facilitate using them for discussion, an accompanying screening and discussion guide was prepared. Though the major focus was on boys, a few girls were included. Children were drawn from schools that catered to a wide socio-economic class and also from the out-of-school sector, coming from an NGO that worked with children from under-privileged circumstances.

Evaluation of the usefulness of the films was process-based. Before the screening, facilitators raised questions to orientate the viewers towards the topic of discussion. The adolescents watched the film, then issues for discussion were raised. Finally, through a series of impact-assessment discussions the facilitators ascertained whether the messages of the film had been retained and internalised, and whether it had changed viewers' attitudes. Evaluation was done immediately post-screening, but should ideally be conducted some weeks later, the better to understand long-term changes in attitudes and processes of reflection, which are both pre-requisites for behaviour change.

Process-based methodologies like these are useful counter-socialisers because they provide a double advantage: messages may be internalised during actual viewing or discussions, but impact assessment also introduces a context where another cycle of reflection can take place and increases the possibility of internalisation. The workshop therefore adopted a participatory approach in recording the responses of the children. A few children wrote down their responses, while what the others said they thought was documented. All the responses were tabulated and analysed.

Pre-screening discussion

Before screening the films, the facilitator asked a few specific questions about the children's understanding of issues of sex, gender, equality, violence etc, based on the guide available. The children were asked at the pre-screening discussion:

- What do you understand by the terms sex and gender?
- Are boys and girls treated as equals?
- Are boys and girls brought up differently by their families? If yes, what are these differences?

An analysis of what the adolescents in the workshop said indicated that they understood that gender bias existed in society. Almost two-thirds of them recognised the need for gender equality. When questioned, many children said that boys were aggressive, strong, dominating and did not show their emotions, while girls were well-mannered, emotional and shy. The impact of gender socialisation processes within families, schools or even in the out-of-school sector was evident.

Post-screening discussion

After the screening, the facilitator used questions from the discussion guide to elicit children's reactions to the film. At both the workshops, children were completely engaged with the films.

> I find this movie (*Listen to the Wind*) very useful. It teaches us many things. The boy who is sent to school is very different from other boys. He likes nature, flowers and he is also a quiet boy. We think boys are not so sensitive as girls but now I think there are also boys who are sensitive. I feel everyone should be treated equally since boys and girls can do the same things. (from response of girl, 15)

After watching *Listen to the Wind*, children in the workshop felt they understood that boys could be kind, helpful and caring and not all are just bullies who are violent towards all kids. Many of the boys in the workshop identified with the main character in the movie, Dawa, who has to deal with bullies, problems in school and loyalty to his friend. The children believed that they would want to become more polite like Dawa and to change their attitudes towards boys who behave like Dawa.

> The film was very useful and had a strong impact on the feeling of being manly and the girlish way of life. The film made me ask myself why can't I be like that? Why do I have to always be powerful? Why can't I understand or feel what another person feels instead of doing what I feel will attract others? The film also gave me ideas to be artistic or just enjoy the nature or beauty of plants or things other than myself. The movie showed ... me a picture of how power could push others to the unwanted side. I think this 'manly' feeling can always change if one understands the thing he is doing. He can question himself if what he is doing is right or wrong, just or unjust. (from response of boy, 15)

After watching *Our Boys*, most boys in the workshop felt they needed to re-examine their opinions about women, taking account of the attitudes of the boys in the film to women. One boy in the film was shy and introverted but he was a good artist and constantly engaged in drawing or creating something, whereas the boys playing in a band were extroverted and outspoken about their futures and their lives, and about girls. The difference between them indicated to the viewers that there are different kinds of masculinity.

Impact assessment

Impact assessment looked at the extent to which the children understood and internalised the issues in the film. Using the discussion guide, the facilitator asked what was memorable: What did the children find useful in the films? Did they identify with any of the characters or issues? How did the children understand concepts of masculinity; and how would they change themselves in light of the film and discussions?

Asking 'Did you like the film?' tells us little; open-ended questions are more useful. So questions in the post-screening workshops included: What did you like in the film? What did you find useful about it? and Did you identify with any character in the film? These encouraged the adolescents to present a deeply thought out response.

Since socialisation creates certain images, the impact assessment set out to ascertain if there was a discernible process of change in the images of masculinities for the adolescents and whether they acknowledged why social change was needed. Since these workshops were exploratory, we did not expect dramatic changes. But the premise was that if even a single boy could internalise the need for change and learn different ways of thinking about his masculinity, the films would have been beneficial. We were trying to identify any new trends of thought by viewers after they had watched the films.

Most children in the workshop said the films made them realise that their success should be a measure of their hard work and honesty and sense of right and wrong, and not because of their gender. They reflected on the characters in the films and realised that they needed to start thinking about their actions for themselves instead of buying into general expectations. Typical comments were: 'Changes can occur only when one recognises one's behaviour and mistakes'; 'The films were very useful; it made me realise that we should think for ourselves – start analysing ourselves'; and 'People are not bad, their ways of thinking and doing things may be bad'.

These teenagers understood that although there were distinct physical differences between men and women, each were important in society. Men could not be considered superior and women's roles need to be respected. They acknowledged the need to ensure more freedom and opportunities for women: 'It is relevant what 'manly' means: not just powerful, superior and rude'; 'There should be no such thing as 'manly'. Men should do what women can and vice versa'; and 'Boys can also be caring and thoughtful'.

The children recognised that the visible gender differences in society were all created by members of society and did not exist as realistic representations. They felt that the roles and expectations of everyone should be equalised, that there was no equality in the world today and that this was wrong. One declared: 'There should be no difference in the ways boys and girls are treated' and another said: 'I understand the concept of equality between boys and girls'.

Conclusion

Adolescent boys need to be encouraged to think about gender-equitable relationships early on in their lives, before socialisation processes have grown rigid and undermined the potential for equalising relationships between men and women. For counter-socialisation to work, an environment is required where there is a culture of discourse between adults and children. In families and elsewhere, adults working with children should solicit their views and enable them to talk about their experiences.

Alternative pedagogies, such as film media, can provide a powerful stimulus for discussions that have the potential to change behaviour by portraying alternative models of masculinity. In Bangalore, the four films that feature in this chapter are being used as part of professional training in around 20 development agencies working with children.

However, film communication is only one aspect of programme development. Using films in process-oriented programmes for children can provide specific objectives for other sessions. The consolidation of the learned message must occur as part of the entire programme. The message needs to be constantly repeated throughout the programme, so that the concerns about gender or masculinity are revisited through various methodologies. Experiential approaches that inform and sensitise children locate them in ongoing process-focused education. In addition, life skills such as health education, building self-awareness and self-esteem and developing decision-making skills need to be built into the school curriculum. Learning should be linked to children's own experiences and should include using film, art and theatre.

Note

The authors would like to thank Ms Sarita Vellani and Dr Meera Pillai for their suggestions and help.

15

Engaging young men in violence prevention: reflections from Latin America and India

*Gary Barker, Marcos Nascimento,
Julie Pulerwitz, Christine Ricardo,
Márcio Segundo and Ravi Verma*

Introduction

In a recent discussion with university students in Lucknow, India, we observed students debating whether young women provoked unwanted sexual comments from young men. A professor asked the men why they often called out sexual innuendoes to young women and then ran away or hid in a group. If harassing women were something to be proud of, he asked, why did they feel they had to hide? And why, he asked, did women students on a university campus believe they had to walk in groups to feel safe? A few young men in the group laughed at the questions; some sided with the women. Some stood up and said that it was the role of men as well as women to question this behaviour and enjoined others to stop using violence against women.

This debate could have taken place in any number of settings around the world. In our work we have observed similar discourses, where some young men support non-equitable views about manhood and views that encourage and accept various forms of violence against women. There are some young men who question this behaviour and encourage others to join in this questioning. However, a large number of young men seem to be somewhere in the middle, mostly silent, sometimes acquiescing to non-equitable gender norms, but perhaps privately questioning them. This chapter reports on some findings from formative research in two very different settings, showing that variation in young men's views about gender norms is not uncommon.

We also discuss Program H. H stands for *homens* (Portuguese for men) and *hombres* (Spanish), an initiative developed in 1999 by a consortium of Latin American NGOs.[1] Specifically, Program H is an evaluated set of interventions that promotes more gender-equitable attitudes and behaviours among young men. These interventions build directly on insights gained from listening to the voices of young men who actively question gender injustice in their communities and societies, including men's violence against women. In this chapter we describe the development of the Program H intervention in Brazil and its recent adaptation in India.

Young men's views about violence against women

In Rio de Janeiro, Brazil, formative research with young men living in low income urban settings was conducted in 2000 for the purpose of developing the Program H operating strategies. Many young men considered some forms of violence against women acceptable, particularly when women were seen as 'challenging their manhood', as in suspected infidelity. In one telling example, a young man in a group discussion said: 'I don't know what a relationship based on respect (between a man and woman) looks like. I've never seen one' (Barker, 2005:119). Overall though, most young men interviewed in Rio de Janeiro were neither completely disrespectful, nor entirely at the point where they would criticise or question the unjust treatment of young women. Many spoke of acceptable versus unacceptable motives for using violence against women:

> *Interviewer*: Do you think there's any time when it's justified to hit a woman?
>
> *João*: ...you have to (hit her) if you see her going out with someone else. That deserves being hit. But if it's just an argument about day-to-day things, you didn't do this, so I'll hit you, I told you to do it and you didn't, for me that's no justification. Only if she goes out with someone else and you find her with the other guy. If it's not that, it's just cowardice to hit her (Barker, 2005:123)

Violence against women was found to be commoner among couples once they had moved beyond a dating relationship, i.e. when they first started cohabitating, which tended to happen between the ages of 20 and 24. This violence emerged, young men told us, when women did not fulfil their part of the bargain, such as not taking care of the children or the house, spending too much time with friends, or being sexually unfaithful.

As part of the process of adapting Program H in India in 2004, research was carried out with young men living in the slums of Mumbai. Young men described numerous examples of violence against women, including un-warranted, unsolicited verbal comments, whistling, jostling, touching, and harassing in public places, often called 'eve-teasing'. Such behaviour was des-cribed as a major pastime for young men, and this was confirmed by a base-line survey of 107 males aged 15 to 24 in which 80 per cent reported having en-gaged in eve-teasing in the past three months. Like the examples from the university campus in Lucknow, these acts of sexual harassment were mostly carried out in the company of other young men, pointing to the important role that peer groups play in modelling and reinforcing certain behaviours. In fact, young men frequently described these incidents with a degree of pride:

> *Rahul*: They (young men) pass comments on passing girls, whistle at them. If a beautiful woman is passing on the road then they comment 'oh, how beautiful, what a fun if I get her!'

> *Mahendra*: Yes, sometimes when we see a good girl, then we tease her...If someone says, 'oh, she looks so heavy', then the other says 'why don't take her and make her light.' (Verma *et al*, 2004: 445)

In some cases, young men acknowledged the powerlessness of the young women being teased:

> *Manish*: I do tease girls. If I am standing on the road then I tease passing girls. But I only tease those girls who are extra smart and to such girls I tease even in front of their parents.

> *Sanjiv*: Some of these youths even go in the crowded area and do finger-ing with the girls. Touch any part of their body. And what can women do? Can they say that this man has touched me here? If they say so, then these boys make fun of them.

Young men in both Brazil and India made clear distinctions between 'good girls' – those considered appropriate for long-term relationships and marriage – and those regarded as sexually available and unsuitable for long term relationships. Girls perceived as sexually available, 'loose' or unprotected were seen as more deserving of being harassed or coerced. Once seen as sexually available – ie as having neither the physical protection of a male around nor the social protection of virginity – they were viewed as having limited rights to refuse a man's sexual advances.

While young men in the two settings described the various forms of violence they believed acceptable, there were always some who questioned it, indicat-ing the complexity in how young men internalise and act on social norms. There were tremendous inconsistencies in the discourses of most young men:

they generally recognised that women should have the same rights as men; or at least perceived that this was the politically correct thing to say. It was also clear that their non-equitable discourses and actions, such as sexually harassing girls with, and before the watching eyes of, their male peers, were partly performative.

Program H: the conceptual background

As these research findings highlight, there are often holes, inconsistencies and resistances in young men's views about manhood that can offer entry points for interventions. In the case of Program H, one key component of the formative research in Brazil was life history interviews with young men who actively questioned non-equitable gender norms. These men showed considerable self-reflection in the interviews, some awareness of the personal benefits of embracing gender equality, and generally had others around them – family members, a valued peer or peer group, or a significant man – who modelled gender-equitable attitudes and behaviours. Sometimes they had seen or experienced gender violence against, say, their mother or sister, or perhaps had themselves been violent against a female partner. The resulting emotional pain to themselves and others had caused them to oppose or question such violence. In sum, most of these more gender-equitable young men had not only reflected personally about such issues but had also found their viewpoints supported by someone in their social context.

These research findings provided the conceptual framework for Program H. They reinforced the need to work at the level of: (1) individual attitude and behaviour change, by engaging young men in a critical reflection of the costs of non-equitable versions of masculinity; and (2) social or community norms, including among parents, service providers and others who influence and/or model these attitudes and behaviours.

Program H in action

With this research base, the Program H partners developed three key components for their intervention: a field-tested educational curriculum for promoting attitude and behaviour change among men; a lifestyle social marketing campaign for promoting changes in community or social norms related to what it means to be a man; and thirdly, a culturally relevant validated evaluation model (the GEM Scale – Gender-Equitable Men Scale) for measuring changes in attitudes and social norms relating to manhood.

The cornerstone of the intervention model is the educational curriculum delivered through a manual and video. It is designed for use in same-sex groups, generally facilitated by men who also serve as gender-equitable role models for the young men. Activities include role-plays, brainstorming exercises, discussion sessions and individual reflections about how boys are socialised, the positive and negative aspects of this socialisation, and the benefits of changing certain behaviours. Specific themes addressed are:

- sexual and reproductive health
- violence and violence prevention (including gender-based violence prevention)
- reasons and emotions, focusing on mental health issues, particularly communication skills, dialogue, emotional intelligence and substance abuse
- fatherhood and care giving, which encourages young men to reconsider their roles in care giving in the family, including looking after children and
- HIV/AIDS, including both prevention and care giving.

The accompanying wordless video, *Once Upon a Boy*, presents the story of a boy from early childhood through adolescence to early adulthood. Scenes show him witnessing violence in his home, interacting with his male peer group, experiencing social pressures to behave in certain ways so as to be considered a real man, having his first unprotected sexual experience, contracting a sexually transmitted infection (STI) and facing a partner's unplanned pregnancy.

The Program H group educational process creates a safe space in which young men can question non-equitable views about manhood. The activities were initially field-tested in six settings in Latin America and the Caribbean and then in two settings in India – Mumbai, with adaptation in 2006 in Uttar Pradesh – and they are being adapted for Tanzania in 2006. These testing and adaptation processes have confirmed that the workshop model and its core principles of promoting critical reflections work across diverse settings.

The lifestyle social marketing campaign aims to promote a more gender-equitable lifestyle among young men. This entails working with men to identify their preferred sources of information and cultural outlets in the community and to craft messages in the form of radio spots, billboards, posters, and plays, to make it cool and hip to be a more gender-equitable man. The campaign is designed to encourage young men to reflect about how they act as men and enjoins them to respect their partners, not to be violent to women and to practise safer sex.

The campaign, originally developed in Brazil and launched in 2003, is named Hora H, which translates as 'in the heat of the moment'. The phrase was adopted by a group of young men who frequently heard their peers say: 'Everybody knows you shouldn't hit your girlfriend, but in the heat of the moment you lose control.' Or: 'Everybody knows that you should use a condom, but in the heat of the moment ...'. Campaign slogans use language and images of young men from the same communities acting in ways that support gender equality. Several major rap artists have endorsed the campaign, which they call a 'campaign against machismo'. More than just another social marketing tool, Hora H creates an alternative identity for young men, one that is non-violent and has the important additional benefit of being interesting and attractive to young women.

In India, the young men adapted the campaign model and gave it the slogan 'The Real Man Thinks Right'. The logo shows a young man pointing to his head, as if thinking. Given the widespread acceptance of violence against women, campaign slogans were designed to reinforce the message that it is possible for men not to be violent to women. One campaign poster reads: 'Raju (a man) never uses violence against Rakma (a woman). This happens.'

Impact evaluation results

In 2005, we completed a two-year impact evaluation study of Program H in Rio de Janeiro, using the GEM Scale. The scale includes 24 attitude questions related to:

- gender roles in the home and child care giving
- gender roles in sexual relationships
- shared responsibility for reproductive health and disease prevention
- intimate partner violence, and
- homosexuality/homophobia and close relationships with other men.

Attitude questions include affirmations of non-equitable gender norms, such as: 'Men are always ready to have sex'; 'A woman's most important role is to take care of her home and cook for her family'; 'There are times when a woman deserves to be beaten'. They also include affirmations of more gender-equitable views, such as: 'A man and a woman should decide together what type of contraceptive to use'; 'It is important that a father is present in the lives of his children, even if he is no longer with their mother'. These questions were tested in a community-based household survey of 749 men aged 15 to 60. This confirmed that the attitude questions held together, meaning that men answered in fairly consistent ways. That is, a man who said he tolerated or even supported violence against women was also likely to show non-equitable views on other questions, such as believing that taking care of children was exclusively women's responsibility. Moreover, young men's attitudes correlated highly with one of our key outcomes: self-reported use of violence against women. The resulting scale was deemed sufficiently reliable (alpha > .80) for use as an evaluation instrument.

The quasi-experimental study included three groups of a total of 780 males aged 14 to 24 in different, but fairly homogeneous, low income communities and compared the impact of different combinations of Program H activities. In one community, only group educational activities were carried out; in another, these were combined with a community campaign. The third community served as a control group, having a delayed intervention. In-school and out-of-school youth were included in approximately equal proportions across all sites. Surveys were administered prior to intervention activities and at six months and one year after the activities ended. In addition, qualitative interviews were conducted with a sub-sample of young men and their steady sexual partners, to explore the impact of the programme on relationships from the perspective of both.

A comparison of baseline and post-intervention results gathered at the intervention sites reveals that a significantly smaller proportion of respondents supported non-equitable gender norms over time (p < .05). A similar change was not found at the control site. Six months after the activities ended, the majority of gender norm items improved significantly in both intervention sites, with ten out of seventeen items improving in one community and thirteen in another. These positive changes were maintained at the one-year follow-up in both intervention sites. In the control group site, only one of the seventeen items significantly improved. In addition, at both intervention sites, reported symptoms of STIs decreased and, in the intervention site where group educational activities were combined with the lifestyle social marketing component, reported condom use at last sex with a primary partner increased; all improvements were statistically significant.

In 2005, the manual was tested with 107 men aged 15 to 29 in Mumbai and the GEM Scale applied before and after the intervention. Although there was no control group for this test, results confirmed a reduction in self-reported occurrences of eve-teasing in the previous three months, from 80 per cent to 43 per cent. In addition, young men's attitudes changed positively, as measured by the GEM Scale, from an average score of 45.5 in the baseline survey (with 100 being the most gender-equitable and 0 being the least gender-equitable) to 49.2 after the intervention.

Final reflections

Program H was not designed specifically for use in school but programme partners often collaborate with, and work, in schools. Group sessions have been carried out in schools, and school staff mobilised to recruit young men for group activities and to participate in community campaign activities. The video is being used as an educational tool in public secondary schools in the state of São Paulo. The manual has been officially adopted by the Ministries of Health in Brazil, Costa Rica, Mexico and Nicaragua, and is used to varying extents with education and public health systems and with community-based partner organisations.

Next steps include developing educational and communication materials to promote young women's empowerment and engage them in a similar, systematic critical reflection about gender norms. Indeed, while empowerment of young women is important in its own right, our community experience has also confirmed that young women directly influence men's views about manhood. In one telling example, boys in a co-educational group session in Brazil wondered whether if they become more sensitive or gender-equitable, they would convince girls in the community to go out with them. They argued – and girls in the group affirmed – that girls often like to go out with the 'bad guys.' This confirms the need to engage both sexes in critical reflections about gender norms.

Another issue in need of greater attention is homophobia. In the impact evaluation study in Brazil, this topic showed least change of attitude. While many young men apparently changed some of their attitudes toward women, they often held steadfastly to homophobic views. Accordingly, in 2005, Program H partners, with support from the Brazilian National AIDS Programme, developed an educational cartoon video called *Afraid of What?* which addresses the issue of homophobia, targeting mostly heterosexual youth.

Program H is constantly evolving, learning and adding new partners and programme components. To date, we have learned that unravelling and questioning non-equitable forms of manhood requires multiple approaches, including:

- explicit discussions of manhood and masculinities in educational activities

■ creating enabling environments in which individual and group-level changes are supported by changes in social norms and institutions

■ incorporation of the diverse needs of young men.

While implementing all these components can be difficult in certain settings, this multi-pronged approach can lead to verifiable changes in attitudes and behaviours, such as the changes confirmed by young men and their female partners. As one young man in Rio de Janeiro stated, after having participated in Program H activities:

> ...I learned to talk more with my girlfriend. Now I worry more about her [worry about what she likes sexually and how she feels]. Our sex life is better ... it's important to know what the other persons wants, listen to them. Before [the workshops], I just worried about myself.

This young man's girlfriend confirmed that he had started to talk to her more, to listen to when and how she wanted to have sexual relations, and to recognise that sex was not the only important part of their relationship. Young men in India who participated in the workshops spontaneously decided to continue activities in their communities which questioned men's use of violence. Some of the original facilitators in Mumbai have appeared on national television condemning men behaving violently to women. Although there is much still to do, these initial results confirm that change at the level of both individual and community norms is possible, and that the violence by young men towards women can be reduced and prevented.

Acknowledgements

The authors would like to offer special thanks to Andrea Provost, Boston University School of Public Health, for her help with editing.

Note

1 The Program H initiative was founded by four Latin American NGOs, Instituto Promundo (Rio de Janeiro, Brazil), PAPAI (Recife Brazil), ECOS (São Paulo, Brazil) and Salud y Gênero (México) in collaboration with International Planned Parenthood Federation (IPPF, Western Hemisphere Region) and the Pan American Health Organization (PAHO). Additional partners in what is now called the Program H Alliance are: SSL International (makers of Durex condoms) (UK), World Education (USA), CORO for Literacy (India), Population Council (USA), PATH (USA) and John SnowBrasil. Information about Program H, including ordering or obtaining the Program H manuals and videos, can be found at www.promundo.org.br.

16

Working not blaming: masculinity work with young African men in KwaZulu-Natal

Robert Morrell and Gethwana Makhaye

Introduction

Violence is a problem for schools and a problem for young men. These are universal statements but they are particularly true in some contexts. Violence is considered to be a particularly serious problem for schools (Wolpe *et al*, 1997) and for young men in South Africa (Morrell, 2001). Yet harmony is more common than violence. There are more men who avoid violence than resort to it. In trying to reduce the instances of violence and limit their impact, governments and NGOs around the world have begun to work with young men. The idea is to help them to avoid becoming involved in violence and to help those already involved in violence to confront it, take responsibility for it and change their ways.

Working with young men entails working with masculinity. It involves working with young men as individuals, helping them understand who they are and why they might be at risk of violence. It also involves working collectively with groups to explore and develop new ways of relating, to develop mutual respect and understanding. The work often takes the form of interventions in institutions, such as schools, where violence takes particular forms. This work involves generating new models of masculinity which reject that of achieving manhood by the use of violence.

This chapter discusses two projects which work with young black men in poverty-stricken areas of KwaZulu-Natal. The province is the largest in South Africa and has among the highest unemployment rates (over 40%) in the country. It has a recent history of civil war in which, from the late 1980s to the early 1990s, 15,000 people were killed in clashes between supporters of the traditionalist Zulu nationalist Inkatha Freedom Party and the African National Congress. Models of masculinity in the region often include martial elements, linked to the days of Shaka's Zulu kingdom (Waetjen, 2004). But this has not been the only model of masculinity. The influence of the church has created a devout, obedient, if patriarchal, ideal (Hemson, 2001) though, equally, the large townships have generated youth cultures which have adopted misogynistic and aggressive masculine styles (Xaba, 2001).

Until recently, having many girlfriends was a sign of successful masculinity. As AIDS morbidity and mortality rates have risen, however, the dangers of numerous sexual partners has begun to be reflected in new representations of masculinity which no longer equate virile sexuality and promiscuity with desirable masculinity (Hunter, 2004). We argue that work with young men can produce alternative understandings of masculinity that help to prevent violence. There is nothing inevitable about young men becoming violent. With help, young men can orient their actions away from violence and develop a capacity for caring and respect which could foster a more harmonious social environment.

Youth masculinities: violence and peace

It is young men who are most likely to be involved in violence. All over the world, but particularly in development contexts, young men die in greater numbers and earlier than their female peers or older men. The main cause of death is homicide. They are 'trying to live up to certain models of manhood – they are dying to prove that they are 'real men". (Barker, 2005: 2). The young men most susceptible to the appeal of such versions of manhood are from poor backgrounds. They use violence 'as a means to cope with their sense of social exclusion' (Barker, *ibid*).

For nearly two decades organisations around the world have been doing masculinity work with young men, frequently with a focus on violence. Programmes have recognised that violence does not occur in a vacuum. Violence occurs because there are discourses that legitimate it, groups that promote and use it, and institutions which permit and sometimes encourage it. Violence occurs because poverty creates conditions of frustration, which in turn provoke violent tensions. At the individual level, there is the recognition that violence is not an automatic response or a natural condition but a conscious act. Working with young men involves getting them to reflect on their actions and to understand them better. The challenge is to help them achieve self-knowledge, give them a language to do this, and, in the process, to generate and support new versions of masculinity.

South Africa – the specific challenge

Two major challenges have spurred work with young men in South Africa: violence against intimates and the HIV/AIDS pandemic. HIV infection rates are rising. A recent national survey indicates that 10.2 per cent of the 15-24 year age group are infected, and that there is increasing gender disparity in rates. Among young adults aged 20-24, 24.5 per cent of women are infected compared to 7.6 per cent of men (Pettifor *et al*, 2004). Rates of infection are highest in KwaZulu/Natal, where over one-third of pregnant women are now infected (Harrison *et al*, 1999). The aggressive sexual behaviour of boys towards girls increases risk of spreading the virus further.

Among the first organisations to tackle domestic violence from a gender angle was ADAPT (the Alexandra Domestic Abuse Prevention and Training Programme), founded in 1994. One of its programmes is directed towards young men who beat their partners (Nkosi, 1998). Another project that works with young men and violence is the EngenderHealth's Men as Partners initiative (Mehta *et al*, 2004). Work that deals with domestic violence and work focused on reproductive health and specifically HIV/AIDS frequently overlap: women who are raped are likely to become HIV positive and South Africa continues to have one of the highest rape rates in the world (Jewkes *et al*, 2002; Kim, 2000). The major difference between domestic violence work and AIDS work is that the former largely deals with the consequences of existing practices and tries to end patterns of violence, whereas the latter aims at prevention. In both cases, the emphasis is on encouraging young men to think about themselves and their actions.

Two case studies

The Shosholoza AIDS Project

The *Shosholoza* AIDS Project was started by the NGO Targeted AIDS Interventions (TAI) in 1998. The name is taken from a popular Zulu song sung in unison as men worked together and now adopted as a kind of anthem at sporting events. The project aimed to raise AIDS awareness by working with young men whereas previously it had been directed at women – and had no discernible effect in reducing the spread of HIV. This project worked with youths of about 16. It focused on promoting safer sexual practices and abstinence by personalising the risk of HIV infection, on examining gender roles and presenting positive visions of masculinity and fatherhood, and it promoted understanding that women's rights are human rights. The project chose soccer as its site of operation since it is by far the most popular sport amongst young African men. It deliberately drew on the language, beliefs and behaviour around soccer, believing this to be a creative medium for facilitating change in the risk behaviours that spread HIV.

Traditional cultural values support the rights of men to have many sexual partners and to dictate the terms of sexual intercourse. In addition, poverty limits the possibilities of young men to express their masculinity in healthy ways. The role of fathers is important because living with a violent father inures young men to violence – while their absence deprives boys of role models and male care, as well as placing extra burdens on the mother.

These factors had predisposed the *Shosholoza* boys to domestic violence. In a 2003 survey of 102 young men (aged 12 to 25 years), seventeen said that they had threatened or beaten their partner, and out of the 35 sexually active respondents, three admitted to forcing a girl to have sex against her will. Similarly, the young men's sexual behaviour placed them at risk. Most had been sexually active for some time, with the majority reporting their sexual debut at age 14 or 15. Of those who were sexually active, 95 per cent had never used condoms; all had had more than one sexual partner, and only 3 per cent said that a woman has a right to say 'no' to sex.

The Inkunzi Isematholeni Project

A second project, *Inkunzi Isematholeni*, was initiated in 2001 to work with younger boys, aged 11 to 15. *Inkunzi Isematholeni* translates as: 'how the calf is raised will determine the quality of the bull'. This captured the spirit of the project – to help guide boys and young men away from violent and destructive behaviour and support their development into good fathers and sexually responsible partners. Extending the masculinity work into the younger cohort aimed to encourage abstinence and delay in the onset of sexual activity and give boys determined to become sexually active accurate information about prevention methods.

All the boys in the project were at school, which provided convenient and organised spaces in which to work. Twenty, mainly rural, schools in the province became involved in the project. Selected teachers were tasked with selecting ten participants from their school to become peer educators, and asked to choose a mixture of extroverted students – for public speaking – and introverted students – for personal discussions. These 200 boys attended a three-day training workshop, which gave information on puberty, sexually transmitted infections, HIV/AIDS and condom use, and encouraged reflection on issues such as culture, masculinity and femininity, personal HIV vulnerability and prevention strategies. Firm emphasis was placed on encouraging participants to think for themselves, asking them questions such as: Where do you want to be in fifteen years' time? What will your house look like? How many children would you like to have? and then asking: How do you think becoming HIV-positive will affect your dreams?

Caring behaviour was fostered by establishing vegetable gardens at the schools to provide food for children identified as in need by the peer educators and the principal. Indigenous trees were planted and left in the care of the youngsters. These activities introduced the participants to aspects of caring for, and supporting others, something not traditionally part of the culture among men in Kwa-Zulu Natal. The aim of these activities was to encourage greater involvement of boys and men in caring for those affected by HIV.

Testimonies

Boys were encouraged to talk about the violence they had seen, experienced or committed. The aim was to assist boys to deal with trauma by talking about it and, in the process, to discuss ways of avoiding violent situations or of dealing with conflict in non-violent ways. The facilitators helped boys to identify the kinds of violence that occurred and to understand how such violence came about. Underpinning all these goals was the goal of interrogating masculinity and presenting positive and constructive models of masculine behaviour.

Virtually all the boys had experienced and witnessed violence of varying severity in their short lives. Some had been involved in serious violence themselves.

> I was once involved in a gang rape. It was New Year's Eve. We were four as males against one girl that was drunk. It was dark and she could not see who raped her. We talked softly amongst ourselves so that she could not hear us. After being raped by the first one, she threw herself to the other one. We did not know whether she realised that she had sex with different people. We all raped her as she threw herself to us as she was drunk and we were not. It was not our intention to rape her but we were there was peer pressure but we also took advantage of that drunk girl.

Many boys admitted that they pressured girls to have sex and sometimes used violence. They explained that this was sometimes due to peer pressure.

> If you tell your friends that you don't have sex, they laugh at you and you start feeling that you are a fool. To prove that you are not a fool, you are a normal person, you start forcing your partner to have sex and if you don't have any partner you will be forced to rape to satisfy your peers' demands of having had sex.

The boys also described being victims of sexual predation. Denying that it was only boys who were sexually assertive, a number told of cases where older, sexually experienced women, forced them to have sex.

> Women will look at a man and if he has beautiful muscles, they want to have sex with him. They wait next to the door and wait for him to go past. They call him to come and help move something that is heavy. When he is inside, the woman close the door and start to undress.

As well as sexual violence, most of the boys had witnessed domestic violence. Facilitators in both *Shosholoza* and *Inkunzi* worked to show how gender inequality, and the claim of men to a superior social status in the home, promoted such violence. The boys readily provided examples of domestic violence from their own lives.

> Most of unemployed fathers spend most of their times in shebeens (liquor parlours) without making any income, when they come back home they demand food and when the mothers are trying to explain that there is no food that is when the man insult and assault the innocent woman.

> A man will come home to find a woman relaxing with the children. He feels jealous that the woman has a nice relationship with the children and he says funny things to the wife. If a man has a love affair with other women, he will beat the wife and pretend he does not want even to spend the night at home meanwhile he wants to visit his girlfriends.

As they analysed the causes of domestic violence, the boys began to identify the failings of men, rather than focusing on alleged female weaknesses. They referred to a lack of communication and understanding within relationships, to infidelity, alcohol abuse and to unemployment. Men who had no source of income were unable to meet familial expectations of provision. They often responded by exerting their power over women or becoming jealous of their successful partners.

The facilitators' approach allowed the boys to perceive the destructive nature of their own and, more generally men's, actions. The consequences of, for example, domestic violence were identified along the lines of collective comments like this:

> Any abuse could lead to suicide; unhappy marriages could lead to divorce that could affect the children; some of the abused children are likely to leave their homes to live on the streets; abused girls are at ease to become commercial sex workers; school, work or sport performance could be badly affected; children, especially boys, who see their fathers as role models could easily imitate their fathers; partners do not talk about issues that arise in their relationship; boys will develop a wrong idea that women must be beaten; if a woman is sexually abused, she may get infected with different illnesses, such as STIs and HIV; a woman might even get pregnant if she is denied use of condoms and contraceptives.

At the end of the process, the boys expressed contrition for their actions and identified positive courses of action for the future. In order to avoid domestic violence, for example, their collective comments can be summarised as:

> Be careful of your actions. Do not be tempted by peer pressure. Avoid lifts, strangers and deserted spots. Encourage communication within the relationship. Men must learn to control their feelings. Men should understand when the woman says 'no' she means it. Be clear on where you are going, especially at night.

With an eye to the future and a critical look back over the past, where many of their fathers were negligent or abusive, they said:

> Parents, especially fathers, should be more responsible for their children. Children should feel safe and not scared of their fathers. Fathers should set a good example for their children. Parents should realise that violence does not solve any problem.

Evaluation

TAI routinely evaluates its programmes via regular feedback sessions conducted with the participants in the programmes, where facilitators listen to stories of significant change as told by the boys. For example:

> When I started in the project I had five girlfriends and I have been able to reduce the number to three.

> I have realised that in order to become a professional soccer player, I must be healthy and this means condomising.

These stories are corroborated in interviews with their partners:

> I can refuse sex without being afraid of abuse.

> He does not mind if I fetch condoms myself from the clinic, unlike before where I would never dream of doing such a thing.

> We talk about other things when we are together and not only about sex as we used to do.

In both projects there was evidence of increased awareness of women's rights and a commitment to the equal distribution of domestic work between boys and girls. By the end of the workshops, most peer educators felt that even if a girl was their girlfriend, they had no right to force her to have sex. The boys have become much more confident about talking about difficult emotional issues so they are more competent to raise complex relational issues with their partners. They have a good understanding of what it means to be HIV positive, appreciate the advantages of sexual abstinence and are clear about the advantages of knowing one's HIV status.

The way some boys view women in their lives is also changing and many have expressed a desire to be more helpful at home to show their gratitude. However, changes in masculinity do not occur without having to face pressures to revert to the traditional ways of acting 'as a man'. Girls often expect boys to take the lead in heterosexual encounters and may ridicule boys who refuse to be sexually active or to endorse traditional male values. Women and girls contribute to the maintenance of the gendered system, even if this is because of their economic vulnerability and need.

Discussion

Shosholoza and *Inkunzi* have succeeded because they involve young men in activities that improve their self-knowledge and analytical skills. They develop confidence in themselves and trust in the facilitators. They are given a supportive environment in which to express difficult emotions. They are not interpolated as oppressors of women or perpetrators of violence. The process allows boys to discuss the difficulties in their own lives and instances of violence and the causes of violence are identified from these disclosures. Boys come to realise that they are themselves victims of poverty, of oppressive masculine stereotypes, of peer pressure and parental neglect. They also come to realise that they can have healthier relationships with other people and lead happier lives by developing new models of masculine behaviour which do not include ready recourse to violence.

The findings of the TAI projects confirm findings made about masculinity elsewhere in Africa which show that poverty is a major factor in constructing masculinity. Fractured families, lack of life opportunities and shortages of resources all dispose boys to demonstrate masculinity in a violent way, often against girls. In their efforts to live lives that are respectful of themselves and of others, boys have difficulty in reconciling peer perceptions of masculine behaviour with their own understandings and those of the traditional community. In this struggle the intervention of outside agencies such as TAI can be critical in helping boys to establish themselves as confident young men, avoiding the temptations of violence and crime. Such support can also come from significant men or from teachers, but this is seldom available.

Secondly, the study shows that in poverty-stricken areas with a recent history of civil strife and ongoing instances of violence, peaceful masculinities can be constructed to replace 'warrior discourses' (Large, 1997: 26-7). This confirms the findings of work with violent men in industrialised countries. By focusing directly on issues of masculinity, it is possible to transform male behaviour and to create positive models of living.

17

Issues of masculinity and violence in Australian schools

Martin Mills

Introduction

There is a worrying tendency in education worldwide to treat boys' violence towards girls and 'othered' boys as normal because of the dominance of boys-will-be-boys discourse in schools (see Epstein *et al*, 1998; Leach, 2003). Although this discourse holds sway in many Australian schools, the feminist movement in Australia has, since the 1970s, had some success in placing issues of gender and violence on the agenda of educational policy. As a result, a number of government reports have been produced and significant government-supported resources addressing gender and violence have been developed for schools at state and national level. However, the backlash against feminism that has been growing in Australia, as elsewhere, has been working to displace concerns about gender and violence from the policy framework in education.

This chapter examines the impact of the anti-feminist backlash in Australian education (Lingard and Douglas, 1999) on policy concerning gender and violence. There appears to be difficult times ahead for those wanting to ensure that issues of gender and violence are not lost in the muddy waters created by attempts to make schools more boy friendly. For although various Australian governments, unlike many elsewhere, are to be praised for having identified the gendered nature of violence in schools decades ago, the issue is still alive, and the current debate about boys threatens to undermine efforts to reduce male students' violent behaviours. The chapter concludes with suggestions as to how matters of gender and violence can be placed on the agenda in Australian schools.

Current Australian policy

As with most societies, violence in Australia is generally perpetrated by men and boys, though this does not mean that women or girls are never violent. As I write, two 14-year-old Sydney girls have been charged with the murder of a taxi driver (see also Brown, 2005). However, such violence is exceptional, as evidenced by the media attention it usually receives. In violence performed by men the victims are often women and girls and the men and boys who are constructed as Other. Whilst the causes of such violence are many and are often contested (see for example Fawcett *et al*, 1996), misogyny plays an obvious role in shaping much male violence, whatever the sex of the victims.

Violence against women and girls by *some* men was identified by second wave feminism as a means by which *all* men maintained their privileges over *all* women (see, for example, Brownmiller, 1976). Whilst post-structural feminisms and sociologies of masculinity have problematised some of the early constructions of gender that tended to treat men and women as unitary categories (see, for example, Gatens, 1996; Kimmel, 1996), men's violence against women clearly plays a major role in policing a gender order that favours male interests over female. However, the more recent theories of gender have enabled a consideration of violence between men as also being gendered and as working to maintain an unjust gender order.

Homophobic violence is clearly grounded in misogynist discourses and is usually deployed in ways that police the boundaries of traditional masculinities. Such violence often works against men, including those who do not identify themselves as gay but who reject forms of masculinity that valorise aggression, hardness and men's superiority over women. This was evident in a comment a 14-year-old boy in a Queensland suburban school once made to me about the difficulties men faced in expressing their feelings:

> Peter: ... like in our society, you like, you gotta be, for men, you gotta be like you gotta be like, you can't be like a little queer. Like a little shy you know like a little softie sort of thing. You can't be like that. Or people start sussing you out. 'Ahh, shit this fella looks a bit suss stay away from him.' ...You know, like that and it's, and like I don't know, it's just a lot, and a lot of pressure's on and stuff and you, I don't know. Oh yeah, and it just wears down the pressure of stuff like that. Men shut their feelings away... and yeah you'll get called a girl 'cause you see that's what girls mainly do. (Mills, 2001: 71)

Peter provides a vivid description of the role of homophobia and misogyny in maintaining particular constructions of masculinity that are harmful to women and girls and to other men and boys.

164

Male-on-male violence that is sometimes motivated by, for example, racist or religious bigotry is also often shaped by misogynist and paternalistic attitudes. For example, in December 2005 there were race riots in Sydney, when mobs of white Australians went on the rampage in the beachside suburb of Cronulla, attacking anybody who looked Middle-Eastern, in order to reclaim the beach for 'Australians'. The rioting and physical attacks on individuals were justified on the grounds that the 'Lebs' did not respect women and had to be driven out to make the beach and its surrounds safe for white women (McIlveen and Lawrence, 2005). Racist violence against othered men can lead them to take up masculinised positions that valorise violence as well as belittling women and supposedly feminine attributes and behaviours. For instance, Archer (2003) notes how many of the British Muslim boys in her study constructed themselves as hard Muslims, as a way to disrupt discourses constructing Asian men as weak and effeminate. As she says: 'The discursive 'talking up' of violence, action and 'hardness' through religious idealism and martyrdom ... evokes a particularly potent, powerful form of masculinity' (Archer, 2003, p. 53). Hence, when schools take up issues of violence, including racist violence, masculinity also has to be on the agenda. To date, it has been feminist concerns that have ensured this to be the case.

When the impact of the feminist movement was felt in education, boys' behaviours towards girls were identified as a major inhibitor of girls' learning (see for example, Jones, 1985). In Australia, this treatment of girls by boys (and sometimes by male teachers) led to a number of government-commissioned reports and policies concerned with girls' education, identifying gendered violence as an important issue for schools to confront (see, for example, Milligan *et al*, 1992; Australian Education Council, 1993; Collins *et al*, 1996). The most recent, *Gender Equity: A Framework for Australian Schools* (Gender Equity Taskforce for Ministerial Council for Employment, Education, Training and Youth Affairs, 1997) identified five strategic directions for schools to take in order to promote gender equity, the third relating to violence and school culture. The stated outcome was that 'gendered violence and sex-based harassment will be eliminated from schools' (1997:17). This was to be achieved through, amongst other things, curriculum programmes and operational practices. They aimed, for example, to: 'promote understanding of the construction of gender and its link to violence'; 'challenge gendered violence and sex-based harassment in schools'; and 'provide girls and boys with opportunities to acquire knowledge and understanding about, and skills to deal with violence, sex-based harassment (including homophobia) and gender based power'.

Various programmes and policies were consequently initiated in schools. For instance, in the State of Queensland, there was an expectation that every government school would have at least one sexual harassment referral officer, although they received very little training. Sexual harassment and violence as an educational concern was also built into various curricula concerning human relationships and personal development. In New South Wales in 2002, as part of the state government's *Strategy to Reduce Violence Against Women*, several school programmes were developed. However, despite the number of initiatives designed to problematise and challenge dominant constructions of masculinity in Australian schools, early feminist concerns about boys' behaviours are still valid. For instance, recent research carried out in Australia noted that:

> Boys emerged as a definite problem for girls in our research. Their sexist, misogynist and femiphobic behaviour and practices contributed in significant ways to impacting detrimentally on the quality of girls' lives and self esteem at school. (Martino and Pallotta-Chiarolli 2005:124)

Although these issues are still of major relevance, policy concerns about gender and violence, alongside other concerns about girls in Australian schools, has steadily been eroded by increasing government-sponsored support for boys' education, which constructs an educational truth that boys are the new victims of schooling.

This truth led to a Federal House of Representatives Inquiry into boys' education, *Boys: Getting it right* (House of Representatives Standing Committee on Education and Training, 2002). The report has been heavily criticised for its anti-feminist stance (see, for example, Gill, 2005). The anti-feminism can be seen in a number of outcomes from the inquiry. One has been the commissioned recasting of *Gender Equity: A Framework for Australian Schools* that grew out of concerns raised by the inquiry team.

The House of Representatives inquiry states that:

> Within the parameters set by the *National Goals for Schooling*[1] the *Gender Equity Framework* needs to be recast as an overarching framework for parallel boys' and girls' education strategies. The overarching gender equity strategy would guard against the adoption of approaches that undermine the achievement of boys or girls.

> This approach casts the educational objectives positively for boys and girls as opposed to the negative approach for boys implied in most of the current policy material – for example, about boys not being violent, not monopolising space and equipment and not harassing girls and other

boys. (House of Representatives Standing Committee on Education and Training, 2002:68)

Because of this concern about the framework, a tender was issued to rewrite it, taking into account the interests of boys. It was issued in November 2003, yet by mid 2006 a draft of a new gender equity framework had still not been distributed for comment. Given the views of those supporting the recasting of this framework that the interests of boys have been ignored in girls' policy documents and that where boys' concerns have been addressed it has been in terms of trying to fix up the boys, there is likely to be little in the new document to assist those in education who are concerned about the persisting issue of gender and violence in schools.

So, whilst educational policy in Australia has so far been supportive of challenging gendered violence through schooling, current moves are unlikely to do so. Although there is a danger of overestimating the impact of previous policies on improving the educational experiences of girls, they did at least provide leverage for placing gender and violence issues upon schools' agendas. Now, though, other avenues need to be found.

A way forward: creating safe schools

The way forward is likely to be problematic. The attacks on a supposed feminised school system and the construction of boys as a disadvantaged group work against problematising constructions of masculinity which are harmful to others. But there are some openings for challenging harmful masculinities.

Ironically, one opening is provided by aspects of the debate about boys. Rejecting any programme aiming to alter boys' behaviour invites a case to be made that it is damaging the educational experiences of other boys and themselves, as well as on those of girls. There is significant literature (see, for example, Francis, 1999; Jackson, 2002; Martino and Pallotta-Chiarolli, 2005) that indicates that some, but not all, boys associate traditional forms of masculinity with opposition to the academic curriculum and the pursuit of academic success. This means that the gender of boys, contrary to the position taken in *Boys: Getting it right*, needs to be put on the educational agenda as a matter of concern in relation to boys' outcomes. In so doing, the ways in which many boys' behaviours inhibit the positive experiences of girls and other boys can also be addressed, as can the issue of creating safe schools for *all* students.

Most people involved in education want schools to be safe places from the fear and the experience of violence. In policy terms this is reflected in Australia in the development of the *National Safe Schools Framework* (Student Learning and Support Services Taskforce, 2003). This document makes little mention of gender and violence, and indeed is silent on gender in the 'guiding principles for the provision of a safe and supportive school environment' (2003:5), but its vision of a situation where 'all Australian schools are safe and supportive environments' (*ibid*) does make the problematisation of violent masculinities a possibility.

This may mean a tactical shift away from the gender agenda, currently dominated by the boys' lobby, to a safe schools agenda. But this agenda is often gender blind, and indeed, like much international bullying literature, it fails to acknowledge the political nature of violence in relation to its defence of the 'patriarchal gender order' (Connell, 1995). This agenda also taps into conservative discourses that demonise young people. However, it is arguably impossible to create safe schools without challenging dominant constructions of masculinity (see, for example, Mills, 2001). That the safe schools agenda can be used strategically by feminist and pro-feminist educationalists concerned about gender and violence in schools is clear in the *Bullying. No way!* website (www.bullyingnoway.com.au), set up to support the *Safe Schools Framework.*

For instance, in the section dealing with gender we see the following:

> Terms such as 'slut', 'whore', 'bitch' and 'butch' are used to regulate girls' behaviour – to suggest that they are not 'doing' their femininity appropriately. Equally, terms such as 'poof', 'wuss' and 'girlie' can be used to deny the legitimacy of boys' behaviours when they operate in different ways from the acceptable or dominant forms of masculinity.

> Sex-based harassment often comes from boys – and some girls and adults – who are stronger, older or more powerful, and whose abuse of power may be condoned by the dominant cultures. Students who suffer this behaviour sometimes find that the harassment is perceived as their individual, personal problem.

> This violence needs to be named for what it is – not the problems of individual students, but part of learned social behaviour that sets up masculinity in opposition to femininity, that devalues femininity, that restricts individual choice and that operates to the detriment of all students.

This website also provides extensive lists of resources and documents that inform schools about developing whole school approaches to gender and violence, offer professional development support for teachers and provide classroom materials. Although the site does not explicitly focus on gender, much aligns with the earlier policy concerns about gender and violence. For example, the website challenges the notion that bullying is due to sick individuals, arguing that much of the violence in schools is the product of unequal power relations that discriminate against girls, women, and marginalised boys and men. Thus it indicates that tackling violence requires exploration of the ways in which boys in schools construct their versions of acceptable masculinities.

Conclusion

This chapter has briefly scanned gender and violence in Australian education. It acknowledges that the feminist movement has made an impression on the educational policy agenda. However, it suggests that the impact of this agenda has been overstated by many within the boys' lobby and that there is still much to be done to challenge forms of masculinity which cause problems for girls and other boys – and also for some teachers – in schools. Those concerned about boys' education are increasingly calling for the employment of more male teachers. Though not covered in this chapter (see Mills *et al*, 2004, for more detail), calls for more male teachers that take no account of how they might perform, colluding with boys' misogynist and homophobic behaviours, will also work against gender-based anti-violence initiatives.

Unfortunately, it is the boys' lobby that currently dominates the Australian national gender agenda in education, as in a number of other countries (Weaver-Hightower, 2003). This domination does not bode well for those attempting to foreground issues of gender and violence as a matter of social justice in education. The concern not to make negative comments about boys can work against any kind of initiative that seeks to problematise their displays of dominant masculinities.

However, the concern *for* boys can be used in ways that contribute to concerns *about* boys. For instance, it can be shown that dominant displays of masculinity negatively affect these boys' academic outcomes, as well as those of girls and other boys, so need to be challenged. Furthermore, a feminist and pro-feminist analysis can be applied to the safe schools agenda so as to ensure that feminist understandings of violence are not removed from the educational agenda. Feminist analyses of schooling that promote gender equity can, and should, be applied to all aspects of education, including the issues concerning boys' education and creating safe schools for all students.

Acknowledgement
I would like to thank Emma Charlton and the Editors for their comments on previous versions of this chapter.

Note

1 Ministerial Council on Education, Employment, Training and Youth Affairs (MCEETYA) (1999), *The Adelaide Declaration on National Goals for Schooling in the Twenty-First Century*, Carlton, MCEETYA

18

'Doing power': confronting violent masculinities in primary schools

Deevia Bhana

Why primary school boys?

> A 13-year-old boy allegedly raped a different 9 year-old classmate each day in front of other pupils in a week-long orgy of violence ... The boy, who stands a good two heads taller than his Grade 1 classmates [in Kagiso] allegedly forced five young boys to hold down the girls so that he could rape them after threatening to assault any classmate who reported him ... the 13 year old was the class bully ... he threatened them [girls] and took their money for lunch ... The girl's father said... 'they're [education department] still in charge of my daughter's safety, but they've failed miserably'. (*Sunday Times*, October 27, 2002).

This newspaper report puts one South African primary school under the spotlight and illustrates the dramatic nature of sexualised and gendered violence. Schools are now recognised as key social sites in the construction of boys' heterosexual cultures (Kehily, 2000) and, in South Africa, are important sites of violence, which constitutes a clear manifestation of gender inequality (Human Rights Watch, 2001). It is speculated that the causes of such violence are due to high rates of economic and social disintegration, and the history of inequities under apartheid, which have led to a brittle emasculated masculinity and a sense of powerlessness on the part of many males (Morrell, 2001). However, while boys' destructive patterns of behaviour have been the focus of research in South African secondary schools (Morrell, 1998), little attention has been paid to the gendered and heterosexualised cultures in South African primary schools, although research in this area is beginning to emerge internationally (see Renold, 2005).

Instances of bullying and the use of force are evident across primary schools (Bhana, 2002). Preventing or reducing the risk of violence in primary schools is critical, yet violence is surprisingly pervasive amongst very young boys, although not all boys behave violently. Other forms of masculinity do exist and some boys are peaceable and gender friendly. Nevertheless, violent masculinity is a particular concern, as it interferes with a school's ability to produce appropriate and safe environments and can be lethal.

It is now well recognised that young primary school children actively construct their gendered and sexual identities (Renold, 2005). Girls should not be seen as passive victims. They are active agents of resistance although violence circumscribes their capacity. Boys, too, are targets of boys' violence. Some of these masculine identities are harmful to gender relations – as illustrated by the newspaper report – but gender identities are malleable and changeable. This malleability combined with current understandings of young boys (Jordan, 1995; MacNaughton, 2000) point to an opportune time to begin work exploring and dealing with violence in primary schools.

This chapter examines the construction of violent masculinities as a signifier of power over girls and highlights how interrogating power itself is central to designing appropriate interventions against gender violence in primary schools. It draws on an ethnographic study which sought to examine the construction of masculinities in schooling amongst boys aged 7 to 9 (Bhana, 2002).

The school context in contemporary South Africa

KwaDabeka Primary School is situated in a poor peri-urban black township area about 16 kilometres from the city of Durban. The apartheid government created the township in 1974 on land adjoining Clermont. The dwellings are mainly informal although there are a few houses. Informal dwellings around the school are mainly tin structures set closely together. Positive changes have occurred in South Africa since the end of the apartheid, and access to basic necessities like electricity and water are improving in the township. Yet poverty among blacks remains endemic as past inequalities keep their hold. Overcrowding, violence and crime, unemployment, inadequate shelter, health-threatening conditions and the scourge of HIV/AIDS challenge family and community life in KwaDabeka.

Many households in the township cannot get adequate food for their children. Fathers are present episodically and may or may not support their children's basic needs. One in five children in South Africa does not live with either parent (Budlender, 1996). The migrant labour system spawned by apartheid has contributed to dislocated family life and many children live with grandparents. In such contexts children are exposed to numerous social risks including apartheid's legacy of inequality and deprivation. Associated with economic hardship are varied forms of violence in the family, in the community and in the school (although physical punishment in schools has been banned since 1996). Children learn to negotiate their daily lives in a climate of intimidation, fear and danger both at home and school.

Age relations complicate matters in the school. As the newspaper report quoted illustrates, the age ranges in a Grade One or Two class are wide. Race and class are determining factors in shaping the current variations in ages. Migrancy, dislocated families, urbanisation and limited access to free pre-school education mean that children who attend Grade One or Two may be under or over age. Both have the potential to exacerbate the situation.

As long as the social arrangements continue to perpetuate worsening poverty for most South Africans (Terreblanche, 2002), children's vulnerability to violence will continue. In dehumanising contexts, boys learn to cope and respond in aggressive ways and are all too ready to react in ways that are reinforced in the family, community and the school (Garbarino, 1995).

How children see the issues

Children carry the heaviest burden of violence in the school. My field notes record the climate of fear and violence in the classroom:

> Teacher hits all children on the head repeatedly as they recite ma me mi mo mu. I am scared. I notice that the children who have been working with the teacher are instructed to leave the group from the board area. They do so quietly, they sit quietly. They are terrified. They do not smile. They are afraid. The teacher walks to the group that has just been seated and slaps a boy on his face. I wonder why. The teacher leaves the class. I enjoy this time. There is shuffling, talk and chat. I can't understand all of it. I talk to Sipho. He says, 'I am afraid of the teacher'.

Later:

> Mrs. H. walks in the classroom. Quiet. She picks on two children. They have not done their work. Mrs. H. shouts. She gets the stick from the table. It's a branch from a tree. She hits them on their back and legs. Stick breaks. Teacher gets another stick. This time it is not a branch. They call it a pipe. Mrs. H. continues where she had stopped. They are crying, sobbing quietly.

My field notes report what happened in the classroom when a parent came to see the teacher about the broomstick her son broke.

> Someone knocks and enters the classroom. A mother. Mrs H calls Sandile. He is shouted at and the mother shouts at him also. The pipe is brought to the mother. It's difficult to understand what she says to Sandile. But slowly he moves towards the desks. The other kids rush eagerly as if they are preparing for an event, and set two desks together. Sandile rests on his stomach across two desks. The kids watch with brightened eyes as if they know what's about to happen. She strikes him with that pipe. I count. Ten times. He sobs. He cries. I discover that Sandile broke the classroom broom and Mrs. H demanded a new one. The mother cannot afford to buy a broom and the mother had come to talk to Mrs. H about that.

Recording this portrayal of violence in the lives of children is not to resurrect discredited notions of a linear relationship between poverty and violence. Using violence to control children creates conditions which allow violence to flourish. Children learn that violence is a purposive behaviour that achieves an end. The more commonplace violence becomes, the more it is seen as a legitimate way of managing conflict. Corporal punishment has an impact on the shaping of identities and it reduces positive relations and affects what is considered appropriate behaviour. The school does not cause violence but it does legitimise it. Neither does poverty cause violence, but the two are inter-dependent and mutually reinforcing. Violence in South African schools occurs across varied social and economic contexts.

Power over girls

Physical violence is a striking characteristic of the young boys' interaction with girls. The ability of the boys to demonstrate their power over girls was evident in the way they could use their greater body size to attack and get rewards. Field notes taken during the play break note how some boys draw on violent masculinity, perpetuating unequal relations of power:

> Thoko had bought a 50c packet of chips and a *vetkoek* [cake]. Sifiso demanded the *vetkoek*. Bullying. Thoko refused. Sifiso pushed her, his voice raised. She refused. He slapped her. She hit him back and ran from him. He went after her and grabbed and hit her again before he ran off with the *vetkoek*.

Boys strongly articulated their use of physical violence against girls. Many boys I interviewed argued that it was the right thing to do. For example, they constantly used threatening words: '*ngizokushaya*' (I will hit you), '*ngizoku-*

bamba' (I will get you), clicking sounds as in '*nx-agh*', as well as actual physical violence. Food insecurity encourages violent social relations. Through the enactment of violence, Sifiso learns that *vetkoeks* or other resources will come to him and will continue to come to him through further enactment of violence. This is in line with Mills' (2001) work which shows how the body is used as a tool for violence. Boys like Sifiso invested in bodily strength and power over girls especially and this dominated gender dynamics in the school.

Other means to demonstrate power over girls also had violent effects. For instance, power over girls was demonstrated by the boys dominating conversations with girls. Girls were expected to show deference and speak little. One of the boys I interviewed said, 'girls are naughty, they talk too much' and so 'I hit them'. Talking too much defied the general expressions of deference that were part of Zulu cultural practices. Thus girls talking too much is perceived as an unacceptable degree of freedom.

Me:	Why don't you like girls, Andile?
Andile:	Girls are rude. They are funny. The girls try to impress the teacher and I hit them.
Me:	Do they get hurt?
Andile:	Yes and I hit them again.
Me:	But why?
Andile:	They must not be rude.

Andile spoke indignantly. Girls, as we have seen, were expected to acknowledge male entitlement and 'not be rude'. Violence is a pattern of behaviour which Andile feels obliged to carry out if silence is not secured. Girls being rude and talking too much, and the freedom such behaviour represents, must be understood as a challenge to male entitlement and to the power males feel entitled to.

Power over girls was also demonstrated through the domination of school space and this is consistent with other research (Thorne, 1993; Skelton 2001). In Thorne's case study of primary schools in the US, she claimed that boys controlled about ten times more space than girls in the school playground. Girls at KwaDabeka Primary School do find a small space in the playground amongst the space invaders and their play often entails small-scale turn-taking which yields a great deal of fun and pleasure. It is highly choreographed and often involves singing and clapping to rhythmic tunes – against the backdrop of violence. Boys often disrupt the girls who play this game of *ije*. *Ije* is the means through which girls find a freer and private space within the public site of the school but that space too is fragile, under constant threat of 'boy trouble':

Rita: When we are playing ije the boys don't like it and they always trouble us.

The boys like to play soccer. I'm asking a question, 'if you [referring to a boy in the group] like to play soccer why do you play with us?'

Gender boundaries are broken through play but the form of play that this generates is unwelcome and abusive towards girls.

The preserve of the male space is actively policed through fear. Power over girls is often achieved through fear:

Me: Do you like boys?

Eli: No.

Me: Why?

Eli: I am scared of them.

Me: Why?

Eli: They are rough.

Me: What do they do?

Eli: They hit. I am scared of him [pointing to Seshishle]. I am scared that he is going to hit me. I'm scared of hitting.

Fear is a major emotion operating within gender relations (Mills, 2001). 'Violent males ... exaggerate, distort and glorify those [hegemonic masculine] behaviours' (Kenway and Fitzclarence, 1997: 121). In a climate of fear, many girls choose to remain silent and their power to resist is slight. Their power and agency diminishes when violence and the threat of violence constructs and limits everything they do or can do.

Power over girls is also evident through the threat of sexual violence. Verbal and physical harassment relating to sexuality against girls is rife:

Me: What do the boys do?

Thulisile: They push us and they swear.

Me: What do they say?

> Thulisile: Like 'I'll find you my man. I'll kill you my man'. Lucs says 'bitch'. He says it to the girls. When the girls are singing some of the boys say 'fuck it, *voetsek* [fuck off] and then they say: 'I'll find you my man, I'll kill you my man'.

In another interview:

> Thulisile: Boys are criminals. They steal our pens and they swear, 'fuck, fuck, fuck'.

> Thabani: Girls smell. They give us diseases. Their armpits smell. Girls tease boys. The boys don't sleep with the girls because the girls stink.

> Thulisile: The boys kick. The boys want to do things with the girls but the girls don't want to do those things.

Heterosexuality is a key indicator of hegemonic masculinity and in this context it was used to construct femininity as polluting. The nature of sexual dominance and exploitation is complex. Distancing from girls who are castigated as polluting creates Thabani's sense of power. Furthermore, the sexual objectification of girls operates to provide Thabani with power over girls. Girls are sexually available to boys, as they see it, but boys choose not to sleep with them because 'they stink' and 'give us diseases'. Is Thabani preparing for sexual harassment activities as he learns masculinity? Evident here are callous sexual attitudes and suggestions that girls are responsible for sexual diseases, creating a climate in which males have power over girls.

Framing interventions on boys, masculinities and power

The classroom interactions described reveal the effects of violent masculinity on girls, suggesting that violence against girls is significant for boys who have little access to resources and support systems. Ending violence and ending violent gender relations are thus inseparable from ending social and economic inequalities. Anti-violence work has to be part of the broader strategy of reform in gender arrangements that will equalise resources and opportunities. The South African government is working hard at poverty alleviation, job creation and addressing the basic needs of all people; but have a long way to go to change the socio-economic situation. Primary schools need to become involved in addressing the issue of power in violence. It is appropriate to recommend that teachers, parents and boys and girls all deal with this problem. Boys cannot be expected to change without frameworks of support.

Teacher development

Firstly, teachers must become more aware of the gender violence in primary schools. There needs to be greater vigilance and more teachers in the playground during breaks. This might help to prevent violent episodes and deter violent patterns of behaviour. To feel able to 'tell on' someone, children must feel safe and comfortable with an adult. By using corporal punishment, teachers alienate children and harm positive social relations with them. Yet teachers not only encourage violence and allow it to flourish but they also make it difficult for pupils to trust teachers and 'tell on' others. Children need to feel that they are taken seriously and that adult teachers care enough for their safety to take action. To do this, teachers need to be more aware of gender in the primary school and boys' investment in forms of masculinity which are seen to be powerful. Moreover, there needs to be greater awareness of the ways in which boys construct their masculine identities. Teachers need to become aware of the ways in which boys struggle to gain power. Garbarino (1995; 1999) suggests that boys who behave violently are struggling, have anxieties and fears and need protection, empathy and positive social support. The primary boys described above are not the enemies. They do have choices but these are limited. Boys are vulnerable to external forces, they lack protection and often live in unstable homes and environments that provide inadequate food and care.

Policy development

Violence prevention policies must be a feature of all primary schools. Those in authority – principals, school governing bodies and teachers – should send a strong message to the entire school community that violence is not condoned and all reports of violent incidents will be acted upon. Ideally this policy should be negotiated and collaboratively written by all the stakeholders in the school.

Support from the Department of Education

The Department of Education should identify programmes and resources which provide information and training about gender violence with particular emphasis on understanding and dealing with boys and girls. They must provide assistance to schools in developing policies consistent with the prevention of violence. This must involve parents and the community.

Whole school development

Finally, the whole school must be placed on alert regarding gender violence. As Jordan (1995: 83) observes:

Changing definitions of masculinity adopted by little boys in the early years of school would not, of itself, destroy gender inequity, nor bring patriarchy tumbling down, but it could broaden the options for many boys and make school more tolerable for girls.

Making schooling safer may offer girls greater opportunities to take risks, to challenge definitions of gender and to foster better gender relations.

19

'Let's be loud! Let's hear your voice!' Exploring trainee teachers' use of theatre to challenge power relations

Lucy Stackpool-Moore and Tania Boler

Introduction

In this chapter, we explore the role of teachers in promoting schools as safe, healthy and empowering learning environments in societies affected by HIV/AIDS. If education is to be the social vaccine to prevent further escalation of the HIV epidemic, teachers, along with students, government officials and educationalists worldwide, will have the daunting but inspiring challenge of figuring out how to do so. Yet teachers are constrained by their own gendered identities and the power relations within the school setting. The great Brazilian educator Paulo Freire argued that, for sustainable change to take place, the people most affected must first become critically conscious of themselves and their environment (Freire, 1972). This concept of critical engagement is central to participatory approaches to adult learning. It has been successfully adapted to address HIV and gender relations through adult learning approaches such as *Stepping Stones* and the *Theatre for a Change* initiative explored in this chapter (Welbourn, 1995; Easby, 2005). It is also relevant to work on addressing gender violence in schools.

Participatory approaches can promote critical self-awareness among teachers as 'reflective practitioners', a process whereby individuals analyse their own practice and behaviour with a view to improving it (Freire, 1972; Schön, 1983;

Chambers, 2000). Such approaches help provide a structured format in which the natural processes of reflection and informal learning can be channelled towards specific learning objectives and bring about directed change in both individuals and their environment (Boler, 2003). Therefore, if teachers are to contribute successfully to school-based interventions to address gender relations and HIV, they need to adopt a participatory and child-centred approach to teaching and learning, and to develop the special skills and sensitivity to do so in a health-promoting and empowering way (Boler and Aggleton, 2005). Despite significant funding for HIV prevention in general, and the pivotal role of teachers in HIV prevention work, it seldom features in training courses.

This chapter showcases an innovative project in Ghana run by a UK-based NGO called *Theatre for a Change*, which uses participatory methodologies to enhance the skills of teachers in promoting HIV prevention within the school. It also evaluates the opportunities and risks of using participatory approaches in pre-service teacher training. Because of the gender dimensions of the epidemic and the power inequalities on which it thrives, some important lessons can also be drawn for preventing gender violence in schools.

Gender, power and teachers-implications for teacher education

To recognise the full potential of participatory approaches in promoting gender sensitivity and reflective practice in teachers, we need to recognise that schools are gendered institutions, and that there is an important distinction between the 'explicit' and the 'hidden' curriculum (Stromquist *et al*, 1998). Applied to HIV, the explicit curriculum refers to knowledge about prevention, testing, counselling and the scientific details relating to the disease itself. The hidden curriculum refers to the underlying gendered, stigmatised and/or silenced opinions that are embedded in the delivery of the explicit curriculum. For any intervention promoting gender equality or HIV prevention to be effective, it must address both the formal (explicit) and informal (implicit) processes of learning within the classroom. One aspect of the latter is providing opportunities for teachers and students to challenge their own gendered identities and power relationships, and to understand how the hidden curriculum influences how these identities are played out within the school environment (Pattman and Chege, 2003).

Much has been written recently about the impact of HIV/AIDS on teachers and the education system (e.g. Kelly, 2000; Coombe, 2002), but very little has looked explicitly at the reverse. A paradox surrounds teachers, gender and

HIV/AIDS: on the one hand teachers offer hope for change in their role as educators; on the other hand they embody the very power inequalities that a prevention programme is seeking to amend. The impact of teachers on gender relations and on HIV/AIDS is closely related to the notion of schools as gendered institutions and to dimensions of power within a school.

It is not so much the 'what' of education but the 'how' that is most important in shaping knowledge and behaviour. Guiding teachers in a reflective process in which they examine their own gendered lives and constructions of identity is likely to enable a similar process of reflection in their students. At the same time, it is important to recognise that, echoing Mills (2000), teachers – and students – need to be empowered as part of the process of addressing the unequal power relations within school settings that contribute to HIV vulnerability. Where teachers may be already feeling threatened or inadequately skilled to teach a subject such as life skills or HIV prevention, this process of empowerment will be vital (Boler, 2003). Moreover, gender equality should be the cornerstone of all HIV/AIDS prevention programmes, targeting change within individuals as well as collectively within the school and wider community (Swainson, 2003). In order to challenge and change existing notions of gender and identity, an educational programme must be directed at individuals *and* at their environment.

Theatre for a Change

In Ghana, *Theatre for a Change* uses participatory methodologies to work with trainee teachers, through pre-service teacher training, in challenging underlying power and gender relations. The NGO targeted this specific group in the belief that trainee teachers are not only young and open-minded but also enthusiastic about teaching and not locked into didactic modes of delivery. The learning process is intensive and sustained; all first and second year students take part in weekly sessions, each lasting about two hours. Trainees are assessed at the end of the year and graded on their achievement. In total, over 4,200 teachers have been trained and the Ghanaian Ministry of Education is slowly taking over co-ordination of the project so that the expertise and responsibility lie clearly with its officials.

The assumption underlying the training package is that vulnerability to HIV infection is fostered by unequal gender relations and that achieving gender equality is therefore a vital way to prevent the spread of the epidemic. The training package is different from the mainstream life skills curriculum in that it does not assume that complex skills such as assertiveness can be learnt in a 45-minute session. Instead, the focus is on promoting critical self-awareness and analysis of power relations through experiential learning; in this case, trainee teachers practise taking on new roles and understanding how to break old patterns of behaviour. Participation is taken to mean experiencing, and the motto is '80 per cent action, 20 per cent talking'! For many of the young trainee teachers, this is the first time they have been encouraged to develop their own opinions. Having been through a conventional education system, they have learnt not to speak out of turn, and that a good student is a silent student. So it can come as a surprise when they are told in the project: 'Let's be loud! Let's hear your voice!'

Trainees explore how power manifests itself in movement, space and voice. For example, eye contact reflects implicit power relations, with those in the weaker position less likely to maintain eye contact. In the training, trainees are asked to maintain eye contact with other trainees and then to explore how they feel. As one trainee recalls:

> Before *Theatre for a Change*'s programme, I hardly maintained eye contact during conversation with people. And now? Of course, I've improved massively on the maintenance of eye contact, which has enhanced my confidence and communicating skills. I was able to maintain eye contact with my father for considerable moments without any ill feeling for the first time. Yes, for the first time! (Male teacher trainee)

Balance can also be used to explore power relations. The trainees work in pairs to find physical balance with one another. After much playful re-positioning, standing on one leg and falling over, they finally find a state of balance. When asked to reflect on what they notice about balance, it becomes clear that being in balance feels good; they feel stronger, more relaxed and happy, and most importantly, being in balance requires them both to be at the same level. Drawing on this, the trainees are encouraged to deconstruct relationships in terms of gender-related power. They try things out physically and are asked to report on what they have experienced. What do they notice about eye contact? What does this mean for balance within a relationship? How does it relate to teaching and learning in the classroom?

Through these participatory activities, trainees experience how power dynamics vary according to the dominant learning methodology. For example, in a traditional formal school setting, the power dynamic often involves one active person – the teacher – while the rest are passive and not in control. *Theatre For a Change* trainees are encouraged to acknowledge that participatory pedagogies which encourage child-centred approaches to learning involve a shift in power but come to realise that handing over power does not mean losing it. Touch tag is one technique used to show how power is not lost but transformed (see box). It is a practical example of how teachers can feel empowered, rather than threatened, in the process of sharing power in the classroom.

In **touch tag** two volunteers (male and female) act out a social interaction based on their own experiences, and the group rate each of them in terms of power. For example, how are women expected to negotiate sexual favours in exchange for material goods? The scoring of status follows from a series of activities on how people have different status in different contexts. In most cases, the woman is the weaker one (score 2 or 3) and the man is in a position of high power (score 8). The group then intervene, touching the person at the point in which they think balance could be improved, and then replacing the volunteer in the improvisation (tag) to see if they can create a more balanced scene. The group continues with the touch tag until the group is content that the power is balanced between the man and the woman. It can take several attempts for the group to agree what is a perfectly balanced interaction. Once the volunteers have achieved balance, they realise that they have both scored higher than the original improvisation; neither has lost anything and both have gained. The men, especially, need to realise that they are not sacrificing their power; indeed, many participants say afterwards how what they previously thought was power they now realise was force. Often the men start off by saying they are going to have to come down to the level of their wives. This is just an early stage of the learning process and usually, by the end, they realise that nobody has to come down to anybody else's level, because they are experiencing a new type of power which is participatory and collaborative. The men are invited to transform power, not into passivity but into balance, so that they no longer feel that they have to control women. The trainees use this exercise to analyse what happens when power in a relationship is in balance: the power doesn't get lost; it is not diluted, but instead there is a transformation in which power becomes strength and division.

Risks and challenges

We have argued here for the need to use participatory methodologies to empower teachers as individuals to challenge their gendered relations with students and with each other. However, the realities of the formal education system conflict with some of the pre-requisites for introducing participatory methodologies successfully (Boler and Aggleton, 2005). The vast majority of teacher training tends to be didactic, non-participatory, inflexible and assessment-driven. In contrast, the participatory methodologies needed to challenge power relations within schools are responsive, raising questions rather than providing clear-cut answers, and challenging teachers to find new ways of relating to one another and to their students. To date insufficient thought has gone into how to bridge the gulf between these two different educational processes and it is often assumed that teachers can easily switch from one pedagogy to another.

One of the challenges faced by all participatory training approaches, such as that espoused by *Theatre for a Change*, is the sustainability and transferability of the techniques into the realities of classrooms. *Theatre for a Change* attempts to pre-empt these challenges by first training 20 facilitators – women and men – who go on to train the rest of the trainees in a cascade approach. Based on the principles of experiential learning, namely that learning is enhanced through direct exposure and repeated practice, this core group of trainers will undergo training themselves on one day and find themselves training on the next. The trainees are encouraged to set up cascade training when they leave the college.

Another tension is around the assessment-driven nature of teacher training and formal education in general. Transformative education is difficult to assess and indeed, given its participatory aims, formalising the approach through assessment may impose excessive structure on something that should be flexible. Participation is therefore a potentially powerful strategy to promote teachers' professional development, gender-sensitive reflective practice and HIV prevention, but it is also problematic. Currently, assessment of the training is mostly through self-assessment. The groups create their own list of training objectives and are encouraged to keep journals on their feelings and reactions during the training. These can be highly personal:

> I would be a liar if I said I have not noticed any changes in my life as a result of *Theatre for a Change*. Like all changes, it crept up on me like a sandstorm in the desert – although this wasn't as harsh. At the moment I cannot say that I welcome these changes but I must say that I appreciate

it. Right now I see myself as more assertive and reflective of my own behaviour and the behaviour of others. (Woman trainee)

The programme has recently been evaluated (Easby, 2005). Among the challenges highlighted were: the demanding nature of the role of facilitator, who is expected to remain neutral when discussing sensitive issues around HIV, sex and sexuality; the risk of dilution in the cascade approach; and the danger that group dynamics may inhibit critical thinking and increase pressure to conform. There is also the possibility that if teacher trainees see theatre as just fun this will impede their connecting with important issues. And, the tendency to promote the idea of men as the problem and women as the victims can create further tension and antagonism. Some teachers also believed that the safe choices acted out by the protagonists were unlikely to be chosen in real life situations because choices about sex are not as rational as they might appear in a role play.

In addition to the challenges outlined by Easby, there remains the issue of what happens once the trainees leave the safe space of the teacher training college and go out to teach in classes of 60 or more students. What happens when they spend most of their day teaching in traditional didactic ways; can they simply switch to a more participatory style in an after-school club? It is assumed that transforming power relations amongst teachers will better equip them for teaching about HIV/AIDS in schools. But there is no evidence that it has and it is far from clear what impact *Theatre for a Change* is having on students' attitudes and behaviours.

Ultimately, if the training does prove to have been transformative, teachers will have shifted to a teaching and learning approach which is both self-critically aware and child-centred. The techniques developed through the programme can provide teachers with the skills to teach life skills lessons in a way that can promote schools as gender-sensitive, safe, empowering and healthy environments. Touch tag and other interactive techniques can be used imaginatively across all subject areas, not just HIV/AIDS education. They are equally valid, for example, when seeking to address gender violence in schools.

Recommendations and conclusions

For change to come about in schools, teachers need to teach in a way that recognises and challenges gendered power relations. To do this skilfully, they first need to recognise their own positions of power, and participate in their own process of transformation. *Theatre for a Change* provides an important and replicable model for equipping large numbers of trainee teachers with the skills to teach in a gender-sensitive and empowering way. Although the approach originates in HIV prevention work, it is well suited to initiatives seeking to address gender violence in schools.

All this implies that participatory teacher education needs to replace the didactic fact-based training which does little to recognise each teacher as an individual with his/her own assumptions about sex and gender. Since theatre and other participatory techniques do precisely this, they should become an integral component of both pre-service and in-service teacher training. The following recommendations are offered:

- For teacher training to be transformative, the process needs to be experiential and sustained over time
- More effort needs to be made to shift to a participatory approach into what is currently a non-participatory system. Teacher training initiatives and expectations need to take into account the realities of formal education systems that may conflict with certain pre-requisites for participatory methodologies
- Local contexts need to be taken into account. Initiatives should always be multifaceted and fine-tuned to the context, and be cognisant of power structures within communities
- Participatory approaches in schools are more likely to succeed in an environment which is child-centred and democratic
- For the cascade approach to be effective, adequate follow-up and support is paramount
- Interventions which confront gender violence in schools need to challenge the structural barriers that affect susceptibility to HIV, including poverty, gender, age and race.

The HIV/AIDS epidemic presents a daunting yet inspiring challenge: re-shaping education so that it becomes central to preventing its spread. Engaging in their own journeys of critical reflection will enable teachers to use education as an effective vaccine against the underlying gender and power inequalities on which HIV and violence thrive.

20

'He put his hands between girls' thighs': using student teachers' memories to tackle gender violence

Fatuma Chege

It is when we, as humans become aware of the inhumanity of violence, of its absurdity and pointlessness, that we discover within ourselves a demand for non-violence, the basis and organising principle of our humanity. (Müller 2002)

Introduction

This chapter draws on a four-month study (November 2004 to March 2005) of childhood memories of violence as documented by a group of African student teachers enrolled at Kenyatta University in Kenya. It was part of the United Nations Secretary General's global study on Violence against Children, which emerged as the UN General Assembly's response in 2001 to a call by the Committee on the Rights of the Child to conduct research on violence against children worldwide. UNICEF Eastern and Southern Africa Regional Office (ESARO), under the guidance of the Regional Education Advisor, was charged with conducting and co-ordinating the sub-project focusing on violence against children in and around schools and other educational settings from a global perspective. The memory work was undertaken to generate complementary data on childhood violence.[1]

Defining violence

The participating students were all agreed that violence constituted any form of physical and/or emotional harm inflicted on any person within the family, community, workplace, school or other social and educational settings. Instructively, apart from the issue of gangs, the memories of Kenyatta University students coincided with the dominant forms of violence identified in the global study, specifically corporal punishment, bullying and gender violence. In this project, corporal punishment was often presented as a gendered experience.

Even though memory work is relatively new among Kenyan researchers, it generated an immense amount of data. This chapter focuses only on sexual harassment and abuse that helps to demonstrate the students' reconstructions of episodes of gender-based violence.

Memory work as a method of generating data

The value of documenting memories is founded on the assumption that our identities, gendered, sexual and otherwise, are constructed continually. They are not formed just around future and present expectations of Self by the Self or Other (Alloway, 1995), but also on the understandings that identities are generated through people's constructions of Self around particular past experiences in relation to significant others. The strength of memory work in this project hinged on the conscious positioning of the subjects, in this case the student teachers, at the core of the research process, providing them with the space and a relatively intimate medium through which to explore their past experiences of violence. This life cycle approach provided a guiding framework within which to map out particular incidents of violence and locate them not only in a specific social context but also in a chronological setting. This approach was defined in terms of the key transit points within the Kenyan education system identified conveniently as: early childhood (before attending formal education); nursery school (4-5 years old); lower primary and upper primary (aged 6-10 and 11-14, respectively); secondary school (15-18 years old) and, for this particular sample, the university (young adulthood, aged 19-25).

The participants

Ten female and ten male students at the University of Kenyatta participated in the study. All were student teachers and – as future parents – had a reasonable stake in the well-being of children. The sampling procedure was based not on the types of violence the subjects were willing to reveal but rather on their willingness to participate in a study of memory work and violence.

Generating data

The participants were asked to record their memories of violence while at the same time positioning themselves in the context of the cited violence, identifying the perpetrators and the sites associated with the incidents they recorded. In addition to documenting their experiences, all the students met at least once a month to share their experiences of doing memory work, to reflect on unfolding definitions and categorisations of violence, and to address the various types of violence that they felt needed group interrogation. At the end of the project, some asked to keep their diaries to help them continue reflecting on their recorded memories, which many were confronting for the first time in their lives. They described as therapeutic the memory work, in which they explored their recollections of childhood violence in a reflexive and constructive way. Memory work seemed to have the edge over more conventional methods such as interviews, as it allowed the integration of the *self-conscious autobiographical accounts* with the *collective understanding of the matter of concern* (Kippax *et al*, 1988). And it allowed the subjects to analyse their shifting identities retrospectively as they reflected on their past selves, projecting them into the future as they constructed themselves as professionals, and proactively in terms of how they responded to the Self and Other in a multiplicity of possible ways as young people preparing to become teachers.

Analysing the diaries

The diaries were analysed thematically according to the emergent types of violence, using the life cycle approach. The findings presented here are those identified as sexual and they manifested themselves mainly in the form of sexual harassment and abuse. Sexual violence at school was mainly experienced as a threat by male teachers against girls – clearly a gendered occurrence. At university, the identified pattern was of male students who sexually harassed their female peers.

Selected findings: memories of sexual violence

Even though sexual violence in the form of verbal and physical harassment featured less frequently in the students' diaries than other forms of violence such as corporal punishment and humiliating verbal punishments or bullying, the sexualisation of girls by male teachers and male peers emerged as a core concern, particularly among female students, whose narratives were corroborated by the memories of their male peers. Such convergence of independent memories between the sexes is an important observation that strengthens the reliability of the data and provides sound grounds upon which to strategise appropriate gender-responsive mixed-sex interventions for combating violence against children.

A discourse of disempowerment was prevalent among female students who experienced sexual violence at school and university in ways that male students did not.

Female students' memories of sexual violence in school
Karen remembered how, in primary Class 5 and 6, one of the male teachers administered punishment in gendered ways that left girls feeling sexually harassed and violated. Karen's memory of gendered punishment (see Box 1) portrays schools as lacking mechanisms for students to channel their concerns about being sexualised, and failing to provide them with the skills for exposing their assailants. It is reasonable to assume that the power relations between adult teacher and girl child, coupled with the cultural objectification of femininity to mean sexual availability for male gratification, did much to silence girls like Karen, and thus helped to perpetuate sexual violence without raising suspicions.

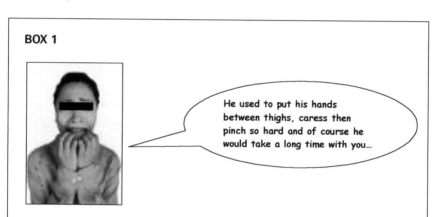

BOX 1

He used to put his hands between thighs, caress then pinch so hard and of course he would take a long time with you...

When we were in Class 5 and 6 there was a teacher who used to teach us English and CRE and his form of punishment for boys was so harsh. He would tell them to put their heads under the desks and then pull their shorts so tightly, then beat them several canes on their buttocks and should they move their hands from under the table, he would increase the strokes. For the girls he used to put his hands between thighs, caress then pinch so hard and of course he would take a lot of time with you. He called you in front at his desk then pull you near him and of course the class not watching he would do that and he did this several times and being the harshest teacher in the school we could not report him and most of us never thought that was a problem at that time. (*Karen, memories of primary school*)

According to Karen, the way the teacher placed his hand between girls' thighs, caressing and then pinching, was personalised and done in privacy behind the teacher's desk, so blocking the goings-on from the view of the class. Further, by physically pulling the girls close to him, the teacher asserted his adult-male power and was able to sneak his hand under the girls' skirts with minimal risk of attracting witnesses should the victim call out. In comparison, the boys received strokes of the cane on their buttocks and in a relatively public way. This was neither personalised nor sexualised, as was the abuse of the girls.

The fact that Karen recorded this memory of ritualistic thigh-pinching punishment in a comparative way yields an identity of teacher-to-be, who is relatively aware and sensitive to the existence of gendered punishments and the potential of these to be sexual. Equally crucial in Karen's recollection is that most of the girls seemed ignorant about the sexual connotations of the teacher's action and the violation of their bodies. Although Karen described the boys' punishment as 'so harsh', her account of the girls' sexualised punishment suggests equally harsh effects on girls such as herself, though she does not place herself in her narrative.

Nancy's memory (Box 2 on page 194) suggests that the girls' memories of sexual violence by teachers tended to gravitate around primary 5 and 6 classes. Girls of this age are in early adolescence as sexual maturation begins. Many girls find this stage of development challenging, as they try to make sense of their physical and sexual changes.

Even though Nancy seemed aware that her teacher was molesting her sexually, her idea that only girls with breasts invited fondling is worrying. Nancy's rationalisation indicates an inability to understand her rights as a child. Young people might be growing up thinking that sexual fondling or other abuse could be right if done to certain sorts of girls. Importantly, Nancy's memory foregrounds the implications of sexual maturation for girls and the dangers of essentialising this maturation as a licence for men to sexually intrude women's bodies.

Clearly, Karen and Nancy were both aware that sexual touch by male teachers was unacceptable. Both noted in their diaries that the teacher's behaviour made them feel violated and uncomfortable. But they were obviously ill-prepared to respond in ways that would expose their teacher assailants. Their testimonies help to invalidate the stereotype that girls enjoy being sexualised and thus invite sexual assault of their person (Robinson, 2005: 28). Of significance is the evidence of the silence that shrouds the female sex and sexuality

---

BOX 2

> This male teacher started touching my chest, but I didn't have breast...

I had gone to school one afternoon on Sunday for music festivals pre-paration when I was in Standard 6. I was the first person to get to school. I got into the class where we used to go to practice. After few minutes, our teacher arrived i.e. the coach. He was very drunk; he greeted me and sat close to me. After few minutes it started raining and there was no other pupil who had turned up. This male teacher started touching my chest but I didn't have breast. He began caressing me but I couldn't understand what he was up to, but I remembered my mother had told me not to allow a man touch any part of my body. I started crying. He requested me to go to teacher's quarter's house and wait for him there, I refused and I told him that I will inform my father who was a teacher in the same school. After that, he allowed me to go home. I was so worried and harassed. I have never told anyone about it. Afterwards when I grew up, I understood that, that teacher wanted to rape me (*Nancy, memories of primary school*)

---

and the girls' fear of being blamed for being the victims. Fear of this sort must not be underestimated, as we can see how it compels girls to remain silent for many years. Almost all the subjects confessed their unspoken conspiracy of silence about their experiences of violence, including sexual violence.

Male students' memories of sexual violence in school

The male students recorded no memories of sexual violence against them. This may have been because of the macho hegemony they needed to main-tain as men in the making (see Robinson, 2005: 29). For example, when a male student revealed in a group meeting that he had been harassed by girls who allegedly touched his genitals, the rest of the students burst into laughter, and some of the men wondered aloud why he was worried about being touched by girls. This response to sexual harassment of boys by girls may explain why the memory project featured scarcely a single entry of boy's reconstructions of being sexually harassed.

However, some of the male students' memories quite distinctly corroborated the girls' claims of sexual harassment by male teachers, giving them further credence. In his diary, for example, one male student recorded several memories of male teachers soliciting sexual relations with girl students in exchange for undeserved examination marks or examination leaks. Apparently, the male teachers' behaviour fanned rivalry between them and the boys, reportedly because they competed for intimacy and attention from the same girls. Teacher behaviour of this kind reflects what Kimmel (1994) and Connell (1996) describe as definitions of manhood that help to maintain the power some men have over other men and which most men possess over most women. This male student, John, wrote:

> I remember vividly when I was in Form Three, there used to be a Deputy Headmaster of the school who used to sleep with (female) students. In fact most of the girls were intimidated to accepting to sleep with him. One time when he snatched the girlfriend of my friend, we protested to the Headmaster, but nothing was done. We organised a strike, which exposed him and made him sacked. (...) In my former secondary school, cheating on the national exam was rampant. Some parents would pay teachers to coordinate the cheating and also bribe the Head-teacher. Girl students would accept sexual advances in order to be assisted. This would cause a lot of anxiety to the other students. In fact in the Geography paper we had to grab material from one of the students (female). Any complaint to the authorities went unheard. When it became worse we had to report to the District Commissioner for action. I remember vividly when I was in form 4 our Kiswahili teacher would assist the students (female) in the national exam in exchange of sex.

By observing that male teachers 'intimidated' girls into having sex, John provides acknowledgement of the powerlessness of the girls whom the teachers exploited sexually. His narrative also demonstrates how the teachers explicitly and practically devalued the girls' schooling by constructing them as sex objects, not subjects with a right to engage in educational endeavours on equal terms with the boys. Such insight from a male student teacher offers hope that, with proper guidance and appropriate life skills education, both sexes can work empathetically to eradicate sexual violence.

University experiences of sexual harassment

On entry to university, the form and nature of sexual violence seemed to change for these students. Most of the sexual harassment was reportedly perpetrated by male students and was directed at female peers. The diaries revealed that even with longer experiences of schooling, coupled with co-education and biophysical development and – assumedly – increased maturity, sexual violence was a reality for young women. The university students constructed themselves as equally vulnerable, helpless and unassertive as the younger girls in the lower levels of education. When sexually harassed, many resorted to making excuses for the abusive male behaviour directed at them, blaming their drunkenness and making resolutions that diverted attention from their assailants' behaviour even when they feared being raped. Mary's memory while at university is an example:

> I remember it was Sept 2003 and I was walking at 10.00pm (still early in KU) towards Eastern (Kitchen) from Nyayo Hostels to visit my friend. When I reached near Nyandarua Hostel, there was a group of young men who were drunk. It was a Friday night. I gained confidence and continued walking assuming them. Unfortunately one of them really felt he must harass me. He shouted at me 'sweetie'... 'matako' (buttocks). The rest laughed and began whistling at me. I assumed them and tried to pass them on the road. They blocked my way but I shed away all my fear and decided to face them. He touched my bottom and another, my breast. Imagine how violated and harassed I felt. Shame on them. I became tough and shouted to them to lay their hands off me and luckily some couple came along and I took the chance to make away. I shall avoid walking alone at night however early it may seem. Some of these drank young men can turn into rapist!

Girls' tendency to make excuses for abusive behaviour from men allowed perpetrators to get off scot-free, whereas they themselves suffered double violence because of its sexualisation and being blamed for it. Although Kenyatta University has an elaborate policy on sexual harassment, it is noteworthy that none of the students in this project indicated that they were aware of its existence, let alone appealing to the university for redress.

Memory work as an intervention in addressing gender violence

The Memories Project confirms that for many girls, schooling has continued to present sexual threats to girls more than boys (see Chege 1998 and 2001; UNICEF Gambia, 2003; Richter *et al*, 2004; Zuberi, 2005). Analysis of the student teachers' memories of childhood violence revealed unequivocally that the meanings communicated to children *in the past* and those interpreted *in the present*, offer invaluable insights into the exploration of self-identities and how these can be de-constructed into relatively more empowering and non-violent selfhoods. As Mitchell and Weber (1999) have argued, memory work can be both a method and a pedagogical tool in teacher education. Student teachers, and veteran teachers through in-service, can reflect on meanings and implications of childhood violence as they position themselves as agents of change in creating non-violent learning environments. The fact that some of the male students verified that teachers actually intimidated female students into accepting sexual relationships is crucial to developing strategies that would facilitate girls and boys to work together empathetically in eradicating sexual violence in educational institutions. Clearly, sexual violence and harassment need to be problematised at all levels of education, including universities, in order to ensure that young people learn how to challenge it through existing institutional or legal mechanisms. Further, there is a need to have not only functioning anti-sexual violence institutional structures but also rights-based education and effective life skills with which to challenge female sexual objectification.

Note
1 Acknowledgements to UNICEF ESARO for funding the memory work project.

21

Ghanaian trainee teachers' narratives of sexual harassment: a study of institutional practices

Gladys Teni-Atinga

Introduction

This chapter is based on an in-depth study of sexual harassment and institutional practices in two teacher training institutions, one tertiary institution and one training college, in Ghana in 2001-2002 (Teni-Atinga, 2005). Participatory methods were employed in the study, including focus group discussions, open-ended interviews and memory work (Mitchell and Weber, 1999). It involved 40 student teachers at the University College of Education in Winneba, located on the coast, and at Bagabaga Training College (BATCO) in Tamale in the Northern Region. The study comes out of my own experience as a former teacher in Ghana. That the teachers who were entrusted with the education of women students were the very people who might abuse them was disturbing. I wanted to understand the factors leading to the sexual harassment of trainee teachers in Ghanaian teacher training institutions and to develop recommendations for policy makers. The chapter focuses on trainee teachers' views of sexual harassment. While I did not specifically set out to study institutional practices, I found that these practices were identified as central to the sexual harassment of beginning teachers, especially the women.

According to the students I interviewed, there are seven key institutional practices around which sexual harassment can occur. These are: 1) promotional exams 2) continuous assessment 3) admission practices 4) exam practices by typists 5) student allowances 6) domestication of female students and 7) study mates. These various practices sometimes involved sexual coercion and the use of power in relationships of unequal status. They correspond to what Shakeshaft and Cohan (1994) term '*quid pro quo*' sexual harassment: the power of authority is used to fulfil sexual desires and non-compliance can mean the student receives no education whatever. The key practices through which sexual harassment permeates educational institutions are described below, as perceived by the participants.

The promotional exam

The promotional exam conducted at the end of the first year of the teacher training programme was identified as the most significant source of students' frustration. To be promoted from the first year to the second year of Post Secondary (PS2), one needs to pass examinations which are both internally and externally assessed. Students who fail more than one subject are withdrawn from the programme. Concerns about this exam were raised in the focus group discussions. A male student observed:

> Presently it is very stressful for some of us because we are due to write the Promotional Exams. At least if you fail in a single subject you know they will give you a second chance to re-write while you are promoted to the second year. When you have to defer two or more subjects to the second year because you could not pass them, you know that you are doomed and will be withdrawn from the programme. (Zandy, 1st year post secondary)

A female student described her fear as the promotional exam approached:

> Some of these tutors dramatise the issue in such a way that makes you panic. Particularly, first year female students are pressured for sex with a promise to offer them better grades in their subject areas. (Serina, 3rd year post secondary)

Another noted that:

> What is serious about the whole thing is that it is not only tutors who use promotional exam to get girls; senior prefects do it as well. As a first year student there is pressure from everywhere. If you are not good academically, you are likely to fall in the trap ... (Lecar, 2nd year post secondary)

For many of these students, refusing to comply with a lecturer or tutor's sexual demands means contesting their authority and that could be potentially devastating to the student. As one of the female students said:

What is dangerous is that these tutors are in collusion, and will do every-thing to protect one another in pursuit of their sexual demands, albeit perverted. To fail you in an exam, one doesn't need to be your tutor, he just has to ask another tutor who teaches you and it will be done without any problem. (Hajiah, 2nd year post secondary)

In the focus group discussions and memory work, the overall reactions of these students indicated that the use of the promotional exam by male lecturers and tutors to threaten female students, particularly those in the first year, has potentially negative and lasting effects on their academic perfor-mance. Even worse, it instils in victimised students an attitude of revenge: they feel they have earned the right to victimise students enrolled after them.

Continuous assessment

Another practice which leads to sexual harassment is the use of continuous assessment. A range of academic activities, such as class assignments, tests, class attendance and final year project work, is regularly evaluated and repre-sents 40 per cent of the final exam. Several students suggested that most lecturers will apply persistent pressure and verbal threats or intimidation when a student refuses them sex. In most institutions, they noted that the return of classroom assignments is often left to the discretion of the lecturer or tutor and done on a one-on-one basis. Lecturers may for example ask stu-dents to pick up their work from their residences and then lure female stu-dents into their rooms. In the group discussion, one woman reported that:

... a lecturer may justify the failure of a female student who refuses to sleep with him by continuous assessment. He can choose to give you a D or a fail and there is nothing you can do about it. (Yali, 3rd year university)

At tertiary level, the power of the lecturer and his ability to use such power overtly or covertly for sexual favours is immense. Continuous assessment is also used as a basis for penalising male students who are in competition or perceived to be in competition with their lecturers for the same woman. One male student told the group in discussion:

I suffered a lot in the hands of a lecturer because of a girl. This lecturer was interested in a girl I was going out with on campus, and when he ap-proached the girl, she had told him openly that she was already dating someone and that it was I. He openly told me he was going to get me with the continuous assessment exam if I didn't leave the girl. Some lecturers have done similar things to other students all because of the power they have from the continuous assessment grading system. (Yacent, 3rd year university)

Admission practices

Candidates hoping to gain entrance to a teacher training institution are made to go through a written test and an oral interview. Here prospective female candidates may be forced by their interviewers to compromise their bodies in order to gain admission and suffer threats of denial of admission. Both male and female participants mentioned in the group discussions that they had been denied admission at least once. As one of the female participants reported:

> The first time I was invited for the interview, I was denied admission because I had refused to meet with the tutor outside the campus the next day. I remember that I had to stay home for two years before finally being able to obtain admission. (Marina, 2nd year post secondary)

A classic case is that of a female student whose admission file was said never to have existed, even though she was interviewed for admission. It turned out the tutor had hidden her file because she refused his sexual advances during the interview. In another example, offered through a memory narrative, a female student wrote:

> I recall that after the interview for my admission I was heading towards home and to my surprise a car stopped in front of me, it was the very tutor who had just interviewed me. I was asked to get into the car and I asked 'for what?' he responded 'Just for a chat'. I refused and he insisted, trying to persuade me. I got into the car and he drove off to the staff club-house and asked that I come inside with him. I refused and said he could discuss whatever he wanted with me in the car. He said he needed to speak to me in private. I came out of the car and began to walk towards the roadside. He drove towards me and said, 'Where persuasion fails, force must be applied. We shall see whether you will get the admission." He made sure that I was denied admission that year... (Mado, 2nd year post secondary)

These students' experiences indicate that sexual harassment starts when candidates are seeking admission and continues after access is gained to the programme. A female third year student wrote in a memory narrative:

> I was told during my admission that my grade in mathematics didn't meet the college requirements, meanwhile, I was going to be offered admission based on the condition that I accept to upgrade my math average. I accepted and registered as a private candidate. When the results were out, I forwarded the original result slip for modification of my academic record; unfortunately it was neglected by the direction ... What was serious here was that some tutors were now capitalising on

that to sleep with me. From all directions, I had advice and propositions, which most often ended up with threats of withdrawal. (Aboskei, 3rd year post secondary)

In effect, admission practices constitute serious obstacles for the young women and represent a barrier to career opportunities.

Student allowances

In the focus group discussions, it emerged that students' allowances were another issue in the colleges, as members of the administrative staff were said to exploit the allowance to get sex. Students who were targets of such attention described how whenever they went for their stipends they were made to believe that their names were not on the pay list, and that this was due to computer errors from the headquarters in Accra. One woman told the group:

> I went in for my allowance one time and was told that they had forgotten to include my name from Accra and so I will have to wait for two weeks. I insisted it wasn't possible because I had no provisions and needed to buy a book for one of my classes. This administrative clerk quickly offered to issue me a cheque to cash if I didn't mind. I said to him that I could wait. His response was that 'I am doing you a favour and you don't even seem to acknowledge it.'... (Aboskei, 3rd year university)

The students' responses indicated that poverty contributes strongly to their vulnerability to sexual harassment and abuse in the learning environment. Male administrators are generally well aware that girls from economically disadvantaged families find it difficult to resist financial favours from administrative staff – a point raised by Leach (2001), Human Rights Watch (2001) and George (2001) in their work on sexual harassment of schoolgirls in Africa.

Exam malpractices by typists

At the time of the study, much of the administrative work in Ghanaian educational institutions had not yet been computerised and secretarial staff still used typewriters. Typists (mostly male) in these institutions have direct access to students' confidential files since they are the ones who create exam lists of students and also input grade sheets. In Ghana, as in some other countries, male typists are considered to be in a position of authority and to have certain privileges. Certain typists are said to use such privileges to sexually proposition female students. According to the participants in this study, they will promise to alter marks for students who did badly in their exams in return for sexual favours. One male participant remarked in discussion:

> The typists are the first to know before you, the student, if you have performed well or not. Sometimes when they want you and you refuse, they will let everyone in the community, including your own schoolmates, know that you have not done well in an exam. They will do all their best to spoil your record. (Zabzogu, 2nd year post secondary)

So clearly, typists are part of the complex power game that characterises sexual harassment in these colleges. Unlike in North America, where typists – where they still exist – have little power, in Africa they are considered to be in key positions. In educational institutions, where they are responsible for compiling the lists of student exam marks, they have great power over students.

The domestication of female students

Participants pointed out that in the training colleges – as in secondary schools – certain chores, such as serving tutors, washing dishes in the staff common hall, cleaning staff offices and carrying water for staff members, are done by female students only. Junior students are made to do the laundry of staff members or cook and clean for tutors and are often sexually harassed or forced to have sex. One student stated in a focus group discussion:

> In this college, female first years are made to serve the teachers during lunch and breakfast in the staff common hall or fetch water or cook for male teachers which often leads to forced sex. (Naomy, 3rd year post secondary)

Female students, particularly in the first year, said they are often so overwhelmed by the many extracurricular activities aimed at pleasing the lecturers and tutors that they have insufficient time for their own academic or personal activities. While their male colleagues use their time for academic work or leisure, or relax in their dormitories away from the hot sun, these young women are busy doing chores.

Study mates

In common with other higher education institutions in Ghana, these two colleges offer boarding facilities for students. Study groups are a formal and compulsory element of training programmes in boarding institutions, and are usually mixed-gender. This often results in coerced sex or sexual harassment, as a female student reported:

> What I find difficult is that, the male study mates expect that you cook for them and this is very common practice. Some go to the extent of trying to sleep with you and I think that is unfair. Where you refuse, they may try to remove you from the study group. (Katia, 3rd year post secondary)

Whether or not this is by consent, a clear policy and enforced rules are needed to prevent such practices. If the objective of the study group is to promote shared learning, it should have nothing to do with sex. What currently prevails in the learning environment is often problematic for the person in the subordinate position.

The challenges of reporting sexual harassment

It is clear that students prefer not to come forward with their complaints because of the consequences associated with reporting cases of sexual harassment. Many female students have come to understand that to acquire a teaching degree and create a career for themselves, they must be ready to compromise their bodies as part of the unofficial programme for their professional certification. As we have seen, female students suffer a great deal at the hands of tutors, lecturers, administrators and male senior prefects. Those who participated in this study experienced feelings that ranged from anger to frustration, helplessness and a heightened sense of vulnerability.

There is also the perception that no suitable avenue for complaint exists, and survivors of harassment can have a misplaced sense of shame. Girls' experiences in school are similar; in one study by Leach *et al* (2003) it was observed that in schools in Ghana girls usually fail to come forward for similar reasons of fear of victimisation, stigmatisation and ridicule, and that their failure to do so has created a climate for perpetrators to act with impunity. Not only do the two institutions in the study appear to have taken sexual harassment of female students for granted, they have also failed to initiate any disciplinary proceeding against lecturers and tutors who commit sexual crimes. No matter how serious the complaint, officials were said to conceal any allegations amongst themselves, and the perpetrators were allowed to continue in their posts.

Survivors of sexual harassment may also be threatened with dismissal from their programme if they draw public attention to an incident. The memory narrative of a post secondary student records how she was made to pay emotionally and physically when she refused to heed the college chaplain's advice and – with unusual courage – brought her case of sexual harassment to her father's attention. But the few survivors who took such risks said they had no support whatever from university officials. Students who came forward with cases of harassment had their cases dismissed and no action was taken. In addition to the emotional consequences they suffered, they were accused of trying to destroy the reputation of lecturers and tutors, and were sometimes punished with physical labour, such as working on the college farm, cleaning toilets or carrying water. Some were even suspended from college for weeks or threatened with dismissal from the college.

Strategies for change

The narratives and testimonies, particularly those of the female students, indicate that the participants in this research were regularly exposed to sexually motivated abuses in the learning environment from lecturers, tutors, administrative staff and senior students. Institutions of learning are hierarchically organised, which means that 'power, might and right' is accorded to lecturers, tutors and administrative staff over the students; senior students over their junior counterparts; and males over females. The victimised suffer severe consequences, which escalate at each step in the hierarchical system of power. The lack of explicit policies to check sexual abuse and harassment in Ghana works in concert with the institutional practices described here to create conditions that facilitate sexual harassment of female trainee teachers. The result is an institutional framework that supports a regime of blatant disregard for the safety concerns of female trainee teachers.

To overcome the problem of sexual harassment and other gender-based forms of violence in Ghana requires a clear policy framework that defines, prohibits and imposes penalties for acts of sexual harassment and abuse. Concerted efforts are needed at all levels. Serious action must be taken against lecturers and tutors who are found guilty of professional malpractice and sexual misconduct such as rape, sexual harassment or physical abuse of students. Case studies such as this one suggest that the conditions of teaching and learning for women are still fraught and more research is needed in the area of women teachers' lives and sexual violence. Above all, the narratives of the beginning teachers suggest that if we want to understand the barriers to reaching the Education For All (EFA) targets for girls and schooling, we cannot ignore the very structures and practices of educational institutions.

22

Eliminating the sexual exploitation of girls in refugee schools in West Africa: what classroom assistants can do

Jackie Kirk and Rebecca Winthrop

Introduction

There is growing awareness of the linkages between political violence and violence against women and girls. In recent conflicts fighting forces have inflicted horrendous sexual violence on women and girls. It happens both consciously, as part of ideological campaigns, as a weapon of war, and informally, as the normalised behaviour of militarised men (Whitworth, 2004). Ongoing conflict and factors such as large numbers of refugees or internally displaced persons, lack of security, precarious economic situations and the skewed relationships created through reliance on humanitarian aid or peacekeepers create contexts for the sexual exploitation of women and girls. The status quo of gender-power inequities in society is reflected in gendered relationships of dependency. In emergency and humanitarian situations different forms of domestic violence against women and girls are also reported with increasing frequency (Inter-Agency Standing Committee Task Force on Gender and Humanitarian Assistance, 2005).

Although less attention is paid specifically to adolescent girls in conflict contexts, many thousands experience sexual violence. This can be rape as a weapon of war, sexual violence and exploitation of girl soldiers and sexual exploitation by peacekeepers and humanitarian workers. In addition, transactional sex[1] may become a necessity for girls who have to ensure their own survival and that of their families. Sexual abuse occurs within close relationships in which challenges to identity and self-esteem as well as shifts in gender roles and power dynamics play out in violent ways. All are fuelled by the prevalence and privileging of aggressive forms of masculinity in times of war. Where conflict has broken down social infrastructures and relationships, and created contexts in which physical male power dominates and violence becomes normal, the gendered power inequities of peacetime are exaggerated and vulnerabilities to sexual exploitation and abuse are intensified.

As the chapters in this volume show, sexual abuse and exploitation of girls in schools is not limited to conflict situations. However, for schoolgirls in conflict-affected contexts the gendered power dynamics of schools *and* of refugee camps converge to create particular vulnerabilities. A report by UNHCR/Save the Children UK (2002) drew widespread attention to the extent of the exploitation of girls and young women by humanitarian workers in refugee camps in West Africa, where NGO teachers were also perpetrators. The report highlighted how teachers were taking advantage of their positions, offering good grades and other school privileges in return for sex.

The International Rescue Committee (IRC) supports education for Liberian refugees in Sierra Leone and Guinea, where, as is quite usual in the region, most of the teachers are men. As refugees, the girls are economically vulnerable and highly dependent on external assistance; because education is so important to them and such a critical means to improving their situation, they are desperate to succeed. Prior to 2002 there were few strategies in place to protect these girls. In response to the report, however, IRC strove to address the issue, establishing preventative mechanisms, including recruiting and training female classroom assistants.[2]

This Classroom Assistant Program is a pilot intervention, now being closely monitored through the IRC Healing Classrooms Initiative, which is a more recent organisational learning project of the IRC, focused on improving teacher support and development to better meet the needs of children and youth affected by crisis. Gender is one of the key focus areas. Since the UNHCR/Save the Children report had raised serious concerns about the professional conduct of teachers and the physical, psychosocial and cognitive well-being of girl students, Guinea and Sierra Leone were specifically included in the Healing Classrooms Initiative pilot assessments in order to learn more about how the Classroom Assistant Program was affecting teaching and learning processes and experiences.

The Healing Classrooms Initiative assessment

Drawing on data collected during assessments of the Healing Classroom Initiative in Guinea and Sierra Leone in October/November 2004, this chapter describes the impact of the Classroom Assistant Programs in two locations. It highlights some of the complexities and tensions in the relationships between assistants, students and teachers and ends with some recommendations for the replication of similar initiatives in other contexts.

The assessment used a mixed method approach to gain qualitative insights into teaching and learning in a sample of the IRC refugee schools in both countries. In Guinea, three schools in the N'Zérékoré area were selected: two in town and one in a camp. In Sierra Leone three camp schools were selected in the Eastern Kenama region. A total of 32 classroom assistants were interviewed in small groups of two or three; 46 teachers were interviewed and 43 questionnaires completed along with 120 student interviews, 46 focus group discussions and 59 classroom observations. Common tools (interview and observation protocols) were used in both sites, but were adapted to fit the specific contexts. Interviews with teachers and assistants were conducted in English, the language of instruction and of the school system, by the principal researcher; interviews with students by research assistants trained as part of the project were conducted in a mixture of mother tongue, Liberian English and standard English. Written questionnaires were also distributed to teachers. Detailed hand-written notes were taken during interviews and discussions, which were also audio-taped. All data were word-processed and analysed qualitatively.

Introducing the Classroom Assistant Program

Soon after the Classroom Assistant Program was initiated by IRC Guinea in 2002, it was adopted by IRC Sierra Leone. Although there was no documentation of actual abuse and exploitation within the IRC programmes, the manipulation of girls into sexual relationships with teachers in exchange for good grades or other in-school privileges was widely acknowledged. It was critical to change the male domination of the schools and create more protective and conducive learning environments for girls, but it was very difficult to find refugee or local women who had the education, time and family support to become teachers.

However, the programme's flexible entry requirements enable more refugee women to become classroom assistants. Those selected take part in a two to five-day workshop, which includes lesson planning, team teaching, tracking girls' grades and attendance, and report writing, in addition to discussion of topics such as sexual abuse and exploitation, child rights and child protection, communication and counselling. The assistants are then deployed to classes in Grades Three to Six to work alongside the teachers.

The classroom assistants (CAs) have an explicit mandate to prevent abuse and exploitation of students, although more broadly the programme was designed to create more conducive, girl-friendly learning environments and support quality learning for all students. One critical task they perform is collecting exam grades from the teacher and distributing them. The students then com-municate with the CAs, which helps avoid situations in which teachers can demand sex in exchange for good grades. The CAs also monitor attendance and follow up on absences by making home visits. They help the girls with their studies and support health education activities, in addition to social club activities such as needlework, games and sports. The CAs are visited regularly by IRC supervisors, to whom they submit monthly reports detailing the girls' attendance, activities and home visits.

Positive impacts of the Classroom Assistant Program
Improving the learning environment for girls and boys
Because of limited data and fluctuating student numbers and refugee returns to Liberia, it is impossible to make a clear assessment of the programme's impact. However, in both countries, available data indicate that, since its in-ception, girls' drop-out and pregnancy rates have decreased, and attendance and achievement (grades, test and exam results) have improved. One CA in Guinea sums it up: 'Before they had many problems in the school like fighting, loving with teachers, getting pregnant, but now it is improving. Before the girls were going down, but now they are improving.'

Girls in Guinea and Sierra Leone describe the effects of the CAs: CAs make them more comfortable and they feel encouraged by the presence of a woman in their classroom, and knowing that she will make home visits. Boys too appreciate the CAs' help in creating calmer classrooms where learning is more effective. The participation of girls in class has improved, especially in English, and interest in library study has increased. In Guinea, girls in a focus group discussion stated: 'Now some of us girls feel more and more safe to ask our teachers any question that bothers us without fear of being provoked by any-one.' Such feelings were expressed by one of the boys too. The presence of another adult in the classroom appears to encourage teachers to present lessons well and try to ensure that all the students have understood.

Elimination of sexual exploitation and abuse

The initial impetus for the programme was to eliminate the sexual abuse and exploitation of girls in schools, and, according to all those interviewed, there has been a change in teachers' behaviour in schools. One cannot state that exploitation of girls by teachers in school – or the risk of it – has ceased, but there appears to be significant positive change to which the programme has contributed. In Guinea, the students talk about there now being 'more respectful' relationships between students and teachers. As one girl says: 'Teachers are no more collecting money from students in school for grades. Students and teachers are now respecting one another.'

The CAs are quick to assert that 'since we came in we put a stop to those things', that 'the teachers can't do anything bad with the students, no, nothing bad like that is happening. I haven't seen anything like that.' CAs in Guinea stress that 'the teachers are careful ... We observe them.' In a number of schools the CAs emphasise the importance of being there to observe and see what is happening in the schools: 'Things have changed. The teachers don't do it [sexually exploit girls].This is why the girls are so serious now. We are there to observe, so the teachers can't say, like, 'This girl is beautiful." One CA is explicit about the difference this makes for the girls: 'The girls are happy that in our presence they know that the teachers cannot do these things. We are there and we can observe them.'

Addressing sexual exploitation in schools: a complex task

These improvements in the quality of the learning environment and of the teachers' engagement with students, and the CAs' role in the system of grade collection and distribution appear to lessen the vulnerability of girls in school. However, the data also suggest that the programme is far more complex than originally envisaged. The introduction of para-professional, unqualified women into hegemonic male spaces cannot on its own address complex protection issues for girls. Significant tensions exist around the teachers' attitudes towards the CAs, the CAs' relationships with girls and the strategies they have for protecting the girls. Although there was no evidence from the research to suggest that this is the case, the potential risk of sexual exploitation and abuse the CAs themselves face, in school as in the wider community, also has to be acknowledged and dealt with.

Teacher attitudes

When the CAs were first introduced, the teachers were generally displeased and considered them to be sex police, hired to report on them. Interview data, however, indicate that most teachers are now more accepting and positive about the impact of the assistants, particularly recognising their help in class management. It appears the teachers have responded to their presence with more respectful behaviour, improved lesson planning and delivery, and interaction with students. However, they assign the CAs relatively menial tasks and ones which maintain their own authority. None of the teachers talk about any real power sharing in the classroom; when the CA is alone with the students, she is merely replacing the teacher. When asked specifically about team teaching, one teacher responds by saying: 'Yes, if the teacher goes to urinate then the CA teaches. When the teacher gives question papers, then the CAs correct.'

The teachers are well aware that the CAs have inferior education and training and some have their doubts about their value. One woman teacher says quite openly: 'According to what they told us, they [the CAs] are there to look after the girls, but I see no use, they can't teach. For example, me, I am handling 13 subjects and if she [the CA] was capable, she should be helping me. The teaching work is tedious, like preparing grade sheets etc. In theory, the CAs are useful, but... I don't know....' Another teacher is equally questioning of the value of the CAs, even suggesting that they add to the teachers' work and have to be managed like the students.

Relationships with girls
The girls, however, are generally appreciative of their classroom assistant, seeing her as a friend, a big sister or a mother figure. However, data also suggest that being relatively uneducated, these women command little respect from students and are not regarded as strong role models. A specific rule in one school in Sierra Leone required the students to call the CAs 'teacher'; the need for such a rule suggests a more problematic relationship between the students and the CAs than might have been expected. Girls interviewed are very aware of the hard work, low pay and the lack of respect for CAs. 'CAs get their fair share of headaches from impolite, rude students,' says one girl. Another recounts: 'Some students are challenging the CA in class and mock the CA outside school.'

Women in both locations describe challenges in gaining the girls' respect. Knowing that the CAs have not completed their own education, the girls can be sceptical of their abilities. As one woman describes it: 'They will test us – just to check we know it, but it is getting better now. At first they were saying things like, 'Oh look at her, she pretends she knows all this', and when the teacher leaves the class, they would raise their hands to ask difficult questions to see if the CAs really do know.'

Perceptions of girls and strategies for girls' education

Although the CAs may act as strong advocates for girls' education, their strategies are somewhat problematic; they tend to put the onus for improvement solely onto the girls and to imply that they are there to make up for the girls' inadequacies compared with the boys. One CA explains: 'Of course, sometimes the boys get angry because we are only helping the girls, but we tell them that the girls are backward and the boys are cleverer and so they [the girls] need more help.' Another says that they focus on the girls 'because they are left behind'. The CAs articulate beliefs that the girls are not serious enough about their education, exhorting them to study hard and to avoid attention from men, including teachers and male students. 'They shouldn't wear false hair or makeup as it attracts men, and short skirt', says one. Another CA in the same school stresses how important it is for her and her colleagues to make sure the girls are well turned out. Another assistant explains: 'Before they were wearing big earrings and polish their lips with colour, but now they are more moderate...' Assistants describe their role in instructing the girls to keep away from the boys: 'We talk to them about not going around with boys,' and 'we always encourage them [the girls] and tell them of the importance of education – that they shouldn't follow men and not to jump with them. We tell them 'you shouldn't wrestle with boys because in doing that it is dangerous."

Discussion

We can see how the programme tends to overemphasise fixing the girls to better fit the school environment. Goetz (1997) highlights the problematic nature of gender equality initiatives which focus on women as the problem, and proposes a shift from 'getting women right for the institution' to one of 'getting the institutions right for women'. Other feminist scholars have also critiqued initiatives in which it is the difficult, messy and unpredictable bodies of girls and women which have to be fixed in order for them to fit into the androcentric institutions to which they desire access.

The position of women teachers has been described as 'tricky', 'impossible' and problematic because of the contradictory experience of power and powerlessness (Walkerdine, 1990; Munro, 1998). Such theories have resonance beyond Western classrooms (Kirk, 2003) and help to articulate the even trickier and more problematic position of unqualified assistants. The CAs have an almost impossible task: they are there to protect and empower girls but they themselves lack status and power.

As refugee women, the CAs are implicated in the overlapping gendered ideologies of different institutions and organisations (Kabeer, 1994). This means that their understandings of the barriers to successful education for girls and the strategies they use tend to reflect rather than challenge prevailing discourses. The CAs' perceptions of the girls, gender equality, protection and empowerment are grounded in their everyday experiences of refugee life. When the programme started, the prevailing attitude was that the girls were seducing teachers with their provocative clothing. Such attitudes shaped the CAs' understandings of the issue and their strategy of monitoring the girls' clothing and appearance.

The CAs' work is circumscribed within the traditional gender-power dynamics of the community, further entrenched in the patriarchal institution of the school. They clearly have agency and have bravely broken new ground in their communities with the support they provide to ensure girls complete their education, but it is not surprising that they ultimately do little to challenge the power and authority of the male teachers. For women whose financial and social security and that of their children may depend on working within the status quo of the community, this could be risky.

Conclusions and recommendations

The Classroom Assistant Program is clearly successful in creating more comfortable learning environments for girls and for boys too. The physical presence of the women, their moral support for the girls and the concern that they show for their well-being and academic success helps to change the classroom space from one in which girls are marginalised and even exploited, to one in which they are given special attention, assistance and encouragement. But it has to be acknowledged that the CAs are in relatively marginal positions in the classroom, and that they cannot eliminate sexual exploitation and abuse on their own. This is dependent on creating a sustained shift in attitudes and the dominant culture of the school, and on empowering women and girls to feel they are fully part of the school and have the same rights, expectations and opportunities as the men and boys.

As the refugees are returning to Liberia, and programmes are scaling down in Guinea and Sierra Leone, lessons learned about effective interventions and factors for success should inform the possible replication of Classroom Assistant programmes in Liberia and elsewhere. Through the Healing Classrooms Initiative, information, programming tools and other supporting documentation on promising programmes are now being widely disseminated. The IRC education team in Guinea is working to develop and improve the programme, and some of the recommendations below are now being piloted, especially with regard to gender training.

Recommendations include:

- Key messages about classroom assistants and their roles in creating girl-friendly, healing classrooms which promote the well-being of all students should be clarified and consistently conveyed throughout programme activities.

- The introduction of CAs should be preceded by holistic gender training for teachers and assistants on dimensions of gender equality in education, including male-female power dynamics in the classroom and team teaching strategies.

- CAs should be linked to women's groups and services in the community, to extend their support base beyond the school and create linkages with programmes from which girls may benefit.

- CAs should be encouraged to continue their education and to enter teaching if they wish through, for example, accelerated secondary school courses, distance learning or complementary vocational and skills training courses. Specific access strategies may be needed, such as childcare provision and study groups.

Notes

1 Transactional sex is a widely used term to refer to situations where girls and women are forced into sexual relationships to gain money, food or other items for survival. The term masks varying degrees of exploitation, coercion and violence, and in some contexts, especially those involving young girls, actually constitutes rape.

2 Another important intervention is the rolling out to all employees of the IRC Mandatory Reporting Policy on Abuse and Exploitation.

23

Gender, AIDS and Schooling in Uganda: a curriculum intervention

Robina Mirembe

Introduction

Gendered power is a feature of schooling and of the spread of AIDS. The school curriculum is used to address AIDS prevention, but AIDS education can be enabling as well as disabling: enabling when it empowers young girls and boys to make informed decisions about sex and its safety, disabling when it helps widen the power gap between them leading to sexual exploitation. This chapter discusses the findings of a doctoral study, *AIDS Education and Gender in Uganda* (Mirembe, 1998), which examined the contradictions inherent in curriculum interventions generated by a school culture which allows societal injustices to be reproduced in the school. The ethnographic component of this study used observations, interviews, focus group discussions, personal accounts and, to some extent, a structured questionnaire, to expose the various complex strands of the school culture which caused these contradictions. The study involved 250 pupils (100 girls and 150 boys) aged 9 to 15 in five mixed-sex schools in Uganda. The main case study was conducted in St. Martins High School.

The ethnographic research concluded that schooling constituted a risk to girls because its systems widened the power gap between boys and girls. A particular aspect of this risk, common to all the schools and explored here, was the sexual harassment of girls by boys. The later stage of the study included an action research component, which adapted the existing AIDS education curriculum to address sexual harassment with a mixed-sex class of 50 pupils (20 girls and 30 boys) at St. Martins. This pedagogical response, as the chapter

217

shows, raises issues around gender inequality, key to both the spread of AIDS and gender violence in the classroom.

Social injustices in school

The study showed that the culture of St. Martins, a competitive, co-educational, secondary boarding school in Uganda, was part of a complex, wider societal culture which promoted patriarchal norms that value women less than men. Both boys and girls in the study associated power with masculinity and male hegemony (Haywood and Mac an Ghaill, 1996) and the practice of masculinity in the school reinforced the informal control of girls and female teachers through sexual harassment, putting them at a disadvantage (Wolpe, 1988).

Informal interaction during the research with young people in class, on the playing fields, in the dining room and in the hall (during a video show and dance) revealed that sexual harassment was common. The practice was often ignored and, if attended to, dismissed by the school authorities as 'playing', 'bullying' or 'discipline'. This trivialisation of sexual harassment is long-standing (Francis, 1997) and, as a collective experience of young women in school, is widely recorded, as this book illustrates. When boys were asked why they harassed girls, they gave reasons such as: 'to control', 'to order the girls around', 'to make girls available for the boys' and 'for fun'.

The girl as victim

Girls in the interviews were reluctant to share their experiences as victims of sexual harassment but they talked about it in groups. Three levels of harassment were identified in these discussions. The first level was straightforward verbal harassment; the second entailed explicit sexual advances; and the third can be categorised as 'criminal assault'. Testimonies from volunteers (girl victims of harassment) and extracts from other informants' accounts (boys and girls who were articulate about what went on in school) are used to illustrate the three levels.

The first, verbal level was widespread. It irritated, humiliated, embarrassed and intimidated the girls. One girl, Carol, reflected in her written account:

> ... boys 'shout at you', 'boo you', 'write' things in your book or your name in textbooks, 'call you names'. For the 'less assertive' ones, this follows them throughout their entire stay at school.

The girls reported being denied language space in class, so that, over time, they were socialised into silence.[1]

The second level of harassment involved more explicit sexual advances in which the girls were treated as sex objects. Examples included boys touching girls' bodies, talking to them about sex, showing their naked chests to them, and forcing girls to dance with them against their will – a particular humiliation for the girls and a victory for the boys. More intrusive and humiliating incidents which the victims were too shy to talk about in individual interviews were referred to during focus group discussions. It was clear that the psychological torture that accompanied such unsolicited physical contact undermined the girls' ability to challenge these acts of social injustice; this allowed the boys to assume greater power, which in turn led to the exploitative third level.

This level amounted to criminal assault; at times the line between sexual harassment and forced sex is a fine one. Girls hardly ever talked about it and so the assailants went unpunished. Esther narrated her experience of being unable to repulse an unwanted sexual advance one Saturday night:

> When we [girls] were going for a video show a friend called me and I went ... He asked me whether we could go to any classroom and talk. We went and talked ... He started touching my thighs. ... I told him to leave me alone but he went on to kiss me and all the rest ...

The female teacher as victim

Young female teachers also suffered harassment from boys and male colleagues without being able to challenge it. Male behaviour ranged from making comments about the way they dressed, to whistling at the sight of a teacher and writing remarks about them on the board. I watched male teachers in the staff room calling the female teachers names, and making advances in a subtle way. Female teachers were also harassed during lessons by boys. One described how:

> They are ever drawing your notice to them especially when they ask obvious questions. Some make their way to the front where you are. One boy taller than I stood besides me and went on to whisper in my ear that he wants to go out. The rest of the boys laughed.

This teacher had not realised what the boys were up to until girls in the class told her. More intrusive harassment was also reported, for example a boy writing an anonymous note asking a young female teacher for sex.

Response to sexual harassment

Interviews revealed that the reaction by women and girls to sexual harassment could take one of three forms: *avoidance* of male harassment – running away to escape the insults; *retaliation* – which might involve facing consequences such as being hit or insulted – or *giving in* e.g. by smiling at the harasser and acquiescing to his demands.

Girls at St. Martins usually discussed their experiences of sexual harassment among themselves and comforted each other. Only intrusive touches – for instance on the thighs or breasts – were reported to staff. On one occasion the harasser was punished but many acts of harassment went unnoticed. Girls complained about female teachers who never challenged sexual harassment.

The curriculum and sexual harassment

St. Martins had introduced a sex education curriculum to address HIV/AIDS. The research showed the delivery of this to be sexist: instead of making the pupils more assertive, it allowed the boys to harass the girls. Informal conversation with the class I was going to teach in the action research phase revealed that they considered sex education lessons boring, irrelevant and a waste of time. As a researcher and teacher (deputy head) in the school, I set out to improve delivery of the lessons, while at the same time addressing the issues of sexism and harassment through a targeted intervention. This involved exploring pedagogies that would facilitate young people's responses to the curriculum and foster their adopting a safer lifestyle. As Aggleton and Warwick (1997) have noted, preventive education only becomes meaningful when it speaks to the lived experiences of actors. The intervention therefore had a dual purpose: improving delivery and learning, and addressing social injustices in the school. Without challenging such injustices, the aims of education are flawed (Osler, 1998). Accordingly, the AIDS curriculum aimed at addressing the power disparities between male and female (Mirembe and Davies, 2001).

The action research approach was based on Bandura's Social Learning Theory, a process-product paradigm (Bandura, 1977), and Freirian Critical Pedagogy, an emancipatory democratic approach that challenges social injustices in society (Livingstone, 1987). Young people were at the centre of the learning, engaging in curriculum development, devising a supportive environment for learning, and evaluating the processes. Three lessons of 60 minutes each, followed by a 30-minute evaluation of the intervention, illustrate how the AIDS curriculum was used to challenge sexual harassment.

Lesson 1: Introduction to sex education: What to teach?
The lesson objectives included: creating a situation for the free and fruitful discussion of sex education topics; allowing pupils to identify friends with

whom to share stories and build mutual trust; and asking each pupil to write down a personal experience of sexuality, thereby laying the ground for a discussion of their concerns.

These objectives required creating a conducive classroom environment for learning, in which the pupils would open up. So for the first ten minutes, pupils held hands in a circle and ran ten times round the classroom, then did stretching exercises followed by relaxation. Only then was there discussion of the sex education curriculum, in which pupils said what they felt about it. There followed a silent period during which each pupil wrote down some experience of growing up, recounting an experience of sexuality at school since the age of 5 and any concerns this raised for them. Once I had collected the papers, the pupils formed single-sex groups (4-5 per group) of their choice, elected a leader and a secretary, then discussed their understanding of AIDS and sex. Finally they got back into a large circle for a ten-minute feedback session from each group.

This lesson showed firstly that when young people participate in the formulation of the curriculum, this not only brings about ownership and improves receptivity and subsequent learning, but also brings on board pupils' concerns. Secondly, being able to talk with others about personal matters is liberating, especially for the harassed, and enhances communication skills. Thirdly, small groups afforded individuals the trust required to discuss personal issues such as sexual harassment. Pupils evaluated the lesson as interesting, as all had participated.

From their written experiences, I deduced a need to include in the AIDS education curriculum topics such as growing up and sexuality. Pupils' anxiety about sex-related disease and infection brought sexually transmitted infections (STIs) into the frame, and the reported harassment in and out of class called for social injustices and human rights to be included in the curriculum. Interestingly, these topics all related in some way to AIDS but did not provoke the negative comments pupils had made about the existing AIDS lessons.

I discovered that pupils wrote about issues they would never have spoken about. I also observed increased pupil participation in the informal learning, as the non-threatening and relaxing atmosphere helped them to open up. This was reflected in the stories they wrote about:

> I hated the way they teased me calling me boys' names (girl)
>
> I let some of my buttons open to show girls my masculinity (boy)
>
> Boys in my class wanted to make relationship with me (girl).

Choosing the group with whom to share their experiences was fundamental in establishing good classroom relationships. Pupils particularly liked the small single-sex groups for discussion and learning.

Lesson 2: Democratic learning

The experience gained during the first lesson informed the next lesson. Since the suggested topics were related to AIDS, it seemed logical to weave them into the AIDS curriculum and highlight the relationship. The objectives were: learning about AIDS; asking pupils to identify inequalities in the classroom; and encouraging pupils to work democratically towards eliminating them.

The sensitive nature of the topic made a supportive classroom environment crucial. As such a climate is best created by the participants (Carr and Kemmis, 1986), I employed a participatory, democratic learning approach, in which pupils were given a chance to effect change for a common good. It has been shown that democratic learning dispels fear (Browne, 1995) and improves the delivery and processes of change in AIDS education (Mirembe, 2002). We began with a key question: 'What makes learning difficult?' to which pupils responded on paper. Examples included: 'fearing each other' (girls and boys), 'harassment' (girls), 'calling names' (boys and girls), 'abusing' (girls), 'belittling' and 'teasing' (girls). Many of the answers pointed to sexual harassment. The second question was: 'Do you have any solution to the problem?' Many solutions were offered and these were written on the board. For example: 'We must respect others in class' (boys and girls), 'Stop shouting at each other' (boys), 'Listen to each other' (girls and boys), 'Respect people's ideas on sexuality' (boys), 'Stop name-calling' (girls) and 'confidentiality' (girls). The third step was constructing class rules and agreeing that everybody, including the teacher, was to abide by these rules. The rules required that all pupils be listened to, respected, and allowed a language space in class. Creating a democratic language space undermines the intimidating effects of, and opportunities for, sexual harassment. Teasing, whistling, calling names, jeering and putting down others was not accepted. It was unanimously agreed that it was everybody's concern to see that the rules were kept and to challenge any contravention. This process of creating ground rules and being committed to enforcing them was empowering for the class and averted the problem of top down monitoring (Harber and Davies, 1997). The fourth step was action. What had been agreed was to become operational in a live situation, the next part of the lesson.

We turned to work in groups of eight to discuss pupils' perceptions of AIDS in the light of the question: 'What views about AIDS are true or false?' Pupils wrote their group responses on large sheets of paper and pinned them up for the rest of the class to read. Perceptions such as 'death', 'red lips', 'thin', 'unfair', 'sin', 'punishment from God', 'prostitute' and 'sex' were noted. In accordance with the ground rules, the pupils were expected to monitor classroom behaviour and control each other. For example, it was agreed that no graffiti was to be drawn on the walls or the work being displayed; nor were pupils permitted to talk about each other during the lessons. The collages on AIDS were pinned up on the wall and each group had a turn to share knowledge of AIDS before a highly attentive class. This too was empowering.

The lesson ended with consolidation of pupils' perceptions of AIDS. I explained the danger of misconceptions about AIDS in relation to HIV prevention and talked about how HIV affects the body. Social inequalities – including in the classroom! – and forms of discrimination such as sexual harassment were highlighted as principal causes of HIV infection and its spread. The pupils were all receptive. Collages illustrating the physical effects of HIV and posters on HIV transmission were pinned on the classroom wall.

Findings from observations and pupils' accounts showed that there was increased participation of girls in the class discussions. During the discussions, pupils came to realise that male domination contributed to the spread of HIV and that sexual harassment was a form of male domination. Young people were asked to ponder the following question at this concluding stage of the lesson: 'Does sexual harassment contribute to HIV transmission?' Pupils discussed values such as the ability to listen to others, consensus, collective identification of a problem and its solution, allowing a voice for all, and accepting that everybody can contribute to knowledge. They learnt that these democratic values are not only relevant to AIDS and its prevention; they also counteract sexual harassment. Thus did pupils begin to relate social injustices such as sexual harassment to HIV/AIDS.

Evaluation by pupils, corroborated later by my observations, provided indicators that sexual harassment was being held down. For example, the class made less noise at the girls' responses, there was no name-calling, pupils listened to each other and complimented each other in discussions, and no graffiti appeared on the collages pinned on walls, something the boys had always indulged in before.

Lesson 3: Biomedical and social aspects of AIDS

The third lesson drew from the first two but was a more formal exploration of the biomedical and social aspects of AIDS, designed to inform pupils further about AIDS and help them work out the social implications through discussion.

The teacher-led discussion covered HIV, its transmission and prevention, and the social aspects of AIDS, especially in relation to inequality and discrimination. The discussion was guided by a statement: 'AIDS is an issue of inequality and discrimination', followed by two questions: 'What form of inequality?' and 'Do we contribute to inequality or discrimination?'

I observed that the pupils paid attention, asked questions and made notes, especially of new facts. They listened to one another's comments and added or responded to them when they got into smaller groups. There was increased pupil participation by both sexes, particularly in the single-sex groups.

Lesson 4: Evaluation of the intervention
A questionnaire was used to test pupils' perceptions of AIDS and to evaluate the intervention. Pupils also assessed the effects of their ground rules and made suggestions for improvement. They recorded improved verbal communication, especially by the girls, reduced sexual harassment, increased confidence among the girls, and improved interaction between girls and boys. But the pupils realised that a sex education class was an island, cut off from the reality of life outside the classroom. Two suggestions were made to improve the effects of ground rules: punishment of culprits and application of ground rules to all classes and dormitories. Neither of these was manageable by the pupils themselves and a school solution had to be sought. Since I was the deputy head teacher responsible for class work including schemes of work, I used the opportunity to draw colleagues' attention to the problem. I invited teachers to contribute new items to the current schemes of work, which we discussed. Discussion with the teachers also created a need to challenge inequality. Since all subjects use a common format for their schemes of work, I inserted gender issues, including harassment, and human rights in the list of scheme items each teacher had to consider when planning and teaching. Early evaluation showed that some teachers were adopting the new approach to classroom teaching and addressing inequalities. Evaluations that went beyond the study would have benefited the intervention.

Conclusion

The curriculum intervention discussed here shows that, even though schooling seems to produce and maintain gendered power relations which can lead to violence, it is possible to address social injustices and inequalities, including sexual harassment, through the curriculum. This is supported when teachers use democratic practices to challenge injustices and when pupils work out possible and manageable solutions by being active participants in curriculum development. The use of schemes of work to address inequalities in lessons, and collaborative action research are two additional ways in which schools can engage with social injustice. The process whereby young people and the whole school system are made to understand individual rights and the consequences of their abuse may be slow but it is certainly worthwhile embarking upon, especially in the face of the HIV/AIDS epidemic.

Note

1 Additional informal interviews with 9-10-year-old girls in two primary schools showed that verbal sexual harassment starts early and progresses to higher levels of harassment. In this way, boys learn at an early age to humiliate females.

Biographical details

Editors

Fiona Leach is senior lecturer in international education at the University of Sussex, UK. She has worked in the field of education and development for many years, and before becoming an academic was a teacher and adviser in Africa. She has published widely in the field of gender and education, and has carried out several studies on gender violence in African schools. She is author of *Practising Gender Analysis in Education* (Oxfam). Her other research interests include cross-cultural knowledge transfer and participatory methodologies.

Claudia Mitchell is James McGill Professor in the Faculty of Education, McGill University, Canada and Honorary Professor in the Faculty of Education, University of KwaZulu-Natal, South Africa. Her research areas include visual and arts-based research methodologies, media studies, youth, gender and HIV/AIDS, gender violence, girlhood and popular culture, and teachers' self-study. She is co-author and co-editor of seven books. Her most recent book is an edited volume *Girlhood: Redefining the limits* (Black Rose Books with Y. Jiwani and C. Steenbergen).

Contributors

Anbreen Ajaib is a human rights activist in Pakistan, working mainly on advocacy in the area of gender, children's rights and girls' education.

Gladys Atinga is currently working with the United Nation's Population Fund as their gender-based violence technical adviser in South Darfur, Sudan.

Gary Barker is Executive Director of Instituto Promundo, a Brazilian NGO based in Rio de Janeiro that works nationally and internationally to promote gender equality and reduce violence, including violence against children and women and between men.

Deevia Bhana is Associate Professor in education at the University of KwaZulu-Natal in South Africa, where she conducts research in the areas of childhood sexuality and HIV/AIDS, gender violence and primary schooling.

227

Tania Boler is senior policy adviser and research coordinator on education and HIV/AIDS for ActionAid International and the HIV/AIDS focal person for the Global Campaign on Education.

Nazish Brohi works with ActionAid in Pakistan as manager of its women's rights unit and is also a freelance researcher and consultant.

Vinay Chandran is Executive Director of the Swabhava Trust, a non-governmental organisation in Bangalore, India, involved in work around sexualities, sexual health and HIV/AIDS.

Fatuma Chege is Senior Lecturer and Chair of the Department of Educational Foundations, Kenyatta University, Nairobi, Kenya, where she is a teacher educator focusing on the areas of gender, sexuality, HIV/AIDS and life skills.

Laxmi Dhital is a freelance consultant currently working for Save the Children Norway in Nepal.

Neil Duncan teaches in the School of Education of the University of Wolverhampton, UK in the area of special needs and inclusion. He is author of a book on sexual bullying in schools.

Erika George is Associate Professor of Law at the University of Utah, USA, where she teaches international human rights and humanitarian law, constitutional law and civil procedure.

Irina Gorshkova is a freelance sociologist in Moscow and author of a number of articles and books on gender issues, including *Violence Against Wives in Contemporary Russian Families.*

Rachel Gouin is a writer, activist and PhD candidate in the Faculty of Education at McGill University, Canada, where she is researching young women's informal learning.

Sara Humphreys is currently based at the University of Sussex, UK. Previously, she worked in Botswana, Ecuador and Namibia as a teacher and teacher educator. Her research interests are in gender and school processes.

Jackie Kirk is a research associate of the McGill Centre for Research and Teaching on Women. She is also advisor to the International Rescue Committee (IRC) and the lead researcher on the IRC's Healing Classrooms Initiative.

June Larkin is the undergraduate coordinator for the Women and Gender Studies Institute (WGSI) and Director of Equity Studies at the University of Toronto, Canada. She is also co-coordinator of the Gendering Adolescent AIDS Prevention (GAAP) project.

Monica Mak is a documentary film maker and lecturer in the Department of Information and Media Studies at the University of Western Ontario, Canada.

Gethwana Makhaye is the founder, fundraiser and director of Targeted AIDS Interventions in KwaZulu-Natal, South Africa, where she is completing her masters in Medical Science at the University of KwaZulu-Natal.

Liz Meyer is a doctoral candidate at McGill University, Canada, where she is investigating how teachers understand and respond to gendered harassment in secondary schools.

Robina Mirembe is a lecturer in the School of Education at Makerere University, Kampala, Uganda, where she has conducted research on adolescent sexuality in the era of AIDS.

Martin Mills is Associate Professor in the School of Education, University of Queensland, Australia, where he teaches and researches in the areas of the sociology of education, gender, social justice and educational reform.

Relebohile Moletsane is Associate Professor in the Faculty of Education at the University of KwaZulu-Natal, South Africa, where she conducts research in the area of girlhood studies, youth and HIV and AIDS.

Robert Morrell is Professor in the Faculty of Education, University of KwaZulu-Natal, South Africa, where he researches and writes in the area of gender, specialising in the fields of gender and schooling and men and masculinities.

Marcos Nascimento is coordinator of the Gender and Health Program at Instituto Promundo, an NGO based in Rio de Janeiro, Brazil.

Sara Parker is Senior Lecturer in Geography at Liverpool John Moores University, UK. She has been involved in Action Aid's REFLECT programme in a conservation area in Nepal, utilising participatory research techniques.

Julie Pulerwitz is Research Director of the Horizons Program at Population Council/PATH, a global HIV/AIDS operations research program based in the USA.

Christine Ricardo is senior gender and health program officer at Instituto Promundo, an NGO based in Rio de Janeiro, Brazil.

Carla Rice is Assistant Professor at Trent University, Canada, where she lectures in culture, psychology, and health, focusing on body image and eating disorders.

Márcio Segundo is co-ordinator of research and evaluation at Instituto Promundo, an NGO based in Rio de Janeiro, where he oversees the evaluation of interventions to promote health and gender equity among youth from local low-income communities.

Shekhar Seshadri is Professor in the Unit of Child and Adolescent Psychiatry, Department of Psychiatry, National Institute of Mental Health and Neuro Sciences (NIMHANS), Bangalore, India, working in the area of masculinities and experiential methodologies.

Shaheen Shariff is Assistant Professor in the Department of Integrated Studies in Education, where she conducts research on school policy and legal boundaries involving cyber-bullying and internet harassment.

Lucy Stackpool-Moore is a programme officer with the HIV/AIDS team at the Panos Institute, London, where she coordinates research on HIV social movements and a global analysis of HIV and TB in the media.

Kay Standing is Senior Lecturer in Sociology at Liverpool John Moores University, UK. She has been involved in the British Council Higher Education Link programme on Gender and Development in Nepal since 2003.

Ravi Verma is a program associate based in the Population Council's New Delhi office, where he works in the area of male sexuality and sexual health concerns, especially in relation to HIV/AIDS risk behaviour and partner violence.

Shannon Walsh is a doctoral student at McGill University, Canada and Research Associate with the Centre for Civil Societies, University of KwaZulu-Natal, South Africa, focusing on participatory visual methodologies in working with youth to support social activism.

Rebecca Winthrop is Education Technical Adviser at the International Rescue Committee, where she has developed education programmes in crisis and post-conflict contexts in over 20 countries.

Olga Zdravomyslova is Executive Director of the Gorbachev Foundation in Moscow, where she conducts research in such areas as gender and the transformation of Russian society.

Bibliography

Abramovy, M. and Rua, M. (2005) *Violences in Schools*. Brasilia: UNESCO

African Rights (1994) *Crimes without Punishment: sexual harassment and violence against female students in schools and universities in Africa*. London: African Rights

Aggleton, P. and Warwick, I. (1997) Young People, Sexuality, HIV and AIDS Education. In L. Sherr (ed) *AIDS and Adolescents*. Amsterdam: Harwood Academic Publishers, 79-90

Aiex, N. K. (1999) Mass Media Use in the Classroom. ERIC Clearinghouse on Reading English and Communication. *Digest #147*. Bloomington: ERIC

Alloway, N. (1995) *Foundation Stones: The Construction of Gender in Early Childhood*. Sydney: Australia Curriculum Corporation

Alston, P. (2005) Ships Passing in the Night: the current state of the human rights and development debate seen through the lens of the millennium development goals. *Human Rights Quarterly*, 27(3), 755-829

American Association of University Women (1993) *Hostile hallways: the AAUW survey on sexual harassment in America's schools*. New York: Louis Harris and Associates

Amnesty International (2005) Nepal: Children caught in the conflict http://web.amnesty.org/library/Index/ENGASA310542005 Accessed November 2005

Amnesty International (2004) *Amnesty International Report 2004*. London: Amnesty International

ANC Women's Caucus Campaign to End Violence Against Women and Children, with assistance from People Opposing Women Abuse (POWA), Sexual Harassment Education Project (SHEP), Rape Crisis and Resources Aimed at the Prevention of Child Abuse and Neglect (RAPCAN) (1998) Fact Sheet. Johannesburg: ANC

Archer, L. (2003) *Race, Masculinity and Schooling: Muslim boys and education*. Maidenhead: Open University Press

Australian Education Council (1993) *National Action Plan for the Education of Girls 1993-97*. Carlton: Curriculum Corporation

Bandura, A. (1977) *Social Learning Theory*. Englewood Cliffs: Prentice Hall

Barak, A. (2005) Sexual harassment on the Internet. *Social Science Computer Review*, 23(1), 77-92

Barker, E. T. and Galambos, N. L. (2003) Body dissatisfaction of adolescent girls and boys: risk and resources factors. *Journal of Early Adolescence*, 23(2), 141-165

Barker, G. (2005) *Dying to be Men: Youth, masculinity and social exclusion*. London: Routledge

Bauer, K., Yang, Y.W. and Austin, S.B. (2004) 'How can we stay healthy when you're throwing all of this in front of us?' Findings from focus groups and interviews in middle schools on environmental influences on nutrition and physical activity. *Health Education and Behaviour,* 31(1), 34-46

BBC (2004) *Week in, week out: The loneliness of Laura* (2004) [TV] Cardiff: BBC Wales 9 November 2004, 6.00 pm

Bhana, D. (2002) Making Gender in Early Schooling. A multi-sited ethnography of power and discourse: from grade one to two in Durban. Durban: Unpublished PhD thesis, University of Natal

Bjorkqvist, K., Lagerspetz, K. M. J. and Kaukainen, A. (1991) Do girls manipulate and boys fight? Developmental trends in regard to direct and indirect aggression. *Aggressive Behavior,* 18, 117-127

Blanco, J. (2003) *Please stop laughing at me ... one woman's inspirational story.* Adams Media: Massachusetts

Bochenek, M. and Brown, A.W. (2001) *Hatred in the Hallways: violence and discrimination against lesbian, gay, bisexual, and transgender students in US schools.* New York: Human Rights Watch

Boler, T. (2003) *The sound of silence: Difficulties in communicating on HIV/AIDS in schools, experiences from India and Kenya.* London: ActionAid

Boler, T. and P. Aggleton (2005) *Life skills-based education for HIV prevention: a critical analysis.* London: UK Working Group on HIV and AIDS

Bright, R. (2005) It's just a grade 8 girl thing: aggression in teenage girls. *Gender and Education,* 17 (1), 93-101

Brookes, H. (2003) *Violence against Girls in South African Schools.* Pretoria: Human Sciences Research Council

Brown, C.K. (2002) *A Study on Sexual Abuse in Schools in Ghana.* Cape Coast: University of Cape Coast/UNICEF Ghana

Brown, J. (2005) 'Violent girls': Same or different from 'other' girls? In G. Lloyd (ed) *Problem Girls: understanding and supporting troubled and troublesome girls and young women.* London: Routledge Falmer

Browne, L. (1995) Setting up a democratic classroom. In C. Harber (Ed) *Developing Democratic Education.* Derby: Education Now, 61-72

Brownmiller, S. (1976) *Against our Will: men, women and rape.* Harmondsworth: Penguin

Budlender, D. (1996) *The Women's budget.* Cape Town: IDASA

Bufkin, J.L. (1999) Bias Crime as Gendered Behaviour. *Social Justice,* 26(1), 155-176

Bullying. No Way! (2004) Available at www.bullyingnoway.com.au/issues/gender. shtml. Accessed on 13th December, 2005

Burman, M. J., Tisdall, K., Brown, J. A. and Batchelor, S. A. (2000) *A View from the Girls: exploring violence and violent behaviour: Research findings.* Swindon: ESRC

Burton, P. (2005) *Suffering at School: Results of the Malawi Gender-based Violence in Schools Survey.* National Statistical Office, Malawi

Butler, J. (1990) *Gender Trouble.* New York and London: RoutledgeFalmer

Caddell, M. (2005) Listening to local voices? International targets and decentralised education planning in Nepal, *International Journal of Educational Development,* 25(4), 456-469

California Safe Schools Coalition and 4-H Center for Youth Development (2004) *Consequences of Harassment Based on Actual or Perceived Sexual Orientation and Gender Non-Conformity and Steps for Making Schools Safer.* Davis: University of California

Carr, W. and Kemmis, S. (1986) *Becoming Critical: education knowledge and action research.* Lewes: Falmer Press

Chambers, R. (2000) *Remarks at the Pan African Workshop on Participatory Approach and HIV/AIDS.* Mwanza: Tanzania, 16 June 2000. Available online at http://www.ids.ac.uk/ids/particip/research/health/partichiv.pdf Accessed on 20

April 2004

Chege, F. (2001) Gender Values, Schooling and Transition to Adulthood: A Study of Female and Male Pupils from Two Urban Primary Schools in Kenya. Cambridge: Unpublished PhD Thesis, University of Cambridge

Chege, F. (1998) *With Our Eyes in Our Own Voices: an interactive role-play and report on sexual harassment.* Nairobi: FAWE and WERK

Chesney-Lind, M. and Shelden, R.G. (2004) *Girls, delinquency, and juvenile justice.* Belmont CA: Wadsworth

Chevannes, P. (2004) *Preliminary Study on Violence in Caribbean Schools, Caribbean Desk Review for the UN Study of Violence against Children,* New York: United Nations

Chianu, E. (2000) Two deaths, one blind eye, one imprisonment: child abuse in the guise of corporal punishment in Nigerian schools. *Child Abuse and Neglect* 24(7), 1005-1009

Chong, E., Hallman, K., and Brady, M. (2005) *Generating the Evidence Base for HIV/AIDS Policies and Programs.* New York: Population Council

Chu, J. (8 August, 2005) You Wanna Take This Online? Cyberspace is the 21st century bully's playground where girls play rougher than boys. *Time.* Toronto: Ontario, 42-43

Citron, M. (1999) *Home Movies and other Necessary Fictions.* Minneapolis: University of Minnesota Press

Clatcherty, G. (2005) *Refugee and Returnee Children in Southern Africa: perceptions and experiences of children.* Pretoria: UNHCR

Collins, C., Batten, M., Ainley, J. and Getty, C. (1996) *Gender and School Education.* Canberra: Australian Council for Educational Research

Connell, R. (1996) *Teaching the boys: new research on masculinity and gender strategies for schools.* Teachers College Record, 98(2), 206-235

Connell, R. (1995) *Masculinities.* St Leonards: Allen and Unwin

Connell, R. (1987) *Gender and Power.* Stanford, CA: Stanford University Press

Connell, R. W. (1989) 'Cool guys', 'swots' and 'wimps': the interplay of masculinity and education. *Oxford Review of Education,* 15(3), 291-303

Coombe, C. (2002) Editorial: HIV/AIDS and Education. *Perspectives in Education,* 20(2), vii-x

Cornwall, A. (2003) Whose Voices? Whose Choices? Reflections on gender and participatory development. *World Development,* 31(8), 1325-1342

Craig, W. and Hymel, S. (2005) Personal communication keynote speakers. *Beyond Rhetoric.* National Conference on Bullying. Ottawa: Ontario

Crick, N. R. and Grotpeter, J. K. (1995) Relational aggression, gender, and social psychological adjustment. *Child Development,* 66(3), 710-722

CWIN (2005) Children in Armed Conflict Fact Sheet, September 2005. Child Workers in Nepal http://www.cwin.org.np/press_room/factsheet/fact_cic.htm Accessed November 2005

CWIN (2003) *Coalition for Children as Zones of Peace: a national campaign to protect children from the effects of armed conflict in Nepal* July 2003, Child Workers in Nepal. http://www.cwin.org.np/resources/issues/cic/coalition4czop.htm Accessed November 2005

Davis, L. (1995) *Enforcing Normalcy: disability, deafness and the body.* New York: Verso Press

DfID (2005) Protecting Schoolgirls from Sexual Abuse. www.dfid.gov.uk/casestudies/files/research/sexual-abuse-africa.asp Accessed on 2 May 2006

DfID (2003) Country Strategy Paper. Department for International Development accessed 12/10/03 http://www.dfid.gov.uk/Pubs/files/cap_nepal_draft.pdf

Dollar, D. and Gatti, R. (1999) Gender Inequality, Income and Growth: are good times good for women? *Policy Research Report on Gender and Development.* Working Paper Series, No. 1. Washington DC: World Bank

Duncan, N (2004) It's important to be nice, but it's nicer to be important: girls, popularity and sexual competition. *Sex Education,* 4(2),137-152

Duncan, N. (2002) Girls, bullying and school transfer. In Sunnari, V., Kangasvuo, J. and Heikkinen, M. (eds) *Gendered and Sexualised Violence in Educational Environments.* Femina Borealis: Oulu, 110-125

Duncan, N. (1999) *Sexual Bullying: gender conflict and pupil culture in secondary schools.* New York and London: Routledge

Duncan, N. (In press) Girls, popularity and power: female identity in high school. In K. Österman and K. Björkqvist, K. (eds) *Contemporary Research on Aggression. Volume I: School violence.* Proceedings of the XVI World Meeting of the International Society for Research on Aggression, Santorini, Greece, 2004. Åbo, Finland: Åbo Akademi University

Dunne, M., Humphreys, S. and Leach, F. (2006) Gender violence in schools in the developing world. *Gender and Education,* 18(1), 75-98

Dunne, M., Leach, F., Chilisa, B., Maundeni, T., Tabulawa, R., Kutor, N., Forde, L. and Asamoah, A. (2005) Gendered School Experiences: the impact on retention and achievement in Botswana and Ghana. *DfID Education Research* No. 56. London: DfID

D'yachenko, T. (2002) Issledovanie prichin gendernogo nasiliya v shkole (Research into the causes of gender violence in school) In V. Artobolevskaya and D.Levitec (eds) *Upravlinie obrazovaniem: opyt, problemy, tendencii* (Conducting Education: experience, problems, tendencies) Murmansk: MGPI, Vol.1

Easby, S. (2005) The Use of Theatre as a Participatory Approach to Behaviour Change in the Field of HIV/AIDS in Ghana: facing the challenges. Masters' Thesis, University of East Anglia

Epstein, D., Elwood, J., Hey, V. and Maw, J. (1998) *Failing Boys? issues in gender and achievement.* Buckingham: Open University Press

Evans, J., Rich, E. and Holroyd, R. (2004) Disordered eating and disordered schooling: what schools do to middle class girls. *British Journal of Sociology of Education,* 25(2), 123-142

Ewald, W. (2000) *Secret Games: collaborative works with children, 1969-1999.* Berlin and New York: Scalo

Fawcett, B., Featherstone, B., Hearn, J. and Toft, C. (eds) (1996) *Violence and Gender Relations: theories and interventions.* London: Sage

Francis, B. (1999) Lads, Lasses and (New) Labour: 14-16 year old students' responses to the 'laddish behaviour and boys' underachievement' debate. *British Journal of Sociology of Education,* 20(3), 355-371

Francis, B. (1997) Discussing Discrimination: Children's construction of sexism between pupils in primary school. *British Journal of Sociology,* 18(4), 519-532

Freire, P. (1972) *Pedagogy of the Oppressed.* London: Penguin

Garbarino, J. (1999) *Lost Boys: why our sons turn violent and how we can save them.* New York: Free Press

Garbarino, J. (1995) *Raising Children in a Socially Toxic Environment.* San Francisco: Jossey-Bass

Gatens, M. (1996) *Imaginary Bodies: Ethics, power and corporeality.* London: Routledge

Gellner, D. N. (2002) *Resistance and the State.* New Delhi: Social Science Press

Gender Equity Taskforce for Ministerial Council for Employment, Education, Training and Youth Affairs (1997) *Gender Equity: a framework for Australian schools.* Canberra: Publications and Public Communication, Department of Urban Services, ACT Government

George, E. (2005) Instructions in Inequality: Development, Human Rights, Capabilities and Gender Violence in Schools. *Michigan Journal of International Law,* 26(4), 1139-1201

George, E. (2001) Criminal Justice? Tackling sexual abuse in schools. *Insights,* special id21 issue, August. Brighton: Institute of Development Studies

Gill, Z. (2005) Boys: Getting it Right: The 'new' disadvantaged or 'disadvantage' redefined? *The Australian Educational Researcher,* 32(2), 105-124

Giroux, H. (2003) *The Abandoned Generation: democracy beyond the culture of fear.* New York, NY: Palgrave MacMillan

Glaser, J., and Kahn, K. B. (2005) Prejudice, Discrimination and the Internet. In Y. Amichai-Hamburger (ed) *The Social Net: understanding human behavior in cyberspace.* Oxford: Oxford University Press

Glover, D., Cartwright, N. and Gleeson, D (1998) *Towards Bully-free Schools.* Buckingham and Philadelphia: Open University Press

Goetz, A.M. (1997) *Getting Institutions Right for Women in Development.* London: Zed Books

Goldfarb, B. (2002) *Visual Pedagogy: Media Cultures in and beyond the Classroom.* Durham [N.C.] and London: Duke University Press

Goldstein, T., Collins, A. and Halder M. (2005) *Challenging Homophobia and Heterosexism in Elementary and High Schools: a research report to the Toronto District School Board.* Toronto: Ontario Institute for Studies in Education, University of Toronto

Gordon, R. (1995) *Causes of Girls' Academic Underachievement: the influence of teachers' attitudes and expectations on the academic performance of secondary school girls.* Harare: HRCC, University of Zimbabwe

Gorshkova, I. and Shurygina, I. (2004) *Nasilie nad zhenami v sovremennykh rossiiskikh sem'yakh* (Violence against Wives in Contemporary Russian Families). Moscow: MAKS Press

Grown, C., Rao Gupta, G. and Kes, A. (2005) *Taking Action: Achieving Gender Equality and Empowering Women.* United Nations Millennium Project. Task Force on Education and Gender Equality. London: Earthscan

Harber, C. and Davies, L. (1997) *School Management and Effectiveness in Developing Countries: the post-bureaucratic school.* London: Cassell

Harmon, A. (26, August, 2004) Internet Gives Teenage Bullies Weapons to Wound from Afar. *New York Times.* http://www.nytimes.com./2004/08/26/education Accessed on 26 August, 2004

Harrison, A., Connolly, C. and Wilkinson, D. (1999) Increasing prevalence of HIV infection among pregnant women attending public sector antenatal clinics in rural KwaZulu/Natal. *South Africa Journal of Epidemiological Information,* 14, 22-23

Hart, J (2001) *Children Affected by the Armed Conflict in South Asia: Nepal Country Report.* Refugee Study Centre: Oxford University accessed November 2005 available at http://www.reliefweb.int/library/RSC%5FOxford/data/region-asia-02.htm

Hart, S. N. (ed) (2005) *Eliminating Corporal Punishment: the way forward to constructive child discipline.* Paris: UNESCO

Hassin, M. (1999) *Our Boys.* Documentary Film. Bangladesh: SCF and UNICEF

Haywood, C. and Mac an Ghaill, M. (1996) Schooling masculinities. In M. Mac an Ghaill (ed) *Understanding Masculinities: social relations and cultural arenas.* Buckingham: Open University Press, 50-60

Heidensohn, F. (1985) *Gender and Crime.* Macmillan: London

Hemson, C. (2001) *Ukubekezela* or *Ukuzithemba*: African life savers in Durban. In R. Morrell (ed) *Changing Men in Southern Africa.* Pietermaritzburg/London: University of Natal Press/Zed Books, 57-73

Herring, S. C. (1999) The rhetorical dynamic of gender harassment online. *The Information Society,* 15, 151-167

Hey, V. (1997) *The Company She Keeps: an ethnography of girls' friendships.* Falmer: London

Hill, A. and King, E. (1995) Women's Education and Economic Well-Being. *Feminist Economics,* 1(2), 21-46

Holdstock, T. L. (1990) Violence in schools: discipline. In B. McKendrick and W. Hoffman (eds) *People and Violence in South Africa.* Cape Town: Oxford University Press

Hoover, J.H. and Juul, K. (1993) Bullying in Europe and the United States. *Journal of Emotional and Behavioural Problems,* 2(1), 25-29

House of Representatives Standing Committee on Education and Training (2002) *Boys: getting it right.* Canberra: Commonwealth Government

Hubbard, J. (1994) *Shooting Back from the Reservation.* New York: New Press

Human Rights Watch (2001) *Scared at School: sexual violence in South African schools.* New York: Human Rights Watch

Human Rights Watch (1999) *Spare the Child: corporal punishment in Kenyan schools.* New York: Human Rights Watch

Human Rights Watch and The International Gay and Lesbian Human Rights Commission (2003) *More than a Name: state-sponsored homophobia and its consequences in Southern Africa.* New York: Human Rights Watch

Humphreys, S. (2005) Schooling Identity: Gender Relations and Classroom Discourse in Selected Junior Secondary Schools in Botswana. Unpublished DPhil thesis, University of Sussex

Hunter, M. (2004) Masculinities and multiple-sexual-partners in KwaZulu-Natal: the making and unmaking of Isoka. *Transformation*, 54, 123-153

Id21 Gender Violence in Schools website, at www.id21.org/education/gender_violence/index.html

Inter-Agency Standing Committee Task Force on Gender and Humanitarian Assistance (2005) *Guidelines for Gender-based Violence in Humanitarian Settings: focusing on prevention of and response to sexual violence in emergencies.* Geneva, IASC. Available at: http://wwwhumanitarianinfo.org/iasc/publications/asp

IRIN (2005) Between Two Stones: Nepal's Decade of Conflict. December 2005. Integrated Regional Information Network (IRIN): UN Office for Coordination of Humanitarian Affairs. Available at http://www.irinnews.org/webspecials/nepal/default.asp

Iyer, D. S. and Haslam, N. (2003) Body image and eating disturbance among South Asian-American women: The role of racial teasing. *International Journal of Eating Disorders*, 34(1), 142-147

Jackson, C. (2002) 'Laddishness' as a self-worth protection strategy. *Gender and Education*, 14(1), 37-51

Jewkes, R.K., Nduna M. and Dunkle K.L. (2004) *Violence against Women and HIV/AIDS: critical intersections. Intimate partner violence and HIV/AIDS.* Information Bulletin Series, 1, The Global Coalition on Women and AIDS. Geneva: World Health Organization

Jewkes, R.,Levin, J., Mbananga, N. and Bradshaw, D. (2002) Rape of Girls in South Africa. *Lancet,* 359(26), 319-320

Jiwani, Y. (2005) Tween worlds: race, gender, age identity and violence. In C. Mitchell and J. Walsh (eds) *Seventeen: Tween studies in the culture of girlhood.* New York: Peter Lang

Jones, C. (1985) Sexual tyranny: Male violence in a mixed secondary school. In Weiner, G. (Ed) *Just a Bunch of Girls.* Milton Keynes: Open University Press

Jones, J., Bennett, S., Olmsted, M., Lawson, M., and Rodin, G. (2001) Disordered eating attitudes and behaviours in teenaged girls: a school-based study. *Canadian Medical Association Journal*, 165(5), 547-552

Jordan, E. (1995) Fighting Boys and Fantasy Play: the construction of masculinity in the early years of school. *Gender and Education*, 7(1), 69-86

Kabeer, N. (1994) *Reversed Realities.* London: Verso

Karki, A. and Seddon, D. (eds) (2003) *The People's War in Nepal: Left perspectives.* Delhi: Adroit Publishers

Katz, J. (1995) Reconstructing masculinity in the locker room: the Mentors in Violence Prevention Project. *Harvard Educational Review,* 65(2), 163-174

Kehily, M.J. (2002). *Sexuality, Gender and Schooling: Shifting Agendas in Social Learning.* London and New York: RoutledgeFalmer

Kelly, M.J. (2000) *Planning for Education in the Context of HIV/AIDS.* Fundamentals of Educational Planning, No. 66. Paris: UNESCO/International Institute of Educational Planning

Kenway, J and Fitzclarence, L. (1997) Masculinity, Violence and Schooling: challenging 'poisonous pedagogies'. *Gender and Education,* 9(1), 117-134

Kim, D., Kim, K., Park, Y., Zhang, L., Lu, M. and Li, D. (2000) Children's experience of violence in China and Korea: a transcultural study. *Child Abuse and Neglect*, 24(9), 1163-1173

Kim, J.C. (2000) Rape and HIV Post-Exposure Prophylaxis: the relevance and the reality in South Africa. Discussion Paper, WHO Meeting on Violence Against Women and HIV/AIDS: Setting the Research Agenda, Geneva, 23-25 October

Kimmel, M. (1996) *Manhood in America: a cultural history*. New York: The Free Press

Kimmel, M. (1994) Masculinity as homophobia: fear, shame and silence in the construction of gender identity. In H. Brod and M. Kaufman (eds) *Theorising Masculinities*. Thousand Oaks: Sage

Kippax, S., Crawford, J., Benton, P. and Gault, U. (1988) Constructing Emotions: weaving meaning from memories. *British Journal of Psychology*, 27, 19-33

Kirk, J. (2003) Impossible Fictions? Reflexivity as methodology for studying women teachers' lives in development contexts. Unpublished doctoral dissertation, McGill University

Kirk, J. and Garrow, S. (2002) *A Facilitator's Guide to the Video: Unwanted Images: gender-based violence in the new South Africa* (French version: *Guide de l'animatrice pour accompagner la video images dérangeantes: La violence fondée sur le gendre dans la nouvelle Afrique du Sud*). Pretoria: Canada South Africa Education Management Program (CSAEMP) and Centre for Developing Areas Studies (CDAS)

Knight, J. (2001) Video. In F. Carson and C. Pajaczkowska (eds) *Feminist Visual Culture*. New York: Routledge

Kosciw, J.G. (2001) *The GLSEN 2001 National School Climate Survey: the School Related Experiences of Our Nation's Lesbian, Gay, Bisexual and Transgender Youth*. New York: Gay, Lesbian and Straight Education Network

Kuleana Children's Rights Center (1999) *Does Corporal Punishment Bring about Discipline?* Dar es Salaam: Kuleana Children's Rights Center

Kumar, K (1994) *What is Worth Teaching: growing up male*. New Delhi: Orient Longman

Large, J. (1997) Disintegration conflicts and the restructuring of masculinity. *Gender and Development*, 5(2), 23-30

Larkin, J. (1994) Walking Through Walls: the sexual harassment of high school girls. *Gender and Education*, 6(3), 263-280

Larkin, J. and Rice, C. (2005) Beyond 'healthy eating' and 'healthy weights'. Harassment and the health curriculum in middle schools. *Body Image*, 2(3), 219-232

Leach, F. (2006) Researching gender violence in schools: methodological and ethical considerations, *World Development*, 34(6), 1129-1147

Leach, F. (2003) Learning to be violent: the role of the school in developing adolescent gendered behaviour. *Compare*, 33(3), 385-400

Leach, F. (2002) School-based gender violence in Africa: a risk to adolescent sexual health. *Perspectives in Education*, 20(2), 99-112

Leach, F. (2001) Conspiracy of silence? Stamping out abuse in African schools. *Insights*, special id21 issue, August. Brighton: Institute of Development Studies

Leach, F., Fiscian, V., Kadzamira, E., Lemani, E. and Machakanja, P. (2003) *An Investigative Study into the Abuse of Girls in African Schools*. Education Research No. 56, London: DfID

Leach, F. and Machakanja, P. (2000) *A Preliminary Investigation into the Abuse of Girls in Zimbabwean Junior Secondary Schools*. Education Research No. 39, London: DfID

Levine, M.P. and Piran, N. (2004) The role of body image in the prevention of eating disorders. *Body Image*, 1(1), 57-70

Levine, M.P. and Smolak, L. (2001) Primary prevention of body image disturbances and disordered eating in childhood and early adolescence. In K.J. Thompson and L. Smolak (eds) *Body Image, Eating Disorders, and Obesity in Youth*, Baltimore: United Book Press, 237-260

Lingard, B. and Douglas, P. (1999) *Men Engaging Feminisms: profeminism, backlashes and schooling*. Buckingham: Open University Press

Livingstone, W. D. (1987) *Critical Pedagogy and Cultural Power*. New York and London: Bergin and Garvey Publishers

Lloyd, C.B. and Grant, M.J. (2004) *Growing Up in Pakistan: the separate experiences of males and females*, Population Council Working Paper 188. New York: Population Council

Lorgelly, P. (2000) *Are There Gender-Separate Human Capital Effects on Growth? a review of recent empirical literature*. Centre for Research in Economic Development and International Trade Research Paper. Nottingham: University of Nottingham

MacNaughton, G. (2000) *Rethinking Gender in Early Childhood Education*. London, Thousand Oaks and New Delhi: Paul Chapman Publishing

Manchester Evening News (2001) Schoolgirl attacked for being beautiful [internet]. Manchesteronline, 28 November. Available from http://www.manchesteronline.co.uk/news/s/37/37438_schoolgirl_attacked_for_being_beautiful.html Accessed 26 January, 2006

Martino, W. and Pallotta-Chiarolli, M. (2005) *Being Normal is the Only Way to Be: adolescent perspectives on gender and school*. Sydney: University of NSW Press

Martino, W. and Pallotta-Chiarolli, M. (2003) *So What's a Boy? Addressing Issues of Masculinity and Schooling*. Buckingham: Open University Press

Mathews, S., Abrahams, N., Martin, L.J., Vetten, L., van der Merve, L. and Jewkes, R. (2004) *Every Six Hours a Woman is Killed by Her Intimate Partner. A National Study of Female Homicide*. Cape Town: University of Cape Town and Medical Research Council

McIlveen, L. and Lawrence, K. (2005) Nation's day of shame. *Courier Mail*, 12 December, 1

McKeown, B. and Thomas, D. (1988) *Q Methodology*. Sage Publications: Newbury Park

McVey. G., Pepler, D., Davis, R., Flett, G., and Abdolell, M. (2002) Risk and protective factors associated with disordered eating during early adolescence. *Journal of Early Adolescence*, 22(1), 76-96

McWilliam, E. and Jones, A. (1996). Eros and pedagogical bodies. The state of (non) affairs. In. E. McWilliam, and P. Taylor (eds) *Pedagogy, Technology and the Body*. New York: Peter Lang

Mehta, M., Peacock, D. and Bernal, L. (2004) Men as partners: lessons from engaging men in clinics and communities. In S. Ruxton (ed) *Gender Equality and Men: learning from practice*. Oxford: Oxfam, 89-100

Mertsalova. T. (2004) *Nasilie v shkole: chto protovopostavit' zhestokosti i agressii?* (School Violence: how to confront cruelty and aggression?) http://ecsocman.edu.ru/images/pubs/2004/09/27/0000178091/

Mgalla, Z., Schapink, D. and Boerma, J.T. (1998) Protecting school girls against sexual exploitation: a guardian programme in Mwanza, Tanzania. *Reproductive Health Matters,* 6(12), 19-30

Milligan, S., Thomson, K. and Ashenden and Associates (1992) *'Listening to girls'. A Report of the consultancy undertaken for the review of the National Policy for the Education of Girls conducted by the Australian Education Council, 1991.* Carlton: Curriculum Corporation

Mills, M. (2001) *Challenging Violence in Schools. An issue of masculinities.* Buckingham and Philadelphia: Open University Press

Mills, M. (2000) Issues in Implementing Boys' Programmes in Schools: male teachers and empowerment. *Gender and Education,* 12(2), 221-238

Mills, M., Martino, W. and Lingard, B. (2004) Issues in the Male Teacher Debate: masculinities, misogyny and homophobia. *British Journal of Sociology of Education,* 25(3), 355-369

Ministry of Education and Training (1998) *The Ontario curriculum grades 1-8: Health and Physical Education.* Toronto

Mirembe, R. (2002) AIDS and Democratic Education in Uganda. *Comparative Education,* 38(3), 291-302

Mirembe, R. (1998) AIDS Education and Gender in Ugandan Schools. Unpublished PhD Thesis, University of Birmingham

Mirembe, R. and Davies, L. (2001) Is Schooling a Risk? Gender, Power Relations and School Culture in Uganda. *Gender and Education,* 13(4), 401-416

Mirsky, J (2003) *Beyond Victims and Villains: addressing sexual violence in the education sector.* London: Panos

Mitchell, C. (in press). Taking pictures and taking action: Visual arts based methods in research as social change. In T. T. Marcus and A. Hofmaenner (eds) *Shifting the Boundaries of Knowledge.* Pietermaritzburg: UKZN Press

Mitchell, C., Moletsane, R., Stuart, J., Buthelezi, T., and De Lange, N. (2005a) Taking pictures/taking action! Using Photo-voice Techniques with Children. *ChildrenFIRST,* 9 (60), 27-31

Mitchell, C., Delange, N., Moletsane, R., Stuart, J. and Buthelezi, T (2005b) The face of HIV and AIDS in rural South Africa: a case for photo-voice. *Qualitative Research in Psychology,* 3(2), 257-270

Mitchell, C. and Kanyangara, P. (2006). *Violence against children in and around schools in Rwanda: through the eyes of children and young people.* Kigali: UNICEF

Mitchell, C., Moletsane, R., Stuart, J. and Nkwanyana, K. (in press) 'Why we don't go to school on Fridays' On youth participation through photo voice in rural KwaZulu-Natal. *McGill Journal of Education*

Mitchell, C. and Mothobi-Tapela, I. (2004) *No Turning Back: youth and sexual violence in and around schools in Swaziland and Zimbabwe.* Nairobi: ESARO UNICEF

Mitchell, C., Walsh, S. and Larkin, J. (2004) Visualizing the politics of innocence in the age of AIDS. *Sex Education,* 3(2) 159-172

Mitchell, C. and Weber, S. (1999) *Reinventing Ourselves as Teachers: beyond nostalgia.* London and New York: Falmer

Mlamleli, O., Napo, V., Mabelane, P., Free, V., Goodman, M., Larkin, J., Mitchell, C., Mkhize, H., Robinson, K. and Smith, A. (2001) *Opening Our Eyes: addressing gender-*

based violence in south african schools, a module for educators. Pretoria: National Department of Education

Morrell, R. (2001) *Changing Men in Southern Africa.* Pietermaritzburg/London: University of Natal Press/Zed Books

Morrell, R. (2001) Corporal punishment and masculinity in South African schools. *Men and Masculinities,* 4(2), 140-157

Morrell, R. (1998) Gender and Education: the place of masculinity in South African schools. *South African Journal of Education,* 18(4), 218-225

Müller, J. (2002) *Non-Violence in Education.* Paris: UNESCO

Munro, P. (1998) *Subject to Fiction.* Buckingham: Open University Press

Nabi, F. and Zaidi, M. (1999) *Now that's more like a man.* Documentary Film. Pakistan: SCF and UNICEF

Naidoo, K. (1998) The men march. *Agenda,* 36, 94-96

Nair, K and White, S. (2003) Trapped: women take control of video storytelling. In S. White (ed) *Participatory Video: images that transform and empower.* New Delhi: Thousand Oaks: London: Sage. 195-214

Naker, D. (2005) *Violence against Children: the voices of Ugandan children and adults.* Kampala: Raising Voices/Save the Children in Uganda

Nasser, M., and Katzman, M. (1999) Eating disorders: Transcultural perspectives inform prevention. In N. Piran, M.P. Levine and C. Steiner-Adair (eds), *Preventing Eating Disorders: a handbook of interventions and special challenges.* Philadelphia: Brunner/Mazel, 26-43.

Nepal News (2004) Maoist terror subverts education in Nepal http://www.newind press.com/news.asp?id=IEH20040526125308 Accessed on 10 June 2004

Newell, P. (1989) *Children are People too: the case against physical punishment.* London: Bedford Square Press

Nkosi, T. (1998) Young men taking a stand! *Agenda,* 37, 30-31

Nussbaum, M. (2003) Women's Education: A Global Challenge. *Signs* 29(2): 325-355

Odaja, A, and Heneveld, W. (1995) *Girls and Schools in Sub-Saharan Africa: from analysis to action.* Technical paper No. 298, Washington DC: World Bank

Olweus, D. (1993) *Bullying at School: what we know and what we can do.* Blackwell: Cambridge MA

Osler, O. (1998) Human Rights, Education and Racial Prejudice in Britain: rhetoric and reality. In C. Harber (ed) *Voices for Democracy: a North South dialogue on education for sustainable democracy.* Nottingham: Education Now, 48-59

Owens, L., Shute, R. and Slee, P. (2000) I'm in and you're out: explanations for girls' indirect aggression. Psychology, *Evolution and Gender,* 2(1), 19-46

Pattman, R. and Chege, F. (2003) *Finding Our Voices: gendered and sexual identities and HIV/AIDS in Education.* Nairobi: UNICEF Eastern and Southern Africa

Peacock, D. (2003) Building on a Legacy of Social Justice Activism: enlisting men as gender justice activists in South Africa. *Men and Masculinities,* 5(3), 325-328

Pettifor, A. E., Rees, H. V., Steffenson, A., Hlongwa-Madikizela, L., MacPhail, C., Vermaak, K. and Kleinschmidt, I. (2004) *HIV and sexual behaviour among young South Africans: a national survey of 15-24 year olds.* Johannesburg: Reproductive Health Research Unit, University of the Witwatersrand

Pink, S. (2001) *Doing Visual Ethnography.* London: Sage

Piran, N. (1999) The reduction of preoccupation with body weight and shape in schools: A feminist approach. In N. Piran, M.P. Levine and C. Steiner-Adair (eds) *Preventing Eating Disorders: a handbook of interventions and special challenges.* Philadelphia: Brunner/Mazel, 148-159

Poran, M. A. (2002) Denying diversity: perceptions of beauty and social comparison processes among Latino, Black and White women. *Sex Roles,* 47(1-2), 65-82

Poudyal, R. (2000) Boys on film: Challenging masculinities in South Asia. *ID21 Research Highlights.* http://www.id21.org/

Pulerwitz, J., Barker, G., Segundo, M. and Nascimento, M. (2006) Promoting more gender-equitable norms and behaviors among young men as an HIV/AIDS prevention strategy. *Horizons Final Report.* Washington, DC: Population Council

Rana-Deuba, A. (2005) *A National Study on Changing Roles of Nepali Women due to Ongoing Conflict and its Impact.* Samanata Studies No 6. Katmandu: Samanta Institute for Social and Gender Equality

Redfield, S.E. (2003) Threats Made, Threats Posed: School and Judicial Analysis in Need of Redirection. *Brigham Young University Education and Law Journal,* 2, 663-742

Renold, E. (2005) *Girls, Boys and Junior Sexualities: exploring children's gender and sexual relations in the primary school,* London: RoutlegeFalmer

Renold, E. (2004) Presumed Innocence: (hetero) sexual, heterosexist and homophobic harassment among primary school girls and boys. *Childhood,* 9(4), 415-434

Reuters (2002) Afghan Woman Attacked with Acid. *Reuters,* April 17, 2002 www. rawa. org/acid.htm Accessed on 26 February 2006

Rhitar, T. and K. Tseten (1999) *Listen to the wind.* Documentary Film. Nepal: SCF and UNICEF

Rice, C. and Russell, V. (2002) *Embodying Equity: working with body image as an equity issue.* Toronto: Green Dragon Press

Rice, C., Zitszelsberger, H., Porch, W. and Ignagni, E. (2005) Creating community across disability and difference. *Canadian Woman Studies,* 24(1), 187-193

Rich, A. (1993) Compulsory Heterosexuality and Lesbian Existence. In H. Abelove, M.A. Barale and D.M. Halperin (eds) *The Lesbian and Gay Studies Reader.* New York: Routledge, 227-254

Richter, L., Dawes, A. and Higson-Smith, C. (2004) *Sexual Abuse of Young Children in Southern Africa.* Cape Town: HSRC Press

Roberts, H. (2003) Children's participation in policy matters. In C. Hallett and A. Prout (eds) *Hearing the Voices of Children: social policy for a new century.* London and New York: RoutledgeFalmer

Robinson, K. H. (2005) Reinforcing hegemonic masculinities through sexual harassment: issues of identity, power and popularity in secondary schools. *Gender and Education,* 17(1), 19-37

Rossetti, S. (2001) *Children in School: a safe place?* Rape Crisis Centre, Botswana/ Comic Relief, UK

Roy, R. (1999) *When four friends meet.* Documentary Film. India: SCF and UNICEF

Ruby, J. (2000) *Picturing Culture: explorations of film and Anthropology.* Chicago and London: University of Chicago Press

Rumak, O. (2001) Perfect breasts. *The Fifth Estate.* Toronto: Canadian Broadcasting Corporation

Safonova, T. (2005) *Pomotsh detiam v usloviiach spetsializirovannogo tsentra* (To help children in crisis centres) In N. Rimashevskaya (ed) *Razorvat' krug molchniya? O nasilii v otnoshenii zhench'in (To Break the Circle of Violence? About violence towards women)*. Moscow: KomKniga, 335-343

Salmivalli, C., Lagerspetz, K., Bjorqvist, K., Osterman, K. and Kaukiainen, A. (1996) Bullying as a group process: Participant roles and their relations to social status within the group. *Aggressive Behavior*, 25, 81-89

Save the Children Norway (2005) *Impacts of the Armed Conflict Pushing Girls and Women into Sexual Abuse and Sex Trade*. Katmandu: Save the Children Norway

Schön, D. (1983) *The Reflective Practitioner: How Professionals Think in Action*. London: Maurice Temple Smith

Schratz, M. and R. Walker (1995) *Research as Social Change: new opportunities for qualitative research*. London and New York: Routledge

Sen, A. (1999) *Development as Freedom*. New York: Knopf

Servance, R. (2003) Cyberbullying, cyber-harassment, and the conflict between schools and the First Amendment. *Wis. L. Rev.* 1213 (2003) at 1215.

Seshadri, S. and R. Poudyal (2002) *Impact Assessment and Opinion Survey of the South Asian Masculnities Film Project*. A Report

Shakeshaft, C., and Cohan, A. (1994) *Sexual Abuse of Students in Schools: what administrators should know in loco parentis*. New York: US Department of Education

Shakya, S (2003) The Maoist Movement in Nepal: an analysis from the women's perspective. In Karki, A. and Seddon, S. (eds) *op cit*, 375-404

Shariff, S. (2004) Keeping Schools Out of Court: Legally defensible models of leadership to reduce cyber-bullying. *Educational Forum, Delta Kappa Pi*. 68(3), 222-233

Sharp, S. and Smith, P.K. (1991) Bullying in UK Schools: The DES Sheffield Bullying Project. *Early Child Development and Care*, 77, 47-55

Shumba, A. (2001) Who guards the guards in school? A study of reported cases of child abuse by teachers in Zimbabwe secondary schools. *Sex Education*, 1(1), 77-86

Sibbons, M (1998) Approaches to gender-awareness raising: experiences in a government education project in Nepal, *Gender and Development*, 6(2), 35-43

Simmons, R. (2002) *Odd Girl Out: the hidden culture of aggression in girls*. Harcourt Press: New York

Skelton, C. (2001) *Schooling the Boys: masculinities and primary education*. Buckingham: Open University Press

Smith, A. (2000) Queer pedagogy and social change: Teaching and lesbian identity in South Africa. In W. Spurlin (ed) *Lesbian and Gay Studies and the Teaching of English: positions, pedagogies, and cultural politics*. Illinois: National Council of Teachers of English, 260

Smith, G.W. (1998) The ideology of 'fag': The school experience of gay students. *Sociological Quarterly*, 39(2), 309-335

Soneson, U. (2005) *Ending Corporal Punishment of Children in Zambia*. Arcadia, RSA, Save the Children: Sweden

Soneson, U. and Smith, C. (2005) *Ending Corporal Punishment of Children in South Africa*. Arcadia, RSA, Save the Children: Sweden

Steffensmeier, D., Schwartz, J., Zhong, H. and Ackerman, J. (2005) An assessment of recent trends in girls' violence using diverse longitudinal sources: is the gender gap closing? *Criminology*, 43(2), 355-406

Stein, N. (2003) Bullying or sexual harassment? The missing discourse of rights in an era of zero tolerance. *Arizona Law Review*, 45, 783-799

Stein, N. (1995) Sexual Harassment in School: The Public Performance of Gendered Violence. *Harvard Educational Review*, 65(2), 145-162

Stein, P. (1999) Drawing the unsayable: Cannibals, sexuality and multimodality in a Johannesburg classroom. *Perspectives in Education*, 18(2), 61-82

Stromquist, N.P., Lee, M. and Brock-Utne, B. (1998) The Explicit and the Hidden School Curriculum. In N.P. Stromquist (ed) *Women in the Third World: an encyclopaedia of contemporary issues*. New York: Garland, 397-407

Student Learning and Support Services Taskforce (2003) *National Safe Schools Framework*. Canberra: MCEETYA

Subrahmanian, R. (2005) Gender Equality in Education: Definitions and Measurements. *International Journal of Educational Development*, 25(4), 395-407

Sunday Times (2002) 27 October, 5

Swainson, N. (2003) Understanding Teacher Attitudes and Behaviour in relation to the AIDS Epidemic in Sub-Saharan Africa, paper presented at the Gender, Sexuality and Schooling Symposium, Oxford Conference on Education and Development, 9-11 September 2003. *Mimeo*

Swart, J. (1988) *Malunde: the street children of Hillbrow*. Johannesburg: Wits University Press

Syvertsen, C. (2001) Ordinary people in extraordinary circumstances: a study of participants in television dating games. *Media Culture and Society*, 23 (3), 319-338

Tabane, R. (1999) A third of schoolgirls are victims of sex attacks. Johannesburg, *The Star*, 8 January, 2

Teni-Atinga, G. (2005) Beginning teachers' perceptions and experiences of sexual harassment in Ghanaian teacher training institutions. Unpublished doctoral thesis, Montreal: McGill University

Terreblanche, S. (2002) *A History of Inequality in South Africa, 1652-2002*. University of Natal Press: Pietermaritzburg

Thapa, D (2002) The Maobadi of Nepal. In K.M. Dixit and S. Ramachandran (eds) *State of Nepal*. Katmandu: Himal Books

Thapa, R (2004) *Gender Experiences in School (a study report)*. Katmandu: CERID, Tribhuvan University

Thompson, B. (1994) *A Hunger So Wide and So Deep: American women speak out on eating problems*. Minneapolis, MN: University of Minnesota Press

Thompson, B. (1992) 'A way outa no way': Eating problems among African-American, Latina and White women. *Gender and Society*, 6(4), 546-561

Thorne, B. (1993) *Gender Play: girls and boys in school*. Buckingham: Open University Press

Tsentr grazhdanskogo obrazovaniia i prav cheloveka: Prava cheloveka v Permskoi oblasti (2005) Center of Civil Education and Human Rights: Human Rights in Perm Region. http://www.pcgo.narod.ru/otchot_2.htm

UNDP (2004) *Human Development Report 2004*. New York: UNDP

UNESCO (2003) *Education for All: the leap to equality. EFA Global Monitoring Report 2003/04*. Paris: UNESCO

UNESCO (2000a) *The Dakar Framework for Action: meeting our collective commitments*. Paris: UNESCO

UNESCO (2000b) The EFA 2000 Assessment country reports. http://www2.unesco.org/wef/countryreports/home.html Accessed on 7 March 2006

UNHCR/Save the Children UK (2002) Note for implementing and operational partners on sexual violence and exploitation: The experience of refugee children in Guinea, Liberia and Sierra Leone. www.unhcr.ch Accessed January 10, 2005

UNICEF (2005) *Progress for Children: a report card on gender parity and primary education.* New York: UNICEF

UNICEF (2001) *Corporal Punishment in Schools in South Asia.* Kathmandu: UNICEF Regional Office for South Asia

UNICEF Gambia and Government of Gambia (2003). Study on the Sexual Abuse and Exploitation of Children in the Gambia, December. www.csd.gm/social research/sexual exploitation study.pdf Accessed 12 April 2005

United Nations (2006) Secretary General's Study of Violence Against Children www.violencestudy.org (forthcoming report, November)

Unterhalter, E. (2005) Fragmented frameworks? Researching women, gender, education, and development. In S. Aikman and E. Unterhalter (eds) *Beyond Access: transforming policy and practice for gender equality in education,* Oxford: Oxfam, 15-35

USAID (2003) *Unsafe Schools: A Literature Review of School-Related Gender-based Violence in Developing Countries.* Wellesley Centers for Research on Women and Development and Training Services, Inc., for USAID, Washington DC: USAID

USAID (1999) *More, But Not Yet Better: an evaluation of USAID's programs and policies to improve girls' education.* Washington DC: USAID

Verma, R.K, Mahendra, V.S., Pulerwitz, J., van Dam, J., Flessenkaemper, S., Khandekar, S., Rangaiyan, G. and Barker, G. (2004) From Research to Action – Addressing Masculinity as a strategy to Reduce Risk Behaviour Among Young men in India. *Indian Journal of Social Work,* XXIV, December, 434-454

Waetjen, T. (2004) *Workers and Warriors: masculinity and the struggle for nation in South Africa.* Champaign, IL: University of Illinois Press

Walkerdine, V. (1990) *Schoolgirl Fictions.* New York and London: Verso

Wallace, P. (1999) *The Psychology of the Internet.* Cambridge, UK: Cambridge University Press

Watchlist (2005) *Caught in the Middle: mounting violations against children in Nepal's armed conflict.* New York: Watchlist on Children and Armed Conflict

Weaver-Hightower, M. (2003) The 'boy turn' in research on gender and education. *Review of Educational Research,* 73(4), 471-498

Weber, S. and Mitchell, C. (1995) *That's funny, you don't look like a teacher: interrogating images of identity in popular culture.* London and New York: Falmer

Welbourn, A. (1995) *Stepping Stones: a training package on HIV/AIDS, communication and relationship skills.* London: ActionAid and Strategies for Hope

Whitley, B.E., Jr. (2001) Gender-Role Variables and Attitudes Toward Homosexuality. *Sex Roles,* 45(11 and 12), 691-721

Whitworth, S. (2004) *Men, Militarism and UN Peacekeeping: A Gendered Analysis.* Boulder, Co: Lynne Rienner Publishing

Wible, B (2004) *Making Schools Safe for Girls: combating gender-based violence in Benin.* Washington DC: US Academy for Educational Development

Williams, S. J. (1998) Malignant Bodies: children's beliefs about health, cancer and risk. In S.W. Nettleton (ed) *The Body in Everyday Life.* London: Routledge, 103-123

Williams, T., Connolly, J., Pepler, D. and Craig, W. (2005) Peer Victimization, Social Support, and Psychosocial Adjustment of Sexual Minority Adolescents. *Journal of Youth and Adolescence*, 34(5), 471-482

Wolpe, A. (1988) *Within the Walls: the role of discipline and sexuality and the curriculum.* London: Routledge

Wolpe, A., Quinlan, O. and Martinez, L. (1997) *Gender Equity in Education: a report of the Gender Equity Task Team.* Pretoria: Department of Education

Wong, L. (1999) *Shootback: photos by kids from the Nairobi slums.* London: Booth-Clibborn

Xaba, T. (2001) Masculinity and its Malcontents: The Confrontation between 'Struggle Masculinity' and 'Post-Struggle Masculinity' (1990-1997). In R. Morrell (ed), *Changing Men in Southern Africa.* Pietermaritzburg/London: University of Natal Press/Zed Books, 105-124

Ybarra, M.L. and Mitchell, K.J. (2004) Online aggressor/targets, aggressors, and targets: A comparison of associated youth characteristics. *Journal of Child Psychology and Psychiatry and Allied Disciplines,* 45(7), 1308-131

Yenikopov, S. (2003) *Osobennosti phsihologicheskoi adaptacii zhenchin k usloviyam perehodnogo perioda* (Peculiar features of psychological adjustment of women to conditions in a transitional period) In O. Zdravomyslova (ed) *Obyknovennoie zlo: Issledovahiia nasiliia v sem'e* (The Usual Evil: research into family violence). Moscow: Editorial URSS, 166-174

Young-Hyman, D., Schlundt, D. G., Herman-Wenderoth, L., and Bozylinski, K. (2003) Obesity, appearance, and psychosocial adaptation in young African American children. *Journal of Pediatric Psychology,* 28(7), 463-472

Zdravomyslova, O. (2003) *Nasilie v sem'e i crisis tradicionnoi concepcii vospitaniya. Po rezul'tatam issledovaniia 'Nasiliie v sem'e glazami uchitelei I vospitatelei'* (family violence and the crisis of the traditional concept of upbringing. Based on the results of the study 'Family violence as seen by teachers and educators') In O. Zdravomyslova (ed), *op.cit.* 152 – 165

Zdravomyslova, O. and Kigai, N. (2005) *Predstavlenie o gendere sviazano s osoznaniem lichnosti. Syzhdenia, otsenki, mnemia russkih zhenshhin I muzhchin* (Understanding gender is linked to the gender understanding of oneself: opinions and evaluations of women and men in Russia). Moscow: Gorbachev Foundation

Zuberi, F. (2005) Assessment of Violence against Children in the Eastern and Southern Africa Region. Results of an initial desk review for the UN Secretary General's Study on Violence Against Children. Nairobi: UNICEF ESARO

Index